WHAT YOU
DON'T KNOW
YOU KNOW

What You Don't Know You Know

Our Hidden Motives in Life, Business, and Everything Else

KEN EISOLD, Ph.D.

Other Press *New York*

Library of Congress Cataloging-in-Publication Data
Eisold, Kenneth.
What you don't know you know : our hidden motives in life, business,
and everything else / Kenneth Eisold.
p. cm.
Includes index.
ISBN 978-1-59051-261-6 (hardcover)—ISBN 978-1-59051-365-1 (ebook)
1. Subconsciousness. I. Title.
BF315.E55 2009
154.2—dc22
2009023475

No question,
this page belongs to Barbara,
who encouraged and supported me,
every step of the way,
with honest criticism, frank comments, and love

CONTENTS

▪

Once, consciousness seemed primary, self-evident. It was through consciousness that the world revealed itself. Below the surface of the mind or beyond its perceptions were the unknown factors that drove human motivation, which were thought to be available for discovery sooner or later—or else were transcendent, supernatural, altogether outside the human.

But in the past century there has been a deep shift in our relationship to the realms of the unconscious. Consciousness, we now know, is variable and contingent. It can reveal only pieces of the world, and distorts what it displays. On the other hand, the territories of the unconscious are limitless and complex. The unconscious is now crucial to our thinking about reality, while consciousness has become problematic. Why do we have it? How can we agree on what it discloses? What is real? The unconscious, a figure in the ground of consciousness, has now become the ground itself.

The unconscious on which Freud concentrated his attention was a small fraction of what we are now coming to understand to be the hidden dimensions of human experience. Freud took a kind of gruff and wary pride in affronting human complacency, which he saw to be based on false notions of conscious awareness and control. For him, the unconscious was an exception to the general rule of reason and awareness. Discovering powerful hidden motivations among the baser instincts, he challenged human pretensions. And all the while he continued to try to redeem the unconscious by making it conscious.

But our new understanding of the unconscious is not just about repressed sexual or aggressive impulses forced into our mental basements. The unknown lurks in every corner of our world, on every level. It pervades relationships not only with our families and friends but also with colleagues and employers. It infiltrates our offices and schools, our businesses, our shops, our clubs—all the arenas of life that appear to be suffused with intention, will, planning, and control. It shapes our economic policies, our politics and international relations. We used to think that the unconscious operated "inside" our minds, the result of essentially private mental actions to avoid, deflect, or censor attention to its contents. Now, however, we know the unconscious is "outside," in social relations, as well, taking part in our every collaborative thought and action.

This "new unconscious," unlike Freud's, is protean and multifaceted. Repression is only one of its mechanisms. It operates through habit and convention as well as violence and fear; likewise, it operates through distraction and avoidance. It is driven by and manifested in the identities we assume, the groups we belong to, the assumptions we inherit, the language we use—all the elements that provide structure to our world. Trauma and terror can play a role in keeping thoughts out of awareness, but so can comfort and familiarity. Consciousness, we are coming to understand, is a thin shell that screens out most of what we could know and much of what might actually help us to know in conducting our lives.

THE BEGINNINGS

The unconscious sprang to the attention of the West a hundred years ago, and we are still struggling to absorb its full impact. People quickly grasped the idea that they were driven by motives they did not understand or dared admit, that they were divided within themselves and suffused with conflict. Intrigued, fascinated by the evidence, they quickly made Freud famous, and the profession he founded grew and gained extraordinary prestige, as psychoanalysts became the recognized guardians of this esoteric knowledge. But it was one thing to understand the concept, to see it and believe it, another to live with it, to take in fully its challenge to our deepest cultural assumptions.

Today, as we expand our understanding of its reach, we are still coming to grips with what it means.

Can it be that we are all driven by the unconscious? Is it always there? At work? In politics? Is it true that it shapes our history just as much as it shapes our personal relationships? Patients suffering from emotional conflicts are obviously confused, and their disorders cry out for mental explanations. Children, before they reach the age of reason, act strangely, impulsively, and display odd forms of logic. We are puzzled by our dreams, and occasionally we say things we don't intend. But are we always in the dark?

Freud correctly grasped that he was one of the intellectual pioneers who has "disturbed the sleep of the world." Coming to America in 1909, he commented that his hosts could not know he was bringing them the plague.[1] Clearly, he understood the immensity of his discovery and its disturbing implications, as he patiently planned to get his message across, amassing the evidence, clarifying his thoughts, and seeking out convincing applications. First, he turned to the explanation of dreams, a universal phenomenon and perennial puzzle, seeing them as the "royal road" to the unconscious. The dream book was published in 1900, followed the next year by his *Psychopathology of Everyday Life*, where he delineated other signs of its presence. In 1902, he assembled a group of colleagues with whom to share his ideas, and, in his early essays on sexuality, he fleshed out his ideas of infant development to account for our profound need to have an unconscious and to maintain it throughout our lives. He expanded his clinical observations and case reports, but then took time to write on how our sense of humor is grounded in our anxiety over barely suppressed, unconscious wishes.

Knowledge of his work spread. His ideas matched all too well the experience that more and more people were unable to deny. At first, neurologists and psychologists, searching to understand the self-defeating behavior of mental patients, were compelled to pay attention because it illuminated what they saw and offered new hope for their treatments. After World War I, the entire world, obviously spinning out of control, was forced to take note of a theory that matched its appalling experience.

Today it is clear that the psychoanalytic concept of the unconscious has infiltrated our culture. A century of cartoons has installed the couch as the iconic representation of our irrational and contradictory selves, the portal to our hidden thoughts. This may be because the couch is where the now booming psychotherapy industry got its start, as psychoanalysis was the first credible means of treatment for mental conflict and disorders. Even though there has been an immense proliferation of other psychotherapies to service our pent-up irrationality and suffering—new outlets that promise faster, cheaper, easier relief—for many the couch still symbolizes the site of our irrationality and the promise of contact with our hidden selves.

The couch today continues to be a good source of jokes, even though, in practice, it is virtually empty. Unused by patients, even scorned by other professionals, in mental health it still symbolizes the furtive disclosures and intimate revelations that we all have come to understand lurk on the margins of daily life. The couch is a reminder that there are things about ourselves that are disconcerting, shocking, unknown.

Today, we also are aware that dreams contain messages we can decode with the help of our glossary of Freudian symbols. If we forget an appointment or an anniversary, we immediately suspect an unconscious wish. If we make a "Freudian slip," now we know exactly what to make of it. No special training is required to see others being anxious or defensive or hostile, especially when they do not see it themselves. People self-diagnose their hysteria, obsessional anality, inferiority complexes, insecurity, and, sometimes even their narcissism. If our minds go temporarily blank, we know we are "blocked"—that is, if we are not experiencing a "senior moment," which makes us a potential target for a competing set of mental health treatments.

These have become clichés of contemporary folk wisdom. But the knowledge gleaned from the couch has penetrated even more deeply into our culture, becoming part of the ways in which we now understand ourselves.

We live, as W. H. Auden said, in an "age of anxiety,"[2] not only because the world has become unfamiliar and threatening but also because we suffer from a special modern form of fear, a vague dread that pervades our lives, a legacy of irrational expectations and frightening reminiscences that we cannot fully recall but also cannot ever completely extinguish.

What we want is never simple, what we do is never aimed at a single purpose, subject to one interpretation. Freud taught us to think that our impulses well up from a powerful and peremptory core: an unregenerate id (or it). Now these warring entities of ego and id have multiplied into a chorus of selves, fragments and bits uneasily co-existing at best. The modern self is discontinuous, contradictory, fragmented. Anxiety arises from many sources. Today we speak lightly of our conflicting "parts" or "sides," our "levels" of consciousness, "layers" of motivation, our "identities," our different "personae." We wrestle with the question of our authenticity, our "true" selves imprisoned within compliant selves, guilty selves, frightened selves—or, at worst, "false" selves.

Many of us take for granted now that while we may want to change, to live more in the present, see things as they are, we also do not want to change. We may feel an urgent need to alter our ways, but we do not want to give up our habits, our established patterns of being. The modern condition is equivocation, ambivalence, oscillation. We do change, but then we slide back; we move forward but then we move sideways.

We have also come to understand that we need the continuous confirmation of others to sustain our identities, to fend off threats to self-esteem, to maintain membership in our communities. Perpetually on the alert, either we avoid situations in which we would be vulnerable to feelings of inferiority or inadequacy, or we cling to communities and relationships that affirm the ways in which we want to be seen. As individuals, of course, we are seldom alert to the specific dangers we face. Indeed, self-esteem requires we avoid knowing just how contingent and fragile our identities actually are. But that obliviousness scarcely makes us stronger.

Today's "political correctness" fosters the fantasy of an ideal community of respect, a belief that we could be simple to each other, accepting and open. But it also supports our sense of ourselves as easily damaged, requiring protection and continuous shoring up by others. Sensitivity training and diversity training are among the techniques that have been developed to proscribe injuries to self-esteem—or to punish those who have transgressed our new norms of vulnerability. Their very existence confirms our fragility.

Today, as a result of a century of the couch, we understand that much of this vulnerability is a residue of our childhoods when, in our prolonged dependency on parental figures, we were often powerless to make ourselves understood or to attain the safety we craved. The fears and disappointments of childhood persist, along with many of its desires, threatening us in adulthood with impressions and impulses we do not recognize and often cannot understand. Side by side with our more mature understanding of the real possibilities offered by the world, limited possibilities we may have worked hard to accept, these fears and desires express themselves in a language we can no longer decode. Bewildered, we know only that we are anxious.

Another legacy of childhood we now also take for granted: the mature ties of adulthood are haunted by the ghosts of old relationships. It is commonly—if somewhat simplistically—understood that the men or women we marry are likely to resemble our fathers or mothers, that is, if we do not just endlessly seek what we are afraid to find and never settle down at all. The familiar alternative strategy, looking for someone totally different, often leads to an unconscious enactment of precisely what we sought to escape. Our employers loom in our minds like distant memories of menacing adults. Fathers and grandfathers hover over the political process as voters seek figures they can trust. We understand we are looking for something we do not know, or fleeing what we no longer see.

As a result we have a new respect for the needs of childhood—and a slew of new concerns about attenuating the legacy of anxiety in the children we raise. In former times, food, clothing, and shelter seemed an adequate listing of life's basic requirements. Parents were expected to provide them for their children. Now we understand ourselves to be far more dependent on the fulfillment of needs that are less easy to detect or define, lacking the status of clear, essential demands: the need for protection, the need for love, the need for recognition and understanding, the need for security, for predictability, for hope.

After a century on the couch, the past is no longer inert for us. It always flickers beneath the surface of the present, never quiet, never gone. We exist on multiple levels, pulled in different directions.

But there is yet another source of psychic vulnerability we are coming increasingly to understand: the mental injuries that result from the insults of the present world. We have always known the dangers of illness, storms, earthquakes, and epidemics, but today we live in a world where cars and airplanes crash, where catastrophic industrial accidents have become common, where economic crises recur. On a larger scale, the modern world is menaced by genocide and terrorism, the threat of annihilation from atomic or biological weapons, or the slow death of pollution and global warming.

What we have now come to understand is that, even if we have escaped or survived such real risks to our lives, we live on with the reverberations of dread that echo in our minds, the psychic shocks that destabilize them. It is not just that we will get sick, suffer accidents, and lose our jobs and our loved ones, but that these incidents will survive indefinitely, repetitively. The world, which seemed to become more predictable and secure with the advances of science and industry, now feels less and less safe, and the threats have penetrated into the recesses of our minds.

The cost of war today includes the perpetual tax of posttraumatic stress disorder (PTSD). Returning veterans may still be heroes to many, but they often cannot resume normal lives. Burdened by fears themselves, they become frightening to others who try to resume normal lives with them. And terrorism, warfare on the home front, all too easily succeeds in making us afraid to take the bus or subway, linger in crowded theaters or stores, cross bridges, or enter tunnels. Ours is not only an age of anxiety, it has become an age of trauma.

Menaced by the dread of internal and external instability, we have become familiar with the defense of denial. Life in the modern world with its accumulating threats almost seems to require the insulation it supplies, and we speak freely of enjoying it when we can, and sometimes of enjoying it too much.

In the past, a few individuals pursued lives of contemplation; others sought detachment as they neared death. Freud told one of his early hysterics she was not responsible for her feelings; she could not help desiring her brother. That was an early example of how the process of the couch introduced a helpful detachment, driving a wedge yet further into the unity of the self.[3] Acceptance and distance have become strategies for coping with our fragmentation and vulnerability.

Psychoanalysis in the twentieth century provided a good part of the psychic glue, the consciousness that helped to hold our shattered selves together, to enable us to endure the dislocation and disruption that increasingly came to characterize our world. It described the "inscape" reflecting our social landscape, the subjective discontinuities reflecting our objective alienation. Not only did it illuminate and articulate the world of desire that was fundamental to consumerist capitalism,[4] it taught us about the anxiety and trauma that were among the costs of industrial competition and the increasing atomization of individual life.

These are some of the many ways that psychoanalysis has seeped into our culture, permanently changing our daily preoccupations and altering our picture of ourselves. It has not acted alone, of course, but has been an integral part of the mix of influences that have made us uneasy and feeling off-balanced in a uniquely informed and modern way. It is clearly impossible to go back to what now seems a simpler world, where things were kept in place and were easier to grasp.

Psychotherapy has become an accepted recourse for those suffering from mental conflicts. We now know there are monsters in the basement. But as Freud correctly saw, the unknown lurks everywhere. This is a difficult message for a century mesmerized by its dazzling technological and scientific advances. Extraordinary scientific and medical discoveries, immense industrial power, the inventions of airplanes and cars, new forms of instantaneous communication, television, computers—all tell us of our increasing power over distance and time, our expanding capacity for knowledge and interaction. The conventional wisdom of our age is that we suffer from information overload. How does that fit with the message of the unconscious? Can we accept the gaps in our understanding, the built-in limits to our knowledge, the shadow of inevitable darkness that accompanies us everywhere?

THE FAILURE OF PSYCHOANALYSIS

The profession Freud founded protected and developed his ideas. But it also restricted their development. It aimed to become a medical subspecialty—just as Freud feared it would—and succeeded in becoming technocratic and insular. Freud went on in the declining years of his life not only to revise his theories but also to write boldly on the conflicts underlying civilization, on religion, on leadership and groups. But his profession focused on rooting out internal dissidents, proscribing new ideas not directly linked to its founder, and slowly moving to consolidate its hold over the field of mental health.

After World War II, psychoanalysts succeeded in establishing hegemony over psychotherapy, controlling departments of psychiatry in hospitals and medical schools, and convincing the public that they were the legitimate experts in this realm to which only they had the keys. Candidates flocked to institutes for training, which expanded and proliferated. New journals were published and new associations formed. To be sure, there were dissident voices and complaints. But in the aftermath of the war, psychotherapy boomed and psychoanalysis was its dominant voice. Even the dissidents profited as the rising tide lifted all boats.

The decline, beginning in the 1960s, became apparent in departments of psychiatry in the 1970s. Alienated by the dogmatic certainties of their psychoanalytic colleagues and suspicious of their claims, many psychiatrists began developing shorter behavioral treatments and aggressively searching for effective drugs. Gradually but inexorably, psychoanalysts who had been heads of departments and deans were replaced; fewer psychiatrists went on for psychoanalytic training. The National Institute of Mental Health (NIMH), which made twenty-eight grants to psychoanalytic projects between 1953 and 1962, after 1978 made none. In 1980, the American Psychiatric Association adopted a new diagnostic framework that entirely eliminated psychoanalytic terminology and concepts. Psychoanalysis, which had claimed psychiatry for its own, lost its grip on the profession.

Then psychologists began to turn away. In 1961, over 40 percent of clinical psychologists had described themselves as "psychodynamic." Fifteen years later, that percentage dropped to under 20, and now it is even less. Gradually, fewer graduate programs taught psychoanalytic theories to aspiring psychologists, and fewer graduate students identified themselves as having a psychoanalytic orientation. By 1999, *The American Psychologist* reported that psychoanalysis was little cited outside of psychoanalytic journals, concluding that it is a self-contained camp. As one researcher recently put it: "Psychoanalysis is now on the fringe of scientific psychology, accepted by few and ignored by many."[5]

In the last ten or fifteen years, this steep decline has become a collapse. Informal surveys suggest that most analysts today have one or two patients in psychoanalysis. A former president of the American Psychoanalytic Association estimates that between 40 and 50 percent of analysts in the association have no analytic cases at all. Candidates no longer seek training in the numbers or with the competitive avidity of the past; in 2001, sixty-five candidates entered training in the institutes of the American Psychoanalytic Association, down from an average of 116 during the previous three years, and way down from earlier years. The circulation figures of journals are significantly depressed, and the publication of books has declined drastically. Professional organizations face aging members and fewer applicants.[6]

Psychoanalysis has lost stature in the scientific community as well. Researchers once committed to finding evidence for its key theories have largely abandoned their efforts. Philosophers of science have attacked it for either failing to verify its claims or for making claims not subject to verification—hallmarks, as they see it, of "pseudo-science."[7]

Why this collapse? The numbers are irrefutable, but what is the reason? The profession of psychoanalysis itself bears much of the blame. It became arrogant and complacent toward other professionals in the burgeoning field of mental health; psychoanalysts' colleagues became resentful and dismissive in turn. Many psychoanalysts, believing they had the final word on the unconscious, alienated patients with their rigidity and smugness. Training institutes, inwardly focused and incestuous, became unwilling and unable to adapt. Psychoanalysts constructed, in effect, a cage of institutions, policies, and habits for itself, a kind of protective imprisonment.

Becoming an end in itself, the profession of psychoanalysis lost interest in the revolution that had spawned it. It became respectable, conventional. Worse, it ossified into a set of dogmas, orthodox beliefs that sapped its ability to generate new ideas. It demanded conformity, and discouraged new concepts. Its practices, more concerned with maintaining control than adapting to new discoveries, became repressive.[8]

But the larger answer to the question of why the profession collapsed is that the world changed, though not in the obvious ways of political conflict or economic depression. Indeed, one of the paradoxes of the history of psychoanalysis has been how it was able to survive and even thrive in conditions of worldwide disaster. The changes that had such a profound impact on psychoanalysis have been subtle and incremental shifts in our economic and political arrangements, shifts that moment by moment were easy to ignore but which cumulatively transformed our social landscape. Operating in the background, these

changes have influenced all the professions, but they have had a particularly devastating influence on the traditional forms of psychoanalytic practice.

There have been three major shifts: first, a collapse of trust in traditional authorities, all the forms of authority essential to managing
social relationships, but particularly the authority required by professionals; second, profound changes in our attitudes toward time,
affecting how we live and work, but also the psychoanalytic requirement for long and frequent sessions; and third, the new economy of
global competition, in which all services are being reduced to commodities forced to compete in the marketplace.

Let me start with the issue of authority, our willingness to accept the control of others as legitimate. As Hannah Arendt pointed
out, authority operates between the extremes of coercion and per-
suasion: it has failed if people have to be forced to obey out of fear.
On the other hand, it is not working if people have to be continuously persuaded to comply. Our communities, organizations, or
governments cannot function without the exercise of a force that is
felt to be legitimate, at least to some degree, a power that can be
taken for granted.[9]

This is a general problem in the modern world as all traditional
forms of authority have been undermined by wars, revolutions, and
economic upheavals. Genuine legitimacy is hard to find. Moreover,
corruption among those entrusted with authority is widespread. In-
dictments of government officials occur frequently. Corporate executives, preoccupied with profit, are seen as indifferent to the needs of
the public, or even as conspirators who subvert the law or thieves
who loot their own coffers. Political figures, notoriously, are controlled
by lobbyists and special interests. It is not clear if corruption or ve-
nality is greater now than ever, but today those who have authority
or who attempt to exercise it inevitably arouse mistrust and skepticism. (The other side of this, of course, is an enhanced gullibility and
a craving for fundamentalist purity and certainty.)

This failure of authority is particularly problematic in the professions. Entrusted with a high degree of control in determining their own standards of competence and ethical standards, professionals depend on the public's perception of their integrity. But recently there are countless revelations of religious leaders who turn out to have been sexual predators, as well as their superiors who have protected them. Increasingly, lawyers and doctors are suspected of putting their own interests ahead of their clients'. Accountants fudge their numbers to accommodate the firms that hire them. Teachers cannot be counted on to teach. And so on. The professions, which painstakingly achieved stability and acceptance over the past century, have lost much of their credibility.[10]

Psychoanalysis has had its own catastrophic failure of authority. The leadership that Freud and his followers exercised over the profession, amounting to authoritarian control as they censored innovation and exiled dissidents, has gradually given way, though not without a substantial legacy of resentment and bitterness. And the idealizations that encrusted Freud have worn thin. Biographers and scholars scrutinizing his life uncovered a number of highly problematic issues: Freud's misrepresentations of his early researches; his strained and seemingly ungrateful relationship with his early mentor, Breuer, the coauthor of the pioneering *Studies in Hysteria*; a possible affair with his sister-in-law; his analysis of his daughter Anna; his condoning of ethical violations by followers; and so forth.[11] Moreover, custodians of analytic history have proved to be secretive and manipulative, as well as foolish and petty, as revealed by Janet Malcolm as well as Jeffrey Masson, former director of the Freud Archives, in his vindictive and iconoclastic behind-the-scenes account. Others have worked to dispel the myths of Freud's uniqueness.[12]

No public figure is likely to withstand the onslaught of such scrutiny, but Freud was particularly vulnerable because his authority had been so absolute. Indeed, for many years it seemed an article of psychoanalytic faith that Freud had anticipated every significant analytic concept, or else it was an error. No one was allowed to challenge or to eclipse the master; no deviation was to be tolerated.

Freud suffered a decline in his stature as a world historical figure as well. No doubt the "Freud bashers" contributed to this development, but larger historical developments sealed his fate. With the lessening and eventual end of the cold war and the corresponding "end of ideology," both Freud and Marx lost their significance as dominant intellectual authorities. If "Freud is Dead," as our mass media have proclaimed, it is partly because all our gods have died.

How, then, to persuade patients to submit to the rather strong and unusual demands of the psychoanalyst? In this climate of mistrust, how can they accept what have been some of the standard conditions of psychoanalytic treatment: confiding their most secretive thoughts to their analyst, accepting that their questions will not be answered, relinquishing control of their statements, allowing their minds to wander while their painful feelings and symptoms become objects of their analyst's scrutiny and they wait for a response? Faith of that kind is harder and harder to come by. To be sure, many analysts have learned to work at earning their authority with patients, developing trust rather than taking it for granted. Recent generations are far more flexible and less inclined to be authoritarian. But that is a shift in what many had come to understand about how psychoanalysis works.

Along with this change in our attitudes toward authority has come a second change: an alteration in our experience of time. The world now runs on one clock, and it runs faster, with instantaneous digital communication and global trade linking us in an expanding community of ideas and images.

These pressures particularly afflict Americans, but as global competition increasingly sets the standards for work life, they are affecting everyone. They disrupt families; they eat into the leisure time required for friendship, and for activities that have traditionally provided opportunities for restoration and reflection. The pace of the modern world no longer seems compatible with the long, drawn-out, open-ended processes of free association and reverie that have long been seen as essential elements of psychoanalytic process. In this context, as the Italian psychoanalysts Antonio Suman and Antonino Brignone have pointed out: "Suggesting four or five sessions a week of psychoanalytic treatment to a patient who does not belong to the profession is increasingly being perceived as being 'out of step' with the times, or as being a request on the part of the analyst for complete submission, or as an implicit acceptance that the analyst is in control of the patient's whole life."[13]

Time is changing in other ways as well. Digital technology makes the reproduction of visual and aural experiences commonplace. As a result, experience itself has become unmoored from its anchorages in time and space. Time is no longer something we feel subject to, some greater force to which we must submit. Today, in the age of TiVo and instant replays, time can be seen as something to be manipulated and controlled.

All of this is making it apparent, as we shall see, that the "new unconscious" is not about time so much as it is about reflection. As Malcolm Gladwell has recently argued in his best-selling book *Blink*, many unconscious processes that lead to insight and understanding— as well as deception and error—occur in a flash. The unconscious does not require time in which to be uncovered; it requires detachment and distance to see what otherwise might remain hidden. It requires attention and insight.

The great benefit of time in exploring the unconscious has been in overcoming resistance to seeing and accepting what is buried. As psychotherapists quickly learn, there is little point in telling patients what they do not wish to know until they are ready to hear; often they need to come upon it themselves. The mere fact that time now is in such short supply intensifies the quest for efficient exploration.

The key fact, though, is that the unconscious is not to be found in time or in space, though we use metaphors of distance and detachment to describe it. It is about the mind, a mind that may be based in the brain but, as we understand now, cannot be precisely located or clearly bounded.

The third major change has been the extraordinary rise of global competition, with the pervasive effect of increasing pressures to cut costs, improve efficiency, and turn services into commodities than can be quantified and controlled.

Today most of us are working harder than ever before, simply trying to maintain our standards of living. Typically, in families with children, both parents now hold down jobs to make ends meet or to acquire the goods and services that have come to seem essential. Corporations relentlessly cut back on expenses, downsizing or outsourcing to meet the expectations of investors. Governments are pressured into curtailing social safety nets. Inevitably the levels of anxiety and stress among workers go up.

Moreover, as services become streamlined and automated, digitized and distributed, we increasingly lose touch with those on whom we rely for help. Robots may not repair our washing machines yet, but computers answer our calls, schedule appointments, follow up with reminders, ask for evaluation, and send our invoices. Increasingly, help is a commodity that business and government are working to produce more and more cheaply.

Psychotherapy is one of the services affected by these trends. It has become one of the major growth industries of our time, no doubt because heightened competition takes its toll on individuals, exacerbating personal difficulties but also creating new sources of strain. People want and need help, and they turn to psychotherapists for understanding and guidance.

Recent studies have suggested that 50 percent of all Americans will suffer from mental illness sometime in their lives.[14] And this matters not only to the individuals who suffer but also to the economy that absorbs the loss of their productivity. Rising conflict and stress produce inevitable effects of physical illness, absenteeism, and burnout. It is also likely that more people today are experiencing depression, anxiety, and rage—and asking for help from an expanding range of practitioners who are being asked, in turn, to provide more effective services at cheaper prices.

At the same time that the strains of heightened competition are creating an increased need for psychotherapy, the same pressures are afflicting psychotherapists, forcing them to become more efficient in the services they provide. It is not just that insurance companies and hospitals are engaged in continuous evaluations and cost/benefit analyses; we are living in a system that everywhere reminds us of comparative expenses, competitive pricing, and cheaper alternative products. For better or for worse, people now want to know—and are pressured to account for—what they will be getting for their money. Indeed, the studies just cited, predicting the increase in the incidence of mental illness, themselves reflect competitive pressures within an industry aggressively seeking to justify costs and increase market share; mental health providers must come up with compelling arguments and statistics to compete for scarce dollars.

In recent years, as we saw, the robust market for psychotherapy has been devastating to psychoanalysis. A survey initiated by the American Psychoanalytic Association found that groups composed of mental health professionals—psychiatrists, psychologists, and social workers—associated psychoanalysis with words like "rigid," "restrictive," "time consuming," and "expensive." Psychoanalysts were seen as "passive," "intellectualized," and "uninvolved." Psychoanalysis was "cult-like," "secretive," "authoritarian," and "esoteric." But the most damning indictment by these mental health colleagues was that no one was inclined to recommend psychoanalysis.[15] In this scenario, drugs may be increasingly attractive as a treatment because they require less time to dispense and monitor. General practitioners and family physicians now routinely prescribe psychotropic medications, a development fueled by the advertising of drug companies aimed directly at consumers. Moreover, consumers often welcome this, embarrassed to disclose their mental suffering to strangers or afraid of the stigma attached to consulting professional therapists.

While drugs can be effective in relieving symptoms and compensating for neural dysfunctions, it is becoming more and more apparent that they are most effective in conjunction with psychotherapies that work to uncover underlying conflicts. If the unconscious meaning of mental suffering remains unaffected by treatment, there can be little more than superficial, temporary progress.[16]

This is true as well for the behavioral and cognitive treatments that have been promoted as brief and effective.[17] As we shall see, psychotherapists who sought shortcuts are discovering the complexities of unconscious motivation and resistances that psychoanalysts have known about all along. Cognitive and behavioral therapists, seeking to work with patients' rational ideas and actual behavior, are rediscovering the impact of unacknowledged aspects of their relationships with their patients and the powerful persistence of suppressed patterns of thought.

In short, the heightened pressure of competition has increased stress in the workplace and undermined established ways of responding to it, but it has called for new and more efficient services. A better understanding of unconscious process can aid those struggling with these heightened pressures, though it is important to bear in mind that the unconscious itself cannot easily be distilled into particular commodities. Consultants often speak of providing services "off the shelf," standardized to meet specific types of problems. They too face pressures to streamline their services, to predict costs and ensure outcomes. But it is the nature of the unconscious to resist prediction and generalization. It requires process and exploration. Can our culture tolerate the difference to gain the understanding it needs?

THE UNCONSCIOUS NOW

This book sets out to refresh and renew our understanding of the unconscious. It seeks to build on new research and recent discoveries, and, in the process, rescue our thinking about the unconscious from the dying hand of psychoanalysis, to make it more widely accessible and useful.

The essence of Freud's radical concept still holds: driven by motives we do not understand, we are not in control of our own behavior. Moreover, as he pointed out, we are divided against ourselves, filled with contradiction and conflict. We dissemble and mislead others, but we start out by deceiving ourselves. We aim to achieve goals we disclaim and, even, at times, sincerely disavow. We collude with each other and we contend against each other, usually without noticing what we are about. But it is also true that the unconscious helps us to adapt more effectively than our conscious minds ever could, detecting information that is vital to our survival and well-being. We are smarter because of it, more intuitive and creative, but, under its influence, we can also be more stupid and venal, prone to disastrous mistakes.

Today, the unconscious is being explored by professionals eager to find explanations for events that elude conventional understanding. Specialists in education are focusing on the social and emotional aspects of child development, not just the teaching of ABCs. They worry about the obscure forces that lead to bullies and to cliques, to pregnancies and school violence. Focusing merely on scores from standardized tests is not enough. Experts in public health today must think of the consequences of psychological trauma for the victims of disaster, not simply broken limbs, bandages, and shelter. Policy experts must contend with how their perceptions and debates can be suffused by unconscious assumptions and their effectiveness undermined.

Economists, who used to rely on the concept of rational decision making to account for the behavior of markets, have become more "psychological" in their thinking as it becomes more and more clear that neither consumers nor producers are entirely rational in their behavior. Politics has also become a fertile field for research, as election campaigns often depend on managing perceptions and feelings voters do not know they have. And so much is at stake. Researchers are getting into the business of political consulting.

Many top business schools here and in Europe have had psychoanalysts on their faculties for years, providing help in probing the hidden dilemmas of leadership. Today, more and more executives, faced with the stress of constantly increasing expectations and changing demands, turn to psychoanalysts and psychologically sophisticated coaches for help. Those working to help businesses adapt to shifting environments, moreover, are discovering hidden resistances to organizational change. Lacking an understanding of unconscious dynamics in the workplace becomes an impediment to the implementation of new designs for work. As a result, a profession of psychoanalytically informed consultants is emerging.

More and more sophisticated services are being developed to respond to our increasingly complex awareness of the layers and the depth of human behavior. And while they increase, new problems and new tragedies leap to the front page, reminding us of how much we still do not understand. What drives some schoolchildren to massacre their schoolmates, and what keeps their classmates from speaking about what they know? How can corporate executives collude in illegal schemes that cannot be sustained, that are doomed to be uncovered or to fail? How can experienced government officials with access to sophisticated intelligence ignore key information and make disastrous decisions? Why are advertisers, media specialists, and spin doctors more influential in our politics than policy makers? What drives a sect to commit mass suicide?

Many psychoanalysts are working to understand such questions. Trained to probe into the murky realms of half-knowledge and denial, the unwanted truths and disclaimed perceptions that form the unconscious layers of human motivation, they see opportunities to expand the scope of their work. Others have trained themselves to work with organizations and schools, government agencies, executives, boards of directors, and others, and they struggle to grasp the paradoxical and self-defeating human behaviors they encounter.

Let me give a brief but prominent example. The U.S. Senate Select Committee on Intelligence, investigating the disastrously misleading intelligence reports about weapons of mass destruction in Iraq, concluded that the failure was the result of an unconscious psychological process, "groupthink." In this process dissenting ideas are discounted and neglected in order to allow for the emergence of a group norm, a dominant idea that, unconsciously, acts to suppress and eclipse all other ideas. Several sets of motivations combine to support groupthink: the desire to please the leader, the drive for group cohesiveness, and the craving for certainty in highly charged and complex circumstances.

Irving Janis, a Yale sociologist, developed this concept originally using research into the decision-making process that led to President Kennedy's invasion of the Bay of Pigs in 1962. He extended it to account for other disasters of inattention such as the run up to Pearl Harbor and the escalation of the Vietnam War, where intelligence and counterarguments were similarly discounted and suppressed; it describes the "bunker mentality" that characterized the responses of President Nixon and his advisors during Watergate. Groupthink also helps to account for many recent corporate scandals, such as Enron, where top executives succeeded in convincing themselves that their illegal manipulation of accounts would go unnoticed.[18]

This work on unconscious collusion in presidential administrations was compelling to the Senate Select Committee and its staff members searching for explanations for this momentous failure. The classic conditions for groupthink were here: a leader who knew what he wanted to hear, pressure to come to a conclusion in the face of ambiguous data, and intelligence agencies that were all too willing to selectively dismiss, forget, or simply avoid thinking about the significant evidence that did not support the case they more and more wanted to make. Unconsciously responding to these pressures, they induced a false certainty among themselves.

Janis is not a psychoanalyst. Many academics and consultants exploring the unconscious dimensions of behavior are not. On the other hand, much of this work goes on under the name of "applied psychoanalysis," a sprawling, jerry-built assemblage of diverse enterprises that has grown up around the margins of the psychoanalytic establishment. Standards vary and are often lax; disputes are rife. And yet there is an undeniable vitality in this burgeoning chaos. Apart from the mainstream orthodox institutions of psychoanalysis, this new world has branched out, expanded and eluded the deadening hand of its control.[19]

This book is a kind of primer to this burgeoning new world of thought, a survey of what is now being done in this dispersed and fragmented field. On the other hand, it is not written by an outsider. I live and work in the midst of the developments I describe. Wherever possible, I include examples from my own work as well as from my knowledge of the work of colleagues. My understanding is informed by personal experience, and my hope is that this experience will make the book's contents clearer and more accessible to the reader as well.

The "new unconscious" is not a new phenomenon. The unconscious aspects of social relations, politics, and organizations have been there all along. The future of work with the unconscious is one of extraordinary opportunity and promise for those willing to face its daunting obstacles and difficulties and able to tolerate its ambiguities and uncertainties. And, who knows, maybe even psychoanalysis will rejoin the effort.

One
THE NEW UNCONSCIOUS
From the Body to the Person

◼

THE PROBLEM OF CONSCIOUSNESS

The study of consciousness—or the "problem of consciousness," as it has come to be known—is highly controversial and contentious. John Searle, the philosopher, noted that when he first became interested in consciousness, now about thirty years ago, "most people in the neurosciences did not regard consciousness as a genuine scientific question at all." He recalled a renowned neuroscientist telling him, "It is okay to be interested in consciousness, but get tenure first."[1] All that has changed; where there was neglect there is now competition and controversy, programs and departments, and libraries of books and journals. Today, the study of consciousness attracts philosophers, psychologists, neurologists, neuroscientists, specialists in artificial intelligence (AI), developmental biologists, computer scientists, and information theorists.

One reason for this change is renewed interest in the unconscious. Consciousness is now seen to sit on top of vast territories of mind in which mental data are silently processed. Even academic psychology, once committed to the study of "behavior" that could be observed and measured, is taking note of this shift in focus. More and more studies detect in observable behavior the critical role played by influences and motives that operate outside of awareness. Such research not only enlarges our understanding of why people act as they do, but also calls into question the data of previous studies, based on the self-reporting of subjects. We are no longer so sure that people can reliably describe their feelings and motives. According to one psychologist, the brain is capable of processing only forty of the 11 million bits of information it receives from our senses each second. Without unconscious screening, consciousness would be overwhelmed.[2]

A new field, cognitive science, forged by an alliance between neuroscientists and philosophers, has staked out a parallel territory for investigation. According to George Lakoff and Mark Johnson, only 5 percent of our ideas reach consciousness: "Moreover, the 95 percent below the surface of conscious awareness shapes and structures all conscious thought. If the cognitive unconscious were not there doing this shaping, there would be no conscious thought."[3]

In another development, the study of complexity or "chaos" expands our understanding of the self-organizing properties of matter. That is, things themselves have a way of organizing into stable patterns. The neurons that make up the brain develop their own structures; individuals working together fall into patterns. Meaning emerges from process. We do not need a creator or a designer in order to make intricate and efficient systems. Indeed, it is becoming more and more apparent, on the contrary, that often it is when we let things take their own course that we find out what actually works. Conscious intent may not always be up to the job.[4]

Paralleling this new interest in the role of the unconscious in understanding consciousness, there is a developing consensus that the development of human consciousness must have helped in our evolutionary struggle. As Antonio Damasio, perhaps our foremost neurologist, has put it, "Consciousness, when it appears in human evolution, announces the dawn of individual forethought."[5] Our ability to generate images of reality in order to guide actions has made the struggle for survival immensely more effective.

Current approachs to consciousness depart significantly from computer-based theories about information processing. At the time computers first became widely available, it seemed a form of common sense to think of our brains as the "hardware" (or "wetware") on which the "software" of programs were inscribed, enabling us to process the input of our senses. That analogy was attractive to those working in AI, who were trying to capitalize on the promise computers seemed to offer of enlarging the human capacity for intelligent thought. But it has become more and more apparent that the analogy does not hold.

Gerald Edelman, the Nobel Prize–winning neurobiologist, for one, has pointed out two major defects in that approach. First, sensory input is not simple and unambiguous data; it is processed and constructed from the start. Second, the ways in which the brain processes data are variable and plastic; we do not have "programs" governed by invariant logic. For Edelman, "the conclusion is clear:"

> The brains of higher level animals autonomously construct patterned responses to environments that are full of novelty. They do not do this the way a computer does—using formal rules governed by explicit, unambiguous instructions or input signals. Once more with feeling: the brain is not a computer, and the world is not a piece of tape.[6]

Thinking of consciousness as an evolutionary development suggests two crucial ideas. First, the brain is an integral part of the body, receiving signals from and sending signals to all parts of it. Emotions alert us to the dangers we face as well as to opportunities that exist for food, shelter, and comfort. Emotions are indicators of vital information about the world. Moreover, they arouse and motivate the body to act on that information. Consciousness not only informs us; it engages us in reality.[7]

Second, the consciousness we employ today is layered, built up on the basis of earlier versions of consciousness that still function, and the layers continuously interact with each other. This layering of consciousness helps us to account for the diversity and contradictory features of conscious phenomena. Human consciousness, on the one hand, accounts for our highest intellectual and cultural achievements, our poems, novels, and philosophical texts. It also underlies our capacity to construct the individual and social narratives essential to our understanding of who we are. At the same time, it is about living in the moment, noticing danger and opportunity as they occur. It is not at all apparent to common sense how these levels relate to each other, and yet we direct our attention across these levels continuously. Just as we do not exist in separate worlds, our awareness of those worlds is not segregated. But different levels of consciousness provide us with different kinds of information that are not always smoothly articulated with each other.

Antonio Damasio conceptualizes a core consciousness and an extended autobiographical consciousness. *Core consciousness* is a continuous processing of images of the world and of the body that corresponds to William James's concept of the stream of consciousness. Most of its contents are continuously refreshed by present experience. Demasio emphasizes (his own italics), *"It is the very evidence, the unvarnished sense of our individual organism in the act of knowing."* Extended or *autobiographical consciousness*, on the other hand, architecturally connected to this core, consists of an extended array of facts and memories that accumulate over time and can be refashioned by experience. To oversimplify, autobiographical consciousness is about who we are, while core consciousness, more simply, reflects that we are and that we keep on being.[8]

Gerald Edelman has proposed a similar distinction between what he calls primary consciousness, focused on the "remembered present," what is happening to us as it is happening, and higher-order consciousness, which uses language to construct more complex meanings.[9] Core or primary consciousness is concerned with our immediate environment and the tangible dangers and opportunities it provides. Extended or higher-order consciousness joins us to our historical and social worlds, monitoring our capacity to fit into our families and work groups, to regulate our identities and self-esteem, providing our lives with meaning, informing us of our links with others.

Along similar lines, Daniel Dennett speculates that human consciousness evolved, first, through the plasticity of the brain, allowing it to learn new adaptive behaviors in its immediate environment and, then, through the development of "memes," complex ideas, often based on language, that provide the basis for cultural evolution.[10]

The interplay between these levels of consciousness helps us to grasp the complexity of our world, but it also provides us with differing and sometimes conflicting sets of information. It is the job of consciousness to synthesize and integrate these different interests and the divergent sets of information each provides, but it clearly is more than can be consistently accomplished. As a result, for all its utility and mysterious complexity, consciousness is full of defects. The commonsense view—largely unchallenged throughout our history— is that consciousness presents us with a picture of how things are "out there" that we are able to view "inside" our minds. Philosophers have called this view the Cartesian theater; the experience of viewing the world in our minds presupposes a division, on the one hand, between the materialistic world of real objects that have substance and weight, and, on the other, the inner, nonmaterialistic mind that constructs representations of those objects and reacts. This dualism no longer sits comfortably with most scientists and philosophers. Moreover, the philosophical dilemma of dualism leads us to two highly practical problems: misleading appearances of coherence in the world and illusions of agency in the self.

First off, the picture we view in our Cartesian theater imposes a false unity on our experience. We see a coherent world, seemingly available for scrutiny and systematic thought, but that world does not actually map onto reality. This is the "user illusion," as it has sometimes been called, based on the analogy of our relationship with our computers where we interface with pictures and programs, not the thing itself. As Edelman has put it, "The take-home lesson is that our body, our brain, and our consciousness did not evolve to yield a scientific picture of the world."[11]

Damasio has endorsed Dennett's multiple-drafts model of consciousness to reflect the complexity of how consciousness is actually constructed. Our experience, in the Cartesian theater, presents a simple and coherent view of the world because the multiple drafts of reality have been invisibly edited and synthesized. We are unaware of the machinery that goes into its construction. To present coherent messages suitable for action, vast stores of information that cannot be processed are discarded. Moreover, what is missing, the gaps, are filled in by inference or memory. What we experience consciously, in other words, is a simulation, a fiction.

Psychologists refer to "accessibility" to describe what gets included in the final edit, but many factors enter into the accessibility of information: how recent and how frequent our exposure to it has been, how relevant it is to the actions we are considering, how frequently it has been used in the past, how it makes us feel. This latter point accounts for the relative ease with which information that makes us uncomfortable or that does not accord with our idealized versions of ourselves tends to be discarded. As the psychologist Timothy Wilson has put it, "We are masterly spin doctors, rationalizers, and justifiers of threatening information."[12]

Dramatic examples of such editing are described in the research on split brains, where neurosurgeons have severed the connections between the left and right hemispheres in order to prevent epileptic seizures. Joseph LeDoux, describing this research, noted that patients inevitably compensated for what they did not understand about their own behavior: "Time after time, the left hemisphere made up explanations as if it knew why the response was performed. For example, if we instructed the right hemisphere to wave, the patient would wave. When we asked him why he was waving, he said he thought he saw someone he knew."[13] The lesson is that, however impaired, the brain does not cease its sometimes heroic efforts to impose unity and coherence on the information it processes.

The second set of illusions has to do with agency. Consciousness fosters the belief that we are in charge of our actions, but the evidence of neurobiology suggests that most of our decisions are made automatically. Our reactions to events are underway before we become aware of them. As Walter J. Freeman has put it, "Taking responsibility for one's self is more like trying to control one's teenager than one's automobile."[14]

Sometimes it is obvious that making something conscious impedes our reactions to events. LeDoux has noted that "prepackaged emotions" quickly elicit reactions to danger that aid survival, a point that Darwin also made. If we see a stick that moves, our bodies do not stop to figure out if it is a snake before starting to flee.[15]

Indeed, our brains often embark on actions or construe reactions to events without our needing to know what we are doing. Almost fifty years ago, Michael Polanyi pointed out the importance of "tacit knowledge," knowledge we take for granted. When we recognize familiar faces, for example, we rely upon such knowledge without knowing we possess it. More recently, psychologists have distinguished between implicit and explicit memory, highlighting the importance in our daily lives of the information we process subliminally, without consciousness. Similarly, they have studied procedural memory, the built-in sets of perceptions and skills that are required for riding a bicycle or driving a car.[16]

But many have argued more broadly that these are merely particular instances of a general truth: consciousness always arises after the fact of perception and response. Freeman notes that awareness "continually runs to catch up with the self, half a second late but backdated." Damasio puts it this way: "We are always hopelessly late for consciousness, and because we all suffer from the same tardiness, no one notices it."[17] In other words consciousness arises from the information we have received, the interpretations we have constructed, and the decisions we have already made. Our bodies and brains have processed that information and constructed a response that is already set in motion when we become aware of it. The evolutionary value of consciousness turns out to be, from this perspective, not in the capacity it provides for us to decide on our actions in advance so much as the opportunity to reflect on the world we perceive and plan new courses of action, after the fact. With it, we can inhibit or alter our behavior, and we can plan better responses for the future. As Damasio put it in the passage quoted earlier, the evolutionary benefit is "forethought."

This brief account of some of the more salient shortcomings of consciousness sets the stage now for a more extended survey of the domains of the unconscious. This chapter surveys the overlapping (and therefore imprecise) areas of exploration where the new unconscious is being mapped out. These are areas of study that are still under construction.

The seven domains identified here are not precisely demarcated. They are domains of inquiry, areas within which specialists have collaborated to do research and build theory; they are not delineated areas in the brain. The knowledge these domains of inquiry contain is distributed and widely available but sometimes not recognized or understood by those working within other domains. The boundaries that limit us today are our own disciplinary or professional definitions.

The rest of this chapter describes the domains more traditionally associated with individual bodies and minds. Chapter Two describes the domains thought of as more interpersonal and social. The distinction is crude and inadequate, as we shall see, reflecting the boundaries around different disciplines rather than the phenomena themselves. The research described in this chapter, by and large, has led to the amassing of considerable scientific evidence in recent years. The interpersonal and social domains have elicited less attention, but are no less real.

How and what can we know about this elusive subject, the unconscious? Can we even define what the unconscious is? (That one author has listed as many as sixteen definitions points to the slipperiness of the subject, which seems to defy our attempts at precision.[18]) In turning our attention to the unconscious, we find ourselves focusing on the permeable and shifting boundary between what is available to thought and what is usually not.

THE AUTONOMIC NERVOUS SYSTEM

Providing for the homeostatic regulation of the body, the autonomic nervous system (ANS) keeps in balance the key functions of our hearts, lungs, digestive tracts, veins, arteries, and so on—automatically, for the most part. Occasionally, actions are required to sustain homeostasis and the system sends signals for action: when we get hungry, we eat; pressure builds up in the bladder, requiring urination; the awareness of cold drives us to find a sweater; and so forth. When acts of conscious intention are required, the need breaks through to awareness, usually through some form of discomfort. Largely, however, the system runs itself without demanding attention.

But consciousness can go the other way. We can tune into this realm of automatic regulation in order to act upon the body. For centuries, yogis and mystics have concentrated on their breathing, using that form of meditation in order to attain transcendent states of mind beyond pain and suffering. Sufis have induced trance-like states through dancing, hermits have cultivated visions through fasting and sensory deprivation, Tibetan monks have achieved astounding control over their bodily temperature and need for food. No doubt in the days when domestic comfort and security were primitive, painkillers limited, and insecurity rampant, a premium was placed on achieving control of the needs of the body through mental agility and manipulation.

The primary purpose of such meditative techniques appears to have been the search for some form of transcendence or detachment, an effort to reach another realm of consciousness where we are less susceptible to the perturbations of insecurity and fear. Perhaps because the struggle to master such techniques required such significant effort and discipline, these techniques tended to be put in the service of long-term religious or spiritual goals. But today science has developed an array of feedback technologies to achieve control over the ANS for more limited purposes. Biofeedback enables patients to manage their blood pressure, heart rate, skin temperature, and muscle tension. It is proving useful in the treatment of such conditions as epilepsy, asthma, incontinence, irritable bowel syndrome, headaches, high blood pressure, and cardiac arrhythmias. Neurofeedback has gained popularity in recent years as a treatment for attention deficit disorder, and is being studied as a potential treatment for anxiety, depression, and drug addiction.

Psychosomatic medicine has sensitized us to the value of intervening consciously to gain more control over blood pressure, headaches, and sleep disorders. Meditation, which now can be studied scientifically through brain imaging techniques, shows powerful influences on bodily processes. Moreover, manipulating consciousness has proven effective in altering the ANS. The so-called placebo effect demonstrates the influence of belief over behavior, and studies have similarly demonstrated that certain convictions affect rates of healing in patients recovering from wounds. In short, the ANS itself is permeable to consciousness and can be manipulated. Even our automatic, self-regulating or "vegetative" systems can be changed through conscious efforts. This finding could be particularly valuable for those who are subject to continual high levels of stress. Greater control of the ANS promises more effective relief. Since the ANS is always involved in our emotional lives, a topic we will get to shortly, such techniques can also be valuable for those seeking better management of their erratic emotional lives.

THE COGNITIVE UNCONSCIOUS

Consciousness may not grasp all the data we receive and the responses we construct, but the cognitive unconscious works constantly to keep us informed, abreast of what adaptation requires that we know about our environment. As the psychologist Timothy Wilson wrote, the cognitive unconscious "plays a major executive role in our mental lives. It gathers information, interprets and evaluates, and sets goals in motion, quickly and efficiently."[19]

Part of this scanning consists of perceptual categorization, whereby the objects or events we encounter are continuously classified into familiar categories. As we gaze across a room, for example, we see chairs, tables, rugs, lamps, and so forth, each object being identified as the visual information we receive is linked with the concepts or generalizations we have previously formed. Such perceptual categories allow us to scan our environment quickly and see what we need to know—and detect what might require exceptional action. It is likely that animals similarly scan their environments and have concepts or categories to identify what they see, such as objects that could provide a meal, for example, or threaten danger. The information received and classified is sent out to other parts of the brain to elicit appropriate reactions, but all of this takes place without consciousness. For the most part, like other animals, we do not know or need to know we are doing this.

The interpersonal environment to which each of us has individually adapted seldom remains constant. As we grow, the learning we have acquired in the earliest phases of our lives needs to be replaced for us to adapt to new relationships as adolescents and adults. Moreover, as we develop, we need new and more flexible categories with which to identify the increasingly complex and differentiated world we encounter. As extended or autobiographical consciousness develops on top of core or primary consciousness, as language comes into play, and as extended consciousness grows more complex through education and experience, old categories and patterns need to be modified or superseded. As Freeman has pointed out, our ability to continue adapting to new circumstances requires that we "unlearn" old adaptations. But it is unclear how unlearning occurs and to what extent old adaptations are fully extinguished.

We know, for example, that the families in which we were reared tend to have an indelible impact on our behavior. Those we fall in love with, the relationships we go on to establish, and the employers we work for all tend to reflect our earlier efforts to get the attention and love we craved and avoid the rejection and neglect we feared. We have a strong predisposition to put new persons in the old categories, to reassert the old assumptions. We may succeed in our unconscious quest to find the match we seek, the one based on those we loved in the past. Of course, our new friend or mate is not the same as the prototype we have made from our past history. And yet often, we assume—and sometimes demand—that they act as we think they should, based on our old expectations. The reflexive and automatic patterns of behavior established at an early age become both guides and barriers to new relationships and the new possibilities they engender.[20]

Psychologists have demonstrated experimentally that people seek out and perceive these resemblances, even when the confirming or "matching" information is presented subliminally.[21] But psychoanalysts have known for years that these transferences occur. Since Freud's original discovery of the power of transference, it has become a key tool in psychoanalytic practice to try to elicit these old categories as they are being applied in the relationship with the analyst, and then help patients to see their anachronistic assumptions. Confronting and challenging these entrenched patterns is essential to helping patients adapt more readily to the real relationships they have in the present.

Psychoanalysts used to assume that transferences required special circumstances in order to be evoked: the detachment and neutrality of the analyst, the absence of real information, the regressive and protective atmosphere of the consulting room. But as many analysts have learned and as our new knowledge of the cognitive unconscious has shown, such transferences are entrenched and robust. Their targets are not just lovers and spouses, but also colleagues, employers, friends, and children. The stripped-down environment of their consulting rooms may help analysts perceive transference patterns, but patients reexperience or reenact them anywhere.

Other forms of psychotherapy also confront the power of entrenched patterns of adaptation. Traditionally, psychoanalysts have tended to favor the method of uncovering old patterns in order to dissipate their strength, though some have emphasized the need for new experience in bringing about change. But as we do not know definitively how the "unlearning" occurs that is essential to new adaptations, or why some patterns are more difficult to unlearn than others, it is likely that other techniques, focusing primarily on current beliefs or patterns of behavior, can also have significant impact. It may be useful to identify the old work of the cognitive unconscious and the way it has determined current patterns of adaptation, but it seems that new patterns can arise and replace the old without identifying such causes in the cognitive unconscious. Nor is reconstructing narratives of the past a guarantee that change will occur.

TWO CASES: AMOS AND MARILYN

Let me give a brief example from my own practice of psychotherapy. Amos was a business executive whose success was hampered by a deep-seated pattern of resisting control by others. Having grown up with parents who were alternately intrusive and neglectful, he had learned as a child to evade their sporadic efforts to discipline him. In his chaotic family environment, he often felt resentful and angry, but I suspect he was also fearful that conforming to his parents' unpredictable and shifting demands would not provide the security he craved; they did not really understand his needs and were not capable of responding appropriately. In his current life, this old pattern of learning to avoid control by others took the form of using time at work to surf the Internet, email his friends, plan trips, and so on—in short, to engage in activities that were clearly just for him and under his control alone. Though he showed that he grasped that it was only by fulfilling expectations on his job that he could achieve his own career goals, nevertheless he found himself unable to manage what he called "distractions." His unconscious adaptation to the circumstances of his childhood was powerful and deep. Moreover, his transference in this case was not to one authority figure; it was generalized to the workplace, to all forms of external control.

Control became an issue in his relationship with me as well. Badly wanting the help he believed I could provide, he knew that he would need to show up for his appointments, pay his bills, and so on. He quickly decided that my services belonged to him, so that he would not need to evade me as he would someone who had a claim on him. On the other hand, neither could he trust me. At the start, under the sway of the mistrust installed in his cognitive unconscious, his solution was to try to be fully in control of the interaction. Typically, he came to sessions with a list of problems he wanted my help in solving, and he would repeat the solutions we came to at the end. As much as possible, I tried to accept his conditions, while also pointing out that often the solutions we came up with turned out not to be as helpful as he had hoped. I introduced the metaphor of raft building to describe the frantic efforts we sometimes engaged in to cobble together strategies for his problems. As he gradually came to see that these strategies did not work, he was able to develop a better appreciation of the underlying problems with which he was contending, and he learned to trust me more.

In my work with Amos over several years, we were gradually able to identify the source of the problem and construct a plausible narrative to account for his fear of being controlled, but change has not been easy. As he gained some mastery over one distraction, another would take its place. Gradually, however, motivated by strong desires not only to please his coworkers but also to achieve financial security, he was able to reduce significantly these distractions and, more importantly, gradually create the internal discipline required to work more effectively.

Marilyn was also the child of a troubled family. As an adult she repeatedly got into abusive relationships with men, often having great difficulty in extricating herself even when she could see the ways in which she was being damaged. We had little difficulty tracing the origin of this pattern to her relationship with her seductive father to whom she had repeatedly turned in childhood for comfort as well as for protection from her cold and punitive mother. Father's empty promises of help together with his physically soothing hugs proved to be a powerful attraction to her, one that she turned to again and again throughout her childhood. The pattern was repeated in her adult life with other men who seemed to promise similar comfort. Though father never delivered on his promises to protect her and leave her mother—a pattern also replicated with the men Marilyn turned to as an adult—she never entirely gave up hope. She did not entirely believe him—as she also seldom believed the men with whom she got involved as an adult—but feeling isolated, without recourse to others, she kept alive the belief that she might succeed at last in finding the strategy that would get him for herself.

Marilyn also became, in her own evocative phrase, a "touch junkie." That is, roughly treated by her mother, while tenderly stroked by her seductive father, she repeatedly sought the soothing and calming effects of physical contact with others. As an adult, she became an adept seductress as a means of gratifying her hunger, and her craving for contact was an additional factor that kept her in abusive relationships. She also sought out massages, colonics, and other forms of physical care that soothed her.

Marilyn's case illustrates how these established cognitive patterns of adaptation, old categories of perception, do not exist in isolation from other unconscious systems. Her autonomic nervous system was affected by these early traumas, arousing in her a persistent need for soothing.

Amos, too, had significant difficulty managing the needs of his body. His sleep was erratic. He wolfed down his food. Frequently ill, he was wracked with anxiety about being able to care for himself, to remember what he needed to do, and to implement his plans. The narrative of his family background that we were able to construct helped us to explain this as well. At an early age, he had almost certainly not experienced the secure attachment to a nurturing figure that would have enabled him to establish his own self-regulating habits. He was still paying the developmental price of being brought up by erratic and inconsistent parents, too preoccupied with their own needs and fears to care for him during that early stage in his life when he was profoundly dependent on them.

Amos also had intense emotional upheavals. The cognitive problem associated with his resistance to control implicated yet another set of unconscious systems that we now need to turn our attention to, the systems of the emotions.

THE EMOTIONAL UNCONSCIOUS

The study of emotions has been hampered by long-standing cultural prejudices that they are not only dangerous but also unworthy of study; they distract us from our goals, they undermine reason, they subvert our values and ideals, and they lead to conflict. Even psychoanalysts, familiar as they are with human emotions through their daily practices, have neglected to incorporate an understanding of them into their theories. Preoccupied with more basic drives such as aggression and libido, they have tended to avoid the more subtle, complex, and nuanced realm of feeling.[22]

Darwin's observation that emotions are present in all higher species and his belief that they were critical in the struggle for survival in effect inaugurated the scientific study of the emotions. Damasio has made this point, more recently: "For certain classes of clearly dangerous or clearly valuable stimuli in the internal or external environment, evolution has assembled a matching answer in the form of emotion. . . . In other words, the biological 'purpose' of the emotions is clear, and emotions are not a dispensable luxury."[23]

It is uncertain how many discrete emotions we have, how best to classify them, or how to determine in what ways they are innate or learned. But there does seem to be increasing agreement that, having developed in the process of evolution, our emotions are not only indispensable but, like cognition, are largely organized outside of consciousness. They shape our behavior, but our awareness of them, like our awareness of our actions, is largely retrospective. As LeDoux put it, "The mental aspect of emotion, the feeling, is a slave to its physiology; not vice versa." He uses William James's example of encountering a bear: we see the bear, we start running, and as we run we become aware of our fear. Our behavioral reaction precedes our conscious emotional awareness. For this reason LeDoux and others have coined the term *emotional unconscious*.[24]

Emotions almost always overlap with cognitive processes because they are set in motion by meanings we construct through perceptions. As Damasio has argued, our "every image, [whether] actually perceived or recalled, is accompanied by some reaction from the apparatus of emotion."[25] In his view, consciousness itself is a product of an interaction between the organism and the environment; as the organism relates to an object in the environment, the confrontation with the object simultaneously effects a change in the organism. Just as our behavioral responses are constructed automatically by the cognitive unconscious, so our emotions are constructed automatically as feeling states linked to the meaning of what we perceive and our need to react. Somewhat like the ANS, our emotions are always in play—and almost always unconscious.

The "feeling of what happens," as Damasio has put it, underpins our awareness of the world, providing an unobtrusive basis for our actions.[26] It does not usually need to become conscious. When we stop to think, it is almost always about what is happening externally and what we should do about it. If there is danger, it is usually out there—along with enticements, puzzles, pleasures, and worries. Emotions, then, can be hard to detect and decode or unravel. For that reason, detecting emotions of which patients are unaware of is the stock-in-trade of psychotherapists.

Our continuing cultural bias against emotions, our belief that they are at best irrelevant and at worst dangerous and distracting, reinforces our tendency to keep emotions out of awareness. Those who focus largely on competition and mastery of the environment tend to neglect the information they receive about their innermost feelings. The negative information about our resistances to this pressure for achievement can be unwelcome, even as we struggle to overcome obstacles to success.

Psychotherapists know well how the arousal of emotion can be more than a distraction or an inconvenient reminder of something we would prefer to forget, becoming a danger in itself. For Marilyn, subject to repeated sexual arousal in her seductive attempts to enlist her father's protection and support, her sexual feelings became a source of fear. Because her father obviously welcomed and enjoyed her attentions, she was encouraged to continue; at the same time she also felt endangered. She did not believe she could count on him to restrain himself, and there is some reason to believe that she was correct. While she became an accomplished seductress and sought out repeated sexual encounters with men as an adolescent and adult, her primary objectives were to get men to protect her and provide soothing sensations of touch. Inside she was numb.

Amos was conscious of a continuing low level of anxiety in his life, a kind of ever-present background noise that sometimes became intrusive and distracting. This noise blocked out many of his other emotional responses, though there were occasional eruptions of rage, brought on when he felt thwarted while waiting for service in a store, for example, or checking in at an airline ticket counter. These tantrums embarrassed him because they were disproportionate to the occasion, and they interfered with his efforts to get the assistance he wanted.

Gradually, we were able to see how this behavior was a kind of transference, and to focus on his underlying fear that the help he needed was going to be withheld or offered in an aggressive or harmful manner. Reviewing these experiences gave us the opportunity to tease them apart, to find the anxiety beneath his rage. His rage, as he came to understand, was a largely futile attempt to reach the person who, he thought, did not care about his plight or understand his desperation.

Damasio has argued that we have essentially three levels of emotional experience: background emotions, analogous to moods or levels of engagement, pervading all our experience; emotions that are unconscious signals eliciting behavioral responses; and feelings, conscious emotions that are useful as a basis for planning. Amos's response to frustration, then, takes place against a background of anxiety and insecurity, which seem constant in his life. Familiar emotions of intense frustration and panic would arise in response to familiar signs of danger in a situation where he begins to feel thwarted. Finally, he would experience conscious feelings of rage as he mobilizes himself in a futile effort to get through to the person perceived as denying help, often resulting in tantrums or other self-defeating behaviors. These feelings of rage were familiar too, and may have gotten results when he was a child. But the full ensemble of reactions did not help him in his current life. They were patently obsolete and childish.

LeDoux's research suggests two ways in which the brain can process its fear responses. Like other emotions, fear can be processed by the cerebral cortex, which provides the opportunity for the response to be more complexly associated with autobiographical or long-term memory and thus lead to more nuanced responses. But emotions can also bypass the cortex; when processed directly by the amygdala, they produce intense and immediate responses, analogous to the danger signal perceived by an animal in the presence of a predator. Such responses are far more difficult to inhibit or control.

In most cases of emotional processing, as we have seen, responses occur without the mediation of consciousness, even when the cortex is involved. But when consciousness occurs, we have the possibility of inhibiting or censoring our first reactions and choosing alternative pathways for action. It was important for Amos to begin to focus on this sense of helplessness associated with his rage. This awareness eventually allowed us to get in touch with the underlying and primary emotion of fear, which in turn allowed us to delineate the sequence.

Many have suggested that each emotion has its own complex set of neurological systems, such as LeDoux has outlined for fear. If that is the case, researchers are presented with a daunting array of complex possibilities for the experience and expression of any emotion: different wiring, different cultural norms, different personal histories—and different levels of consciousness.

The pioneering work of Paul Ekman and his colleagues in analyzing how facial expressions reveal emotions consistently across different cultures suggests that there are seven basic emotions, rooted in our evolutionary development: surprise, happiness, sadness, fear, anger, disgust, and contempt. His work suggests that emotions are not only valuable in preparing us to make quick responses to events, based on what he calls "autoappraisers" that detect the situations eliciting appropriate emotional responses, but also that our ability to read the emotional responses of others has assisted the development of our communities. The existence of a set of basic core emotions, revealing themselves in largely invariable facial gestures, enables us quickly to communicate with each other preverbally, sharing information and also inducing common reactions. We bond and respond together before we become fully aware of what is happening.

He suggests that we consider each basic emotion shaped by evolution as a theme, but that each theme has variations in its expression depending on cultural and personal differences. Moreover, the variations overlie each other in complex ways, as we seldom feel one pure emotion without some admixture of others. Adding to the complexity are emotions that are ambiguous or mixed. Ekman notes, for example, that there is little evolutionary or personal advantage in communicating guilt, shame, or embarrassment, as these are precisely the emotions we do not want others to detect in us. He also notes that the emotion of envy does not seem to have a clear signal, again a circumstance that can be seen as aiding our ability to carry off successful envious attacks on others.[27]

This touches on a point made about Ekman's work that adds immeasurably to the complexity of the picture. Culture and civilization significantly increase our skills in masking emotions or misleading others into believing that we are experiencing emotions different from what we actually feel. Just as language makes it easier to lie and to deceive others, so can emotional signals be manipulated. Unlike language, to be sure, emotional expressions tend to be involuntary, but the motives to control the impressions of others are also very strong, and it would be a mistake to underestimate them or even to assume that they are under conscious control.[28]

The understanding of our largely buried emotional responses to events is largely a practical matter, depending on our sensitivity to signals, our capacity to decipher contradictory signals, and our empathy to those experiencing emotions. Ultimately, our ability to identify the seven—or eight, nine, or ten—basic emotions may matter less than our capacity to detect and discriminate among the ones we experience in ourselves and others. Some people, with intuitive skill and sensitivity, are good at it. Everyone can be better.

UNCONSCIOUS SELF-ESTEEM

Early in his career, Freud stressed our powerful need to ward off awareness of motives damaging to self-esteem. He and Breuer used the concept of censorship to account for hysterical symptoms. Perceptions about oneself that were unacceptable because they conflicted with social norms—most notably sexual desires in women—were banished from consciousness but enacted in symptoms. A few years later, in his book *On the Interpretation of Dreams*, the concept of censorship was extended to account for thoughts banished from daytime consciousness because of their danger to self-esteem, but reappearing in disguised form in dreams.

Freud moved on to articulate a more complex set of dangers, outlined in his concept of the Oedipus complex, but his initial conception retains a certain commonsense value. We sense intuitively how much we resist thoughts that are too difficult to entertain, either because they would force us to give up well-established, cherished beliefs or because they would compel difficult actions we are not confident we could carry out. These efforts to preserve self-esteem have been noted by psychologists who have studied the disparity between our self-image and our actual behavior as measured by our actions. David McClelland, for example, has studied the gap between people's implicit motives, which he sees as shaped by needs developed in childhood, and their conscious self-attributed motives, shaped by their self-images developed in adulthood. David Kenny has studied the disparity between people's self-reports and the generally more accurate reports of others. Summing up this research, Timothy Wilson notes, "There is a good deal of evidence that people see themselves through rose-colored glasses and that, within limits, it is healthy to do so. What is the harm in thinking we are a little more popular and extroverted and kind than we really are?"[29]

Harry Stack Sullivan, the American psychiatrist, made our struggles to preserve self-esteem the cornerstone of his theory. At a time when most psychoanalysts looked to Freud's drives to account for human behavior, he believed that we were more actively but unconsciously engaged in maneuvers to safeguard the stability of our self-regard than we were in seeking to satisfy our deeper sexual or aggressive urges. For him this was not so much a matter of enhancing self-esteem through rose-colored glasses, as Wilson put it, as maintaining the stability of our self-image.

He coined the term *self system* to describe the array of virtually automatic defensive maneuvers or "security operations" that we employ to ward off threats to the stability of the self. He was not interested in the self itself, conceptualizing it simply as everything we experience as belonging to us. Conceptions of the self as unique or separate or even coherent were, for him, illusions. What mattered was how we defend this collection of attributes and images we call our own from the threat of anxiety. As he put it, "Anything which would seriously disturb the equilibrium, any event which tends to bring about a basic change in an *established pattern* of dealing with others, sets up the tension of anxiety and calls out activities for its relief." Or as Donnel Stern has clarified, "The task of the self system can be described even more simply as the refusal to perceive or formulate novelty, because novel experience may be dangerous. Safety lies in familiarity."[30]

In our terms, anything that threatens the stability and consistency of the cognitive and emotional categories we have established and upon which we rely to live in the world will arouse anxiety. Not only will we have to discard an old adaptation, establishing a new pattern, we will be forced to acknowledge that we do not understand things as well as we thought, that we are not as much in control of events as we had thought, and that we cannot be sure of what we are currently planning to do. As a result, the self system will be invoked to protect the integrity of the status quo. For Sullivan, there were different intensities of threat. On the routine level of everyday experience, we simply "selectively inattend" to information that is inconsistent with what we want to continue to believe about the world and ourselves. More dangerous threats bring about dissociation, blanking out the information entirely. But the point is that this monitoring of experience is a continuous and largely unconscious activity.

These edits for the sake of our self-image extend to understanding our motives. What we have learned about the cognitive and emotional unconscious makes it clear that we usually do not know why we act as we do, though that fact may be difficult to acknowledge. As we have seen, people make up explanations to avoid the psychological injury of not appearing to be in control of their own actions. This is amplified considerably when the motives are unattractive or socially unacceptable. Unlike Freud's hysterics, we may be more willing today to own up to our sexual desires, but there are many other motivations or feelings or thoughts we would prefer not to acknowledge, even to ourselves. It is difficult to admit being vindictive, spiteful, envious, competitive, mean-spirited, or nasty. But it is also often embarrassing to acknowledge ignorance, dependency, confusion, poverty, or simple errors. We don't want others to know such things about us, but often we also don't want to acknowledge them to ourselves.

An example from Amos, my distracted businessman, will help to illuminate this point. He had a colleague and friend whose advice and company he frequently sought. At an earlier point in their careers, Amos had been very helpful to his friend in getting him a job where he himself worked, and in defending him from critics. But more recently, when Amos lost his own job at the firm, he felt betrayed that his friend had not warned him that some of his careless and socially inept behaviors had put him in jeopardy. To be sure, Amos's colleague could have been a better friend, but it struck me that he was, nonetheless, a reasonable and somewhat typical friend who did not go out of his way to tell Amos things that Amos would not have wanted to hear. Over several years, however, Amos became repeatedly obsessed with his friend's "betrayal," working hard to keep these feelings hidden because he felt that they were exaggerated, inappropriate, and dangerous, in that they would only irritate and bewilder his friend, who continued to be, in many respects, helpful and responsive.

Amos and I did know several things that could help to account for this obsession. We knew how much Amos longed for unobtainable friends during his isolated and unhappy childhood, and how during that period he had formed exaggerated and idealized ideas of what friendship could be and, indeed, did appear to be for others. Moreover, he was somewhat jealous of his friend's good looks and greater social skills. His friend appeared to have a large circle of acquaintances, and he had had several long-term relationships during a period when Amos had few or none. These disparities were only exaggerated during the time Amos was out of work, while his friend was thriving at the job Amos helped him obtain. But Amos's sense of betrayal did not abate when he got another job. In fact it increased on several occasions when, under repeated questioning, his friend revealed more information about how their coworkers had criticized or disparaged Amos in front of him before Amos was fired. His friend did strike me as somewhat insensitive, but none of these factors seemed able to account for the intensity and persistence of Amos's feeling of betrayal. And our discussion of these ideas did not bring any relief.

What did bring relief was the gradual awareness that, in blaming his friend, Amos was avoiding blaming himself. It was not that Amos failed to reflect on the factors leading to his dismissal, including both what he had done wrong or failed to do. Over time, I think we had arrived at a fairly balanced and realistic picture of these events, including his own role in being fired. But Amos harbored deep-seated fears of being defective and inadequate. Like most children, he had blamed himself for his isolation and unhappiness, and though he had been able to become quite successful as an adult, those thoughts and feelings from his childhood persisted underneath his adult adaptations. Being angry with his friend served several purposes, but the most important purpose, we came to agree, was in sparing the activation of those old feelings of worthlessness and inadequacy. His self system found a safer target.

This example points to the fact that, often, there *is* harm in such self-deceptions—harm to ourselves. Amos's difficulty in acknowledging his core beliefs about his unworthiness not only posed a threat to his friendship, it caused him to live continuously with a barely contained level of dread. Even in protecting himself, he knew what he did not dare to face.

Two

THE NEW UNCONSCIOUS
The Interpersonal and the Social

■

The influence of the unconscious does not stop at the boundary of the self. In the previous chapter we focused largely on the domains traditionally associated with the personal unconscious. Now we move into the realm of relationships, the interpersonal world of families, the social world of groups, and the larger worlds of intergroup and international relations.

The domains of the "new unconscious" we are about to explore are not inherently different from those we explored earlier, nor are they entirely discrete and distinct. They rely on more complex memory systems that arise later in childhood development. The brain is plastic, as we saw, and neurons grow and connect as needed. The architecture of the brain is integrative, built more around pathways and linkages than barriers. The domains identified here, though, have more to do with the communities of inquiry that have arisen to explore three different aspects of the unconscious: language, group and organizational process, and larger social communities.

I will be describing research that has been done within a variety of professions and disciplines. Much of it stems from pragmatic efforts to solve problems and find avenues for action by social psychologists, linguists, philosophers, sociologists, political scientists, organizational consultants, as well as those involved in conflict resolution—the many and varied professionals who have struggled to understand the more puzzling and paradoxical aspects of human behavior. They, too, have found the unconscious to be indispensable as a way of accounting for what does not otherwise add up.

Partly because the processes I will describe in this chapter are more complex, and partly because the theories that have been devised to account for them are more speculative, less supported by hard evidence, these domains should be thought of as being under development. The unconscious is at work here, but we have much to learn about the mechanisms of its functioning.

UNCONSCIOUS LANGUAGE, UNCONSCIOUS MYTH

Language, the primary medium we use to communicate, is also the best means we have to conceal and deceive. Without our capacity for language and our skill in using it, the unconscious would have less power and influence than it does. But within language itself, the unconscious works to shape our experience. The tool of language is not neutral. Language itself is infiltrated with unconscious processes in two ways: language frames discourse, so that our social conversations are structured in ways of which we are usually unaware; and language confers meaning on our private acts, meaning that inevitably and invisibly suggests—as well as excludes—other meanings.

Both the cognitive and emotional unconscious, as we have seen, are based on our ability rapidly to discriminate and categorize perceptions. We often do not know what defines these categories, since we infer them from the behavioral responses they elicit in us as well as others. However, when it comes to behavior, the categories appear to possess neuronal consistency. Researchers in this field express this in a slogan: "Neurons that fire together wire together."[1]

Language, when it comes along in our development, adds immensely to our capacity to find ever more subtle and varied categories to make sense of our perceptions. Those who have studied these processes believe that the neural pathways representing those earlier categories remain architecturally linked with later pathways in the brain, not supplanted or replaced. As a result, earlier categories that are triggered by images—shapes, specific movements, colors or shadows, sounds, et cetera—are enlarged, modified, or supplemented as higher order consciousness comes into play with its sophisticated language abilities.

Our everyday experience of "Freudian slips," for example, illustrates the primacy of such categories in creating meaning. Despite our best efforts to express the appropriate thoughts we want to convey, we sometimes find ourselves reverting to the old categories, revealed as our conscious intentions falter and fail us. Language lifts us to another realm of abstract thought, and provides more complexity to our thinking, but, erected upon the categories that have already been established in our brains, it does not preclude earlier experience, nor does it always successfully elude it.

Clearly the person who said, "There were lots of little orgasms floating in the water," no doubt meant to say "organisms." The male student who told his girlfriend, "Don't consider this an erection on my part," meant to reassure her that he did not intend a rejection, but, just as clearly, something else was on his mind. While many slips of the tongue can be explained as mere verbal accidents, others clearly seem to have meaning. I have heard many patients frequently use their mother's name to refer to their wife, for example, or exchange their wife's name with their daughter's. I have done the same myself, far too often to be able to pass the incidents off as mere mistakes. The slips tell me about an underlying similarity in my feelings or perceptions.

Such a slip can be thought of as a kind of metaphor where one thing is juxtaposed with another to highlight an unexpected or unusual similarity and suggest additional meaning. In the case of such slips of the tongue, where the link is personal, the metaphor is private. But the language we all share is suffused with metaphors that we take for granted and that we share, usually without noticing them.

George Lakoff and Mark Johnson, in an extended body of work, have argued that language is essentially metaphorical, grounded in embodied experience. They offer many examples of "primary metaphor," the building blocks of conceptual thought: the metaphor "More is up," for example, can be seen in such phrases as "Prices are rising," "The stock market is down," or "He set his sights too high." The metaphor "Time is motion" leads to such expressions as "The meeting went quickly," or "How fast the day passed by." Another example: "Knowing is seeing," as a result of which we say "I see what you mean," "His reasoning is obscure," or "He left me in the dark." Normally, we do not stop to think that these are metaphors in which a conception is mapped onto an experience of space. The analogies feel built in, essential, because they are built into our neuronal pathways. Though each language and culture has its own metaphors, these primary ones are fairly widespread, no doubt because they are rooted in early sensory motor experience that orients all of us to the physical world as children.

Lakoff and Johnson also argue that each culture has its own complex metaphors, extended elaborations of such basic building blocks, serving to embody and perpetuate its norms.[2] They use the example of "A purposeful life is a journey," an extended metaphor that invisibly binds a number of thoughts together and shapes our thinking. The logic behind this metaphor is that life, like a journey, requires planning, will run into obstacles and detours, needs resources and resourcefulness, will come to an end, and so on. The point is that such a complex metaphor is not constructed by individuals in response to particular situations. It is provided by our culture and assimilated, activated by neuronal connections that we develop as we grow, acquire language, and engage in conversations with family and friends.

They comment that such cultural metaphors deeply influence how we think about our lives: "There are cultures around the world in which this metaphor does not exist; in those cultures people just live their lives, and the very idea of being without direction or missing the boat, or being held back or getting bogged down in life, would make no sense."[3] Such cultures may develop other extended metaphors that express their own underlying beliefs, but this one very much belongs to us. Subtly, imperceptibly it reinforces our culture's emphasis on striving for achievement and on separation from family as essential ingredients for a satisfying life. It also reveals a form of individualism that is specific to our culture: the journey is not a group effort, as competition and isolation are implicit.

This basic metaphor is repeated in our fables, our bedtime stories, our novels, our commercials, our old epics and new films. In no way does the metaphor force us to live our hectic, pressured, and isolated lives. Our competitive economic system is far more responsible for that. But the images and metaphors embedded in our language add a subtle and invisible pressure to conform to our cultural norms. Implicit, taken for granted, reified in our habits of speech, these ideas become part of a linguistic unconscious that reinforces and sustains our adaptation to our culture's dominant values and attitudes. They direct our thoughts and actions without our conscious awareness, as we pass up the chance to formulate alternatives. Potential alternative pathways go entirely unformulated because existing pathways are easier to follow.

Michel Foucault made a similar point, noting the power of our terms of discourse to promote particular social and political ends. As he wrote in his foreword to the English edition of *The Order of Things: An Archaeology of the Human Sciences*, his work aims "to reveal a *positive unconscious* of knowledge," an unconscious not of repression and hidden defects, driven by anxiety, but of influence and intention, driven by opportunity.[4]

Let me give an example he has used: the concept of mental health, which, throughout the eighteenth and nineteenth century, extended social control over many patients previously seen as crazy, degenerate, or morally defective. The concept led to the reform of old institutions, the network of local prisons, workhouses, and religious homes that warehoused or tended to the population of village idiots, vagrants, incompetents, beggars, vagabonds, the antisocial, the possessed, or perhaps merely eccentric individuals living on the margins of society, often in anarchic conditions. It extended the control of the state over populations that were previously neglected or left in the care of others, and it also led to the development of new hospitals and institutions to contain them. Not only did it move such persons out of the public realm of daily life, it advanced the profession of medicine, helping to promote other professions such as psychology and social work. The new professionals became the instruments of social control. It is fair to say that the discourse of mental health, simple enough on the surface, has had immense effects as ways of thinking about mental disorders have gradually shifted and shaped political and economic processes in ways that now are perceived as reasonable and right. Once the new terms were accepted, the experience of reality changed.

Another example offered by Foucault's archaeology is the term *homosexual*. Before that term became accepted in the nineteenth century, there were sexual acts between members of the same sex, of course, but those acts had not been crystallized into a distinct typology or social identity.[5] Now, however, the existence of this linguistic category inevitably evokes questions for us that other cultures do not necessarily ask. It seems impossible today for children who engage in random acts of sexual experimentation not to worry about whether they are gay.

Foucault's perspective on the creation of such categories was political from the start. His archaeology of the human sciences aimed to stake out a radical critique of the social order and identify those who have benefited from such forms of linguistic imperialism. In contrast, Lakoff and Johnson's perspective on language has been descriptive and anthropological, more academic than practical. More recently, however, Lakoff has put his linguistic analysis in the service of American electoral politics. He has argued that the Democratic and Republican parties in America offer competing myths about the family that are embedded in the issues they emphasize and the language they use. The Democrats' governing metaphor is of the nurturent family, concerned to protect and foster the development of its members, while the Republicans see the family, particularly the strong father, preparing its members for a tough and unforgiving world. In the light of these underlying metaphors, their differing social policies are more coherent than they might otherwise appear: the Republican vision of the family is characterized by the need for a strong national defense, firm law enforcement, a strict moral code, and a reduced emphasis on social insurance programs and entitle-

ments. The Democrats, on the other hand, come across as more ma-
ternally oriented, trying to lend a helping hand to the disadvantaged,
promoting social justice, and offering insurance. Following on these
ideas, Lakoff has offered his consultant services to liberal politicians
to help them frame their issues more successfully.[6]

Lakoff's views have spawned significant criticism, as is to be expected in the highly contentious political realm where so much is at
stake. Not everyone agrees with his analysis of these particular frames
or with the extent of their influence on the public. Yet there is no doubt
about the general influence of metaphorical frames on political discourse. And other academics have since entered the fray, employing
their understanding of unconscious mental activity in the service of
politics.[7]

Clearly language has an immense power to shape thought by shaping the categories we use to see and describe the world. It structures
perceptions and elicits reactions—a fact not lost on the advertising
and public relations industries as well as the growing profession of
"spin doctors." But there is an important question about how strong
or inflexible that power actually is. We are all now familiar with the
idea that the Eskimos have almost twenty different words for snow,
suggesting that in their world, shaped by their language, they see
twenty different things where we see one. The linguist Benjamin
Whorf is largely responsible for the idea that we can experience only
what our language allows us to identify, that language determines our
experience of the world. But language—and our ability to think—
probably offers us more flexibility than Whorf's theory suggests. The
very fact that we make slips of the tongue points to a flexible connection between thoughts and words. Those of us who speak English
and have just a few words for snow may actually be able to discriminate more than a few kinds of snow, though we would have to struggle
to describe them a bit more than Eskimos do, given that our language
has fewer resources for that task.[8]

Still, it clearly makes a difference if we call the Iraq war an "act of
liberation" or an "invasion," or if abortion is referred to as "infanticide"

or "choice." How our discussions are framed by language and how those framings enter into our public discourses not only shapes our thinking in ways we seldom pause to think about but also invisibly proscribes other ways of thinking.

Such frames work by becoming embedded in conventional discourse, becoming part of a cultural legacy that seems inevitable, unquestionable to members of the culture. The tool of language also structures the unconscious on a smaller scale. Individual families construct metaphors and myths that exert a powerful influence on the way members form their identities and life goals. Such myths bind generations together in shared narratives and common purposes. Particular attention has been paid to Holocaust survivors and the intergenerational transmission of trauma, based on stories or fragments of stories that are conveyed indirectly because the victims cannot bear to tell their experiences, or sometimes even to remember them. Families often have other secrets—failed pregnancies, tragic deaths, scandals, crimes, abuse and incest—recollections of which have been avoided, denied, or buried, except for hints that can be detected in fragmented stories or odd suggestive behaviors that have survived. We "read" such stories by indirection, absorbing and transmitting their messages.[9]

Selma Fraiberg and her associates put this eloquently in a study they conducted over thirty years ago:

> In every nursery there are ghosts. There are the visitors from the unremembered pasts of the parents; the uninvited guests at the christening. . . . Even among families where the loved ones are stable and strong the intruders from the parental past may break through the magic circle in an unguarded moment, and a parent and his child may find themselves reenacting a moment or a scene from another time with another set of characters.[10]

A common example of such haunting from the past is the "replacement child," the child who was conceived to take the place of another who died. Unknowingly, the new child plays a role in a drama of which he is unaware, his life an unconscious metaphor for a life cut short, a life only he can live. Often, even if the replacement child knows about the earlier sibling, he has no idea of how his life has been shaped by the meaning he has been assigned and his parents' inability to let go of the child who has died.

Vamık Volkan has given us several dramatic examples of how trauma can be carried forward from one generation to the next. He describes Peter, for example, the stepchild of a survivor of the Bataan Death March in World War II, in which over 11,000 American soldiers died. As an adult, serving in Vietnam, Peter reversed the story of his stepfather's helpless suffering, inflicting it on others rather than enduring it himself, by killing many civilians, including women and children. After the war, he went on to become a big-game hunter who enjoyed exterminating large numbers of animals, sometimes using machine guns. But Peter was completely unaware of how his actions were influenced by his stepfather's story, how he had made it into a virtual scenario of the life he was perpetually negating as his own unfolded. Volkan's account of Peter's analysis reveals the difficulties involved in undoing the influence of such stories, but also strongly suggests how frequently people incorporate such stories into their lives without awareness.[11]

In the early years of psychoanalysis, Freud offered us the myth of Oedipus as a representation of the universal story perpetually re-created in the repressed unconscious. Each of us went through a stage of incest and parricide, a kind of imagined trauma. Freudians thought of this as an "unconscious fantasy," a kind of daydreaming, off-limits to consciousness, in which we repeated the Oedipus story again and again, each with our own cast of actors. Jungians, in contrast, looked for a different set of stories in the unconscious, archetypes of the hero, the great mother, senex (the wise old man), or puer (the young child). In recent years, Freudians have become more critical of unconscious fantasy as a concept that was applied too glibly and carried too much freight. Similarly, many Jungians have distanced themselves from their traditional reliance on archetypes. But it is still true that we absorb stories from our families and our culture, constructing narratives out of our experience, using language to extend and develop the categories established by our cognitive and emotional unconscious.

Nowhere is the presence of unconscious stories more evident than in our dreams. Freud argued that dreams use a different kind of language, compounded of images, symbols, allusions, and associations— what he called a primary process, to distinguish it from the secondary process of logical discourse. Freudians today often call that distinction into question, but there is no doubt that dreams organize the material of experience in a way that is different from ordinary language, where associations and metaphors dominate the logic of time and space.[12]

Dreams reveal the recurrent metaphors that structure individual worlds, which could be called personal myths. The dreams my patient Amos reported, for example, endlessly recycled a few familiar elements. He was always trying to get from one place to another, but something interfered. The train was late or his information was incorrect. Sometimes the car broke down or he took a wrong turn and got lost. There were different particulars in each dream, but the main story line was the same: his attempts to move around the world were always defeated. Usually the thing that defeated him came as a surprise, something he had failed to anticipate, for which he had not made allowances. If our culture offers the implicit metaphor that life is a journey, as Lakoff and Johnson have argued, Amos's personal take on his journey was that he could never succeed at reaching his destination. The underlying message of his dreams was constant: he was incompetent.

Marilyn's recurrent dreams were of repeated threats to her life: a thief had broken into her apartment, threatening to kill her; a car suddenly veered onto the pavement where she was standing; a mass murderer sprayed her office with machine-gun fire. The world was filled with random aggression, and she had no one to protect her. Clearly the dreams reflected her childhood experience of being exposed to danger and her largely futile efforts to protect herself.

These personal myths are consistent because, in each case, there was a particular overwhelming fear that dominated these dreamers' childhoods, a familiar set of events along with a recurrent sense of helplessness. Most dreams are more varied, however, and more difficult to decipher. No single story line dominates, and the images and events are without the words or labels that might help the dreamer identify how the dream links to other experience. They are like incomplete metaphors.

Mark Blechner[13] has proposed that the subjects of our metaphorical sentences are stripped away in dreams, leaving us with what he calls "subjectless predicates," embodied activities without the clearly identified bodies that are performing them. This removes the imagery of dreams from their context, not only the real-life situations which provoked the dreams in the first place but also important information about who is doing what to whom, which accounts for much of their baffling and elusive quality. Once the contexts of a dream is restored— the identities of the characters in the dream as well as the incidents that gave rise to it—the meaning of the metaphors out of which the dream has been constructed can become instantly clear.

Verbal frames, myths, metaphors—all these meanings buried within our everyday language—immensely complicate our efforts at communication. It is disconcerting to see how much language itself is infiltrated by unconscious processes, how much it is itself a part of what we rely upon but cannot fully understand. Here again, it behooves us to be alert, reflective, and willing to question not only what we take for granted but what we may believe we have finally come to understand.

UNCONSCIOUS BELONGING

This is the domain of the unconscious that is perhaps least recognized and appreciated in our culture. Our historic, embedded focus on the individual has meant that we idealize and reward our leaders, our winners, our geniuses and heroes. Seldom are committees singled out for praise. Indeed it is a widespread conviction among us that groups thwart the individual, impede action, and waste time. And, often, that is true—mysteriously and unfortunately true. We continue to work and meet in groups, which are indispensable for accomplishing work, and we seldom understand how their unconscious actions get in our way. I said "their" actions, but, obviously, their actions are also our actions, our actions under the constraints and invisible pressures of group membership. Groups provide insidious opportunities for us to thwart our own best intentions and derange our well thought out plans. In the Introduction, we saw an example of "groupthink" at work in the disastrous decisions of President Kennedy's advisors preparing for the Bay of Pigs invasion. A group of brilliant men with access to extraordinary information as well as exceptional resources blinded themselves to simple facts and obvious dangers. Not taking into account their own vulnerability to the difficulties and dangers of group membership, they brought on a near catastrophe.[14]

Somewhat as "security operations" work in individuals to protect self-esteem, groups collectively neglect to pay attention to the information and ideas that threaten their cohesion, that contradict what they want to believe or are afraid not to believe. In this case, differing points of view were minimized, disparaged, ridiculed and finally just ignored. Something resembling a delusion state took over.

Here we are in the presence of the deepest paradox of group life: working together, group members can be creative and productive, achieving far more collectively than they possibly could working as separate individuals; on the other hand, groups can lead their members to be out of touch with reality, destructive, and deluded. We can have, on the one hand, brilliantly functioning teams, pooling their thoughts, spurring each other on to new and better ideas; on the other, we can have what happened among Kennedy's advisors in the Bay of Pigs debacle or among executives at Enron.

Should we think of the processes that produce these different outcomes as a piling up of individual motives, a concatenation of parallel factors operating in the separate group members? Or as a process engaging the group as a whole, a kind of social or tribal instinct?

Darwin argued in *The Descent of Man* that if members of a tribe were always ready to aid one another, sacrificing themselves for the common good, they would inevitably be victorious over other tribes.[15] He believed that such a social instinct aided natural selection, especially when operating within the family unit. It may be true that we have a tendency to submerge our individual interests for the sake of a larger goal. His concept of a social instinct remains an interesting hypothesis.

It may also be that the size and complexity of the groups we inhabit add a challenge to cognition, as Howard Gardiner noted in reminding cognitive scientists of George Miller's seminal essay, "The Magical Number Seven, Plus or Minus Two." Miller observed that there are limits to our ability to keep complex streams of information distinct in our minds. Faced with too much complexity, we "chunk" the bits together into wholes we can process, at the expense of precision or even accuracy. In groups, particularly larger groups, such chunking means that we lump people together as we try to grasp the shifting complexities of group dynamics.

On the other hand, as we chunk others, inevitably others chunk us, with the result that we are all more likely to feel that we are in the presence of strangers, unseen and alone. Such anonymity easily leads to counterproductive forms of regressive behavior, resentment, and impulsiveness in larger groups. As a result, not only do we fear large groups, our own behavior in large groups gives us ample grounds for being afraid. Mobs and crowds have provided all too many illustrations of the power of coordinated destructive mass behavior.[16]

More recently, there has been significant interest in applying complexity or chaos theory to understanding group processes. Chaos theory notes the self-organizing properties of large systems, suggesting that there may well be ways in which individuals interacting with each other, under certain conditions, produce spontaneously emerging patterns of integration. Schools of fish appear to coordinate their movements spontaneously, as do flocks of birds. Ants, termites, and bees have evolved extraordinarily intricate societies, clearly without consciousness or central planning. Perhaps comparable tropisms or mechanisms underlie our group dynamics.

Ralph Stacey, a professor of management in the United Kingdom, has argued that groups can be viewed as complex responsive processes, a point of view that helps to account for their creative capacity to develop new ideas. If we conceptualize groups as occasions in which collections of individual minds engage in common projects, we highlight the processes through which the interactions of conversation, what George Herbert Mead called "conversational gestures," produce emergent structures. From this perspective, groups are neither simple collections of individual minds, nor are individual minds merely contained in groups. Paradoxically, minds shape the process of the group at the same time that they are shaped by those very processes as individual gestures interact. From interaction, new integrations continuously occur.

Stacey refers to the work of Ilya Prigogine and his concept of "dissipative structures":

> Models representing a critical degree of micro diversity . . . take on a life of their own, in which their future is under perpetual construction through the micro interactions of the diverse entities comprising them. The "final" form to which it moves is not given in the model itself, nor is it being chosen from outside the model. The forms continually emerge in an unpredictable way in the interaction of the entities comprising the system.[17]

A similar point has been made recently by James Surowiecki, in accounting for how groups, free to process information randomly, generally arrive at astonishingly accurate results. He gives the example of a contest to judge the number of jelly beans in a jar. Time and time again, while the individual guesses vary tremendously, the average of the guesses turns out to be correct. The collective is able to generate wisdom—or, at least, an amazing degree of accuracy.[18]

Chaos theory, cognitive chunking, and social instincts may work to describe processes that occur when they are free to move of their own accord, without interference, without disruption or "noise." Theories of emergent structure or automatic computation might well explain how flocks of birds fly in formation or schools of fish dart about in the water with exquisite coordination, or how a group of separately acting individuals who are not bumping up against each other or competing for attention can come up with the correct number of jelly beans in a jar. When it comes to human behavior, however, movement without turbulence is the exception. Individuals who feel threatened will oppose processes of synthesis, or joint resistances will arise within subgroups promoting different agendas and disrupt the prevailing flow toward integration.

Two kinds of motives can arise in individuals that profoundly disrupt group processes, introducing perturbations that derail a group's capacity for cooperation and synthesis. Briefly, they are anxieties that individual members feel about being included or accepted in the group, and anxieties about failing at the task they have come together to perform.

The desire for approval is likely to be stronger among members of a teenage clique or gang than in a group of presidential advisors, but few people are immune to the pressures of feeling included or, worse, the danger of being excluded. Without consciously trying to adjust our behavior, we attend to the subtle signs of opportunity or danger in being accepted and belonging. Confronted with the existence of such a motive, many of us would deny it, try to suppress it, or try to correct it unobtrusively. Such motives may seem childish, stupid, and embarrassing, but they are there.

A related set of individual motives has to do with identity. More adult or sophisticated group members may not be satisfied with mere inclusion, requiring recognition for their specific identities in order to feel secure. I suggested that Kennedy's advisors had identities as cold warriors to sustain, identities embedded in their former roles, outside connections, and public positions. If a group fails to affirm such identities or, even, if it raises the possibility that they may be threatened or challenged, members will fight to protect and reaffirm them. Threats to an existing common identity in a group can become experienced as a danger to the group itself, eliciting an unconscious collusion to act together defensively.

Typically, groups find ways of accommodating different identities, providing a sense of security to members as a precondition to active engagement. Only when a group has gone through a stage of formation, in which the identities of members have been established, recognized, and accepted, can the group usually feel secure enough to work at its purpose. We will get a better appreciation of the complexity of such processes in Chapter Four, when we explore more fully the meaning of identity and its different forms. The identity needs of group members can also lead groups to subdivide, each subgroup offering its members a sense of belonging, though often at the expense of the cohesion of the whole or its ability to pursue its task. Often a quick glance around a roomful of people engaged in a meeting will show the group divided by gender, age, or ethnicity, as coalitions emerge and form unconsciously around issues of identity. The women sit together, for example, or minorities in the back.

Also, there are the anxieties that the group will not be able to succeed at the purpose for which it was established, especially if the task itself is challenging or risky. Moreover, work can be impeded by a lack of needed resources, poor organization, incompetence, changes in the external environment, and competing versions of the task that cause members to work at cross-purposes. The group's inability to work at its task will render it demoralized and anxious, searching for scapegoats or for some means of escape from its dilemma. Desperation provokes a vicious circle: groups unable to function get more anxious, which causes them to seek stronger defenses, which, in turn, renders them yet less able to face reality and function at their task, and so on.

In Chapter Five, I will give a number of examples to illustrate more thoroughly how unconscious anxiety and defenses permeate organizations. But let me give an example here, a consultation to a hospital in which a variety of unconscious processes was exposed in the process of trying to understand what lay behind an atmosphere of contentiousness and blame. This problem was particularly serious as the hospital was in a precarious financial state, requiring more than usual amounts of cooperation and creative effort to improve performance and survive. Staff members needed help in getting to the root of their internal conflicts.

Bill Kahn, the consultant, found that the present state of affairs originated in the hospital's response to a surgical error that had occurred five years previously. Back then, under the forceful leadership of the hospital's nurse manager, brought in to prevent such errors from recurring, the hospital enacted a defensive preoccupation with avoiding errors. In a way that turned out to be all too congenial to the personality of the new manager, according to Kahn, a kind of informal tyranny was imposed, using hypervigilant strategies of blame for those she did not trust and favoritism for those she did. The policies and procedures she implemented, though disliked and complained about, were supported by the administration and staff because, at the time, they seemed to provide the staff's only protection against future errors. Much of this strategy operated unconsciously. As time passed the origins of the defensive strategy were forgotten, though the error was sometimes recalled and invoked to justify the need for certain particularly objectionable procedures.

It eventually became clear to Kahn that he had been brought in to provide the evidence for firing the nurse manager, who had now come to be viewed as the problem. The hospital's use of her and her tyrannical reign in a defensive strategy had run its course; the fantasy of finding safety through blame was exhausted. The hospital administration now needed to address a different problem, survival through enhanced performance, and the old culture of blame undermined the new strategies of cooperation and teamwork that were now seen as essential to success. The danger now appeared to be outside, in the form of competition from other institutions.[19]

This case allows us to see two distinct sets of fears and two different defenses operating at different times in the same group. Initially, of course, the fear was of mistakes and injuries to patients, the kind of risk that is inherent in the mission of any hospital. In the appointment of the nurse manager we can see, perhaps, a related worry: doctors cannot be relied on to police themselves. Bringing in a second profession to monitor those originally in charge, as a result, may have seemed a better way to ensure standards, but it may also have aroused professional rivalries, not only stirring up resentment among the physicians but also encouraging the nurse manager to be harsh and punitive in response. Five years later—and perhaps with higher standards and tighter controls in place—the hospital had to be more competitive, more efficient, and more effective in carrying out its mission. Now the new conventional wisdom about the benefits of decentralized control and self-managing teams replaced the older concept of top-down management. The nurse manager and what she stood for had to go.

Kahn worked hard to forestall management's solution, arguing that without a better understanding of the structures and roles they now needed in order to face their competitive environment more effectively, merely disposing of the nurse manager was insufficient. But, as is often the case, the hospital management had gotten what it wanted from its consultant, and it went on to offer the nurse manager a severance package.

In fact, throughout, the hospital was contending with two overlapping, mutually interpenetrating but distinct problems: how to become more effective and how to manage the anxiety of those who work there. At first, a form of authoritarian leadership was imposed to deal with lax procedures. But there was also the need to reassure those in the system that something was being done about the hospital's problems. Anxiety could be reduced because someone was now firmly in charge. Five years later, the problem was the need for the hospital to survive by becoming more competitive. Removing the nurse manager did address the real problem, to some extent, in that it made room for a new climate of cooperation, but it also created a scapegoat who was blamed for what was not happening. Removing the obstacle and heaping her with blame reduced anxiety, but, as the consultant argued, the hospital was not engaging the more complex task of forging a new collaborative climate and engaging the resistances that such a new plan would inevitably entail.

Such defenses against anxiety can often look like rational responses to problems, and they can be indistinguishable from them. Bringing in a strong supervisor, for example, may be an appropriate response to a crisis, as quick and firm new actions are needed. Such actions also provide emotional reassurances, which are also needed to help people calm down and get back to focusing on their work. The need to adapt and respond and the need to provide defenses may overlap, but they are still separate goals. The problem arises when they do not overlap and work together. The defense persists as a norm or a standard, a procedure or a policy that comes to be seen as the way that things need to be done, the way they have always been done, when in fact its primary purpose was always to instill a sense of safety. Such defenses are most effective when they are not questioned, when this purpose of relieving or containing anxiety operates unconsciously.[20]

If we look at the hospital system through the lens of social instincts or chaos theory, we can discern the potential for the system to organize itself in an effective manner. Without anxiety, without competing needs for different subgroups in the system, without external threats and the danger of internal accidents, the system might have functioned smoothly. It contained all the information and resources it needed. But anxiety elicited perturbations in the system, profoundly affecting its ability to function.

The lesson in the management of groups, then, is the importance of paying attention to anxieties in the group and the various defensive maneuvers to which they give rise. Unblocking defenses is the key to restoring the emergent processes, allowing the group more fully to engage its work.

THE UNCONSCIOUS AT LARGE

Let me start with a dialogue between representatives of two warring populations: In 1980, a group of Israelis and Egyptians were convened in the United States in an attempt to reduce the political tensions in the Middle East. For a time, the discussion was dominated by a professor of history from Cairo, vehemently asserting the necessity for a Palestinian state. Eventually, he was interrupted by a child psychiatrist from Jerusalem who asked him how he could convince her not to fear a Palestinian state. She recollected an attack on her community by Arabs in 1929, an attack that took place despite promises of protection by the British. The Egyptian historian answered, "I do not believe that you Israelis are afraid; Israelis are never afraid."

This is just one incident that illustrates how political and ethnic conflicts bring about a process of dehumanization. I could have cited an example of political and ethnic conflicts between Israelis and Arabs, Serbs and Croats, Tutsi and Hutu, black and white, or Shiite and Sunni. Erik Erikson coined the ungainly term *pseudospeciation* to describe the all too familiar process through which we come to believe we are members of a different species, apart from other groups of human beings, and that different racial, religious, or ethnic communities no longer deserve our respect or understanding.

In this case, the professor from Cairo reported that, after a sleepless night, he consulted the Qur'an and found three passages that spoke of Moses' fear. "I never thought that Moses was afraid. But now I know that since Moses was afraid, you can be too. So I believe you." In the context of the group that had come together for this unusual purpose, he could not sustain the contradiction of his experience through a sleepless night.[21]

Prejudice is a universal process, rooted in normal development. On the simplest level, it stems from the ways in which our brains create

categories as part of our adaptation to reality. We saw in the operations of the cognitive unconscious how we automatically prejudge
when we assimilate new perceptions to old categories, which is, essentially, what prejudice is—the assimilation of new perceptions to
old categories. When we use our cognitive unconscious to automatically prejudge on the basis of ethnic or racial categories, we can see
how unfair or distorted such categories inevitably end up becoming,
but we cannot stop ourselves from doing it. At a more advanced level,
normal prejudice is based on our ability to discriminate strangers from
caregivers, those we know and have come to rely upon from those
we don't. The normal two-year-old in our culture will cry in the presence of a stranger; the adult will simply stiffen or become more re-
served. But as Peter Fonagy and Anna Higgitt have observed in their
studies of normal attachment, "However socially noxious the strategies adopted by some individuals may be, prejudiced responses are
basic to coping with insecurity in attachment."[22]

Prejudice, then, will never be done away with. It is built into how
we normally function. Those who claim to be free of prejudice can
only be speaking a half-truth, at best. The most they can validly affirm
is that they do not act on their prejudices. This is clearly a place where
consciousness needs to intervene, to help us suppress or reformulate
our automatic, unconscious reactions and chart alternative courses
of action.

Malignant prejudice, when normal processes of discrimination are
amplified and acted upon, often occurs when identity is involved. Thus
the identity of a group and its members is preserved, as members deny
the existence of unwanted attributes among themselves, purifying
themselves by disposing of such thoughts and perceptions, and then
projecting those attributes onto the group that is despised. Often it is
only an aspect of the humanity of others that is disowned or distorted
into exaggerated caricatures. Jews, for example, have been seen as
avaricious, blacks as lazy, Arabs devious, Orientals inscrutable, and
so forth, in a process that sustains racism and makes room for discrimination against women, the disabled, the old, and others.

But then there are the even more virulent forms that lead to ethnic cleansing and genocide. Usually we see this more clearly at a distance. But the ubiquity of terrorism today brings this process closer to home. We see how easily whole populations can be proscribed as "dogs" or "vermin," easing the way for suicide bombers to decimate crowds of citizens going about their daily business. In turn, we have difficulty grasping the humanity of those who resort to such desperate, extreme measures. They seem indifferent to life, driven by fanatical pride or hatred, disenfranchised—as if those attributes did not exist in substantial measure among their victims as well.

The process of dehumanization does not stand alone as the cause of our devastating conflicts and genocidal campaigns. Economic self-interest, pressures for national security, the need to distract local populations from their discontents—all of these and more are among the factors that account for the provocation of conflict. But neither can the persistence of such profound and destructive conflicts be accounted for simply in terms of self-interest. Deeply irrational and delusional processes inevitably accompany and sustain them.

So far, this account has stressed the negative and blatantly destructive aspects of these processes. There are idealizing effects of prejudice as well. Indeed, our entertainment and advertising industries are based on the manipulation of such perception and feelings, creating celebrities and stars, trusted brands, strong candidates, and TV series that inspire identification and loyalty. Immense research is devoted to testing the audience appeal of such products, and those who appear to have their pulse on the taste of the public are handsomely compensated. This is inevitable in a consumer-oriented society, where those who have products to sell seek out the means to manipulate perceptions and create positive prejudices.

These are not the only examples of how unconscious processes infiltrate the larger world. It follows from our knowledge of the cognitive unconscious that we absorb information from all dimensions.

In order for us to make sense of larger social, national, and international issues, they have to be linked to images and metaphors that are immediate and concrete, that make them a part of the world to which we automatically adapt. In an age dominated by instant communication and global media this happens constantly and relentlessly. Wars, earthquakes, famines, plagues, hurricanes, assassinations, and terrorist attacks—all the ways in which life continues to be precarious and uncertain despite our scientific and technological advances and sometimes because of them—are brought to every home daily. Our local communities no longer insulate us from such events.

Even without the assistance of the media, we pick up more than we know. For example, in a retrospective research study into the dreams of ordinary Germans during the Third Reich, it became overwhelmingly clear that the average German had some form of awareness of the Holocaust. The imagery of trains and camps in dreams demonstrated that some information about the extermination of the Jews infiltrated their minds. No doubt, of course, all Germans knew about the brutally restrictive policies and laws, and many could not escape knowing how Jews were rounded up, how gradually they disappeared from the streets. But apparently, the dreams put it together, even if consciousness did not grasp the message.[23]

What might be found in our dreams today if we were to search them for signs of global warming, nuclear threats, torture, and plagues? What might be found in our email communications, listservs, and Web sites? We do not need our dreams to prove the existence of those problems, but our dreams might provide valuable information of the impact they are having on us, the psychological and social cost of living with such threats at the margins of consciousness. Cyberspace is an ideal location for unconscious communication as it combines anonymity with the possibility of impulsive actions and reactions. We know the immense potential of digital technology to move information. We have yet to learn about its impact on the unconscious.[24]

THE NEW UNCONSCIOUS AND THE OLD

How is the new unconscious different from the old? How can we learn to live with it? The old unconscious was disconcerting and intrusive at the start, an insult to human pride, Freud thought. But after it had been mapped and publicized, we came to know what we were likely to find in its depths. The new unconscious is protean and ubiquitous. It will never be mapped conclusively. It will always catch us by surprise.

We can, however, locate much of Freud's unconscious within the territories we have identified. Most of it is in the cognitive and emotional unconscious, of course, where early learning about primary attachments as well as persistent emotional expectations are encoded. As we saw above, this is where transferences take root, the perceptual categories of childhood that persist into new adult relationships, and this is where the repetition compulsion gains its force, the tendency to duplicate again and again old behavior patterns, hedged about with the danger signals of anxiety. These are among the major contributions of psychoanalysis to the study of human behavior, ratified by generations of psychoanalysts and psychotherapists in their work, and now confirmed by the contemporary research of neuroscientists.

Much of the new unconscious falls under what Freud called the preconscious, thoughts and perceptions of which we are unaware unless we turn our attention to them. To be sure, much of this preconscious is a form of what is now called procedural memory, memory that cannot be easily retrieved, as it is the basis for much of our automatic behavior. Often when we become aware of procedural memory, such as driving a car or speaking a foreign language, our self-consciousness renders us momentarily inept; our actions seem to depend on our keeping our knowledge of those skills implicit. Still, there is no great emotional barrier to knowing it.

Freud's dynamic unconscious is about knowledge we do not want to have, knowledge that is disavowed, denied, repressed, avoided, or otherwise defended against. The substantial work that has been done

on the emotional unconscious provides ample evidence of how fearful, unpleasant, or enticing emotions shape our behavior: murderous
rage, vindictive hatreds, envious attacks, as well as seductive enticements. Those motivations, including the motivations not to know
about our motivations, are largely buried.

But there is an important point to make about Freud's discrimination of two principles of mental functioning: the rational principle
belonging to consciousness, and the irrational and largely associative principle governing the unconscious. His attempt to dichotomize
the conscious and the unconscious into such camps does not stand
up. All mental processes are associative, which is why free association remains such a valuable tool as it allows us to trace our thoughts
and feelings wherever they lead and discover the inherent logic of
experience. Drew Westen has noted that Freud appears to have been
"constrained by an unconscious assumption that several antinomies
could be reduced to a single distinction: conscious/unconscious,
rational/irrational, mature/primitive, and civilized/instinctive."[25] Such
an assumption helped to make the old unconscious intriguing and
exciting, an adversary to progress. But the new unconscious we are
coming to know does not lend itself to such drama. Less extreme, it
turns out to be more useful.

Freud, a clinician and a self-described "conquistador," unrestrained
by the ideological demands imposed on his own followers, stumbled
on many of the domains of the unconscious we have identified. He
took note of the importance of self-esteem, particularly in his early
work where he stressed the role of censorship in banishing thoughts
that were threatening to one's reputation. It is fair to say that he probably never lost sight of the dangers self-esteem posed to emotional
stability. He began his public career by focusing on the discontinuous narratives presented by our dreams, the tricks played by language
in the unconscious, and he noted as well the power of myth to shape
behavior. He was interested in group behavior, and though his theories could account for a relatively small part of it, he claimed it as a
valuable and important area of inquiry. Moreover, he was ceaselessly

interested in the larger world and the role of unconscious forces in history. It is fair to say that the new unconscious was richly foreshadowed in his accounts of the old.

But how do we live with the certainty of there being so much we do not know? Clarity and consistency are not to be found—but that we have been well aware of for some time in our skeptical and relativistic age. There are many truths, and no Truth. The scope of the unconscious makes it clear that even our truths are constantly shifting: we can never know the full extent of what we do not know. What has been left out? Neglected? Unexplored? All knowledge is hypothetical, but all hypotheses are certain to be supplemented, reworked, or disproved. When can we say, "Enough"? There can appear to be no ground beneath our feet. Paradoxically, our understanding of the many domains of the unconscious forces us to be more attentive to the surfaces of things, the ground that conceals so much in its depths but upon which we need to walk in order to reach our goals.

Perhaps the surface of water is a better metaphor for the boundary between the conscious and the unconscious, since we cannot traverse a body of water without breaking the surface or getting wet. Nor can we often see far into its depths. We can dive more deeply into it, and sometimes we can walk around it. But there is seldom an alternative to becoming, at least, partially immersed.

Swimmers learn to relax in the water. Staying afloat and moving around, we too have to become comfortable in this fluid and murky element. We need to sense the currents and ride the waves. Sometimes the tides will take us where we need to go. An occasional heroic sprint may be required to get us out of a danger spot and avoid a whirlpool or an undertow. But fighting the water or trying to set rigid goals will exhaust us, and in the end we will be defeated. Steady breathing, regular rhythms will take us further.

On the other hand, we need to cultivate an attitude of receptivity and mindfulness, working to stave off premature conviction, to remain curious. Our body will often tell us what we need to know, if we can hear its itches and whisperings. Faint signs will often point us in the right direction. Changes in the light, shifts in the wind, sudden silences will hint at presences we cannot know directly.

As we proceed through the following chapters, we will get a better sense of how to live in these realms—and what is to be gained by being more attuned to their messages.

Three

A SHORT ACCOUNT OF THE SELF

■

This chapter and the next examine some of the concepts that we use to refer to ourselves as actors at the center of our experience, the "I" we think and feel ourselves to be. Here I focus on the "self," our contemporary idea of what it means to be a subject. My aim is not only to show how the concept of self reflects deeply ingrained cultural and historical assumptions, assumptions that can no longer be justified, but also how it leads us away from grasping the actual complexity of experience and action, particularly in the light of the new unconscious. Typically, we use words like *self*, *person*, *charac-ter*, and *individual* interchangeably. But, as we shall see, they refer to somewhat different concepts that do not easily sit together.

If our mental processing is as loosely assembled, as various and as multitracked as it now appears to be, we cannot hold on to tradi-tional notions of an integral and consistent self, a unitary site of con-sciousness and thought. Descartes is often credited with inaugurating modern philosophy with the statement, "I think, therefore I am." For us, now, the question is, "I think, but where is this thinking taking place?" Moreover, "Who or what is actually doing the thinking?"

This question was troubling to explorers of the old unconscious, as the self was seen as the site of several often competing sets of motivations. But these days the question is even more urgent, as mental processing can no longer be seen as contained within indi-vidual minds. Not only do we need a new view of the subject that accounts for the gap between the conscious and unconscious portions of our minds, we need some way of thinking about the links between and among us, the ways in which we are inherently social beings who think and act together. The social basis of our existence is to be seen not only in our collective efforts; it is hidden in our accommodations and adjustments to each other, our basic assumptions and collusions, our conscious acts of cooperation as well as all the collective pre-suppositions and preconditions buried in the unconscious that underlie individual thought and social action.

THE HISTORY OF THE SELF

There is an important moment in the lives of young children when they first realize they are somebody. They come to grasp that just as the word *cat* refers to the furry, four-legged pet that purrs, *I* refers to the unique person who has their name and lives in their body. "I am 'me.' I am someone too."

We view this experience as indispensable to our psychological and moral development. It prepares us to develop a sense of agency, which in turn is essential for assuming responsibility. Without believing one is a distinct self, one cannot be truly accountable for what one does. It is important, then, to understand our separateness and to disengage from our need to rely on others, to act on our own behalf. Beyond that, though, contemporary culture encourages us to hold on, tena-ciously, to that infantile sense of our own unique importance. For us, that childhood experience of possessing a self has become the basis for our reigning concept of what it means to be a human being.

At the simplest level, our concept of the self denotes a container that holds everything belonging to us, the organs bounded by our skin, the thoughts inside our minds. From this point of view, we speak of "ourselves," "myself," "himself," and so on. Our selves belong to us, as do their contents. This is why the discovery of the self in young children is of such central importance. They grasp for the first time that they are not the possession of anyone else; they assert owner-ship over their bodies and their thoughts, their feelings and their in-tentions. Over time, experience teaches that this possession is partial and provisional. To insist upon one's autonomy and independence can become impoverishing. But this is where we start to become re-sponsible agents and assemble our cultural identities.

William James took this idea of the self as his point of departure: *"In its widest possible sense . . . a man's Self is the sum total of all that he CAN call his*, not only his body and his psychic powers, but his clothes and his house, his wife and children, his ancestors and friends, his reputation and works, his lands and horses."[1] This generous and expansive definition bears the earmarks of James's historical moment, of course: today, in an age where women have at least legal grounds for claiming full social and economic equality, few men would risk referring to their wives as a part of themselves. But all definitions are historically bound, reflecting the fact that our thinking emerges from a particular social context. This is especially true of the self.

The concept of the self could only begin to emerge in our history when the idea of possession became central to our common experi-ence and the acquisition of possessions become an important social focus. The importance of possessions, in turn, depended upon a significantly increased social mobility. Those who did not have wealth and status conferred upon them by birth sought the opportunities to acquire them in order to take their place in the world, to become some-body. These developments roughly overlapped with what is often re-ferred to as the rise of individualism, the idea that each person in society had inalienable rights as well as independent economic inter-ests. Throughout the eighteenth century, society came to be seen as arising out of a consensual contract of free men, and the growth of the economy, the wealth of nations, was attributed to unfettered competi-tion among free agents. Under these conditions, shorn of traditional meanings and inherited roles, individuals in our culture began to feel the need to find some basis for their value, some purpose to fulfill. External possessions gradually came to be seen as achievements that mirrored internal characteristics of taste, intelligence, and style.[2]

This helps to explain how we came to think of the self as unique. Just as children in our culture come to see themselves as possessing themselves, not being possessed by others, and go on to become increasingly aware of their separateness, we responded collectively over time to increasing social pressures to make ourselves into sites of special qualities and attributes, to assume our places among other unique selves. The self entered the social competition to become somebody. Or, failing to do so, the self could be reproached for lacking the ability to succeed at that project.

In previous ages, most people were members of local communities, following well-established pathways in life as their parents and grandparents had. Or they were members of classes, set apart from other classes if they possessed land or titles, or bound together in guilds, merchant leagues, and orders that enforced standards and conferred meaning. Some were citizens of communities that defined their obligations to one another; some were serfs, some vassals of lords. The course of life was ordered, for the most part, identities imposed, boundaries set. This is not to say that life in those days was secure or stable; wars, migrations, plagues, and other disasters continually afflicted human life, forcing painful and dramatic changes. But then conceptual order was reestablished, and life fell back into familiar categories. God in heaven, or the mythic presences living beyond the world of appearances, sustained the meaning of things, reaffirming the sense of each person's place in the world.

Modern history is the story of the breakdown of such traditional orders, among other things, and the introduction of dynamic change pervading all social relations. Identity, no longer provided by stable social structures, has had to be created. What was once the prerogative and privilege of the few became an imperative for all. Cut loose from the grip of traditional relations, we all had to become somebody.

The more recent history of our culture has worked to augment the importance and centrality of the self with relentless consistency. Enlightenment philosophy took authority away from traditional and established groups, placing it into the hands of a reason that was the property of independent, self-reflective minds. Romanticism enlarged the inner world of sentiment and imagination, dreams and fantasies, and gave birth to the notion of the creative artist as hero. From that perspective, social pressures to conform were seen as obstacles to fulfillment. Entrepreneurs and individualists became the engines of economic development and took conspicuous places on society's stage. They seized the political and economic initiatives that became more available to those outside the established social order, and they conspicuously celebrated their accomplishments. Psychoanalysis excavated and enlarged the interior realm of the self. Consumerism worked to develop insatiable appetites for material possessions. Over the past three hundred years, virtually every significant social and economic development heightened our belief in the significance of the self and added to the growing list of the achievements and possessions it has been asked to contain.[3] It has now come to seem that if the self is composed of the qualities and attributes it possesses, at its core must be something that possesses the self itself, an original source, an essence.[4] The self has come to seem something like the secular version of the soul, a precious and unique primal gift.

Our culture supports this belief in individuals who can develop this gift of selfhood and enforce their destinies. We give Oscars, Nobel Prizes, "genius" awards, honorary degrees, distinguished medals, and trophies to those we single out for their exceptional achievement. At the same time, we know, as the recipients themselves often know, that it is a distortion to isolate them from the collective efforts that made their accomplishments possible.

In fact, our culture today appears to have reached a kind of crisis as the container of the self spills over its expanded boundaries or even breaks up under the stress of its own demands. The burgeoning psychotherapy industry caters to clients who feel themselves to be fragmented or depleted, inadequate or self-deprecating. Narcissism presents selves with inflated self-esteem, while, on the other hand, depression arises in selves that are neglected or insufficiently appreciated. The middle ground is not only difficult to establish but difficult to locate. What is important about us? What are reasonable expectations and normal desires? Self-esteem seems to be required, but can narcissism also be essential to our well-being? The importance of the self is widely acknowledged, its defects and ills frequently discussed, but today it cannot be defined with much specificity, nor can we assert with any confidence a curative process or an ideal state to strive for. In a culture grounded in competition and boundless ambition, there can be little lasting agreement on such questions.

Our society is organized around production and consumption, efficiency and growth. People struggle to pay sufficient attention to anything else. Moreover, because of our society's extraordinary emphasis on ownership, on goods, and the competitive accumulation of possessions, issues concerning the environment, social welfare, education, and health are neglected.[5] The concept of self implies little about ourselves as beings that, among other things, long to love others, not just be loved, that hope to get something out of admiring others, not just the hope of being admired in turn, that strive as agents to accomplish more than the piling on of skills and attributes. It encourages us to become fixated on an early stage of infantile development.

This stress on the self in our culture has received much comment from a wide array of social critics. Some years ago, Christopher Lasch wrote of our having become a "culture of narcissism." More recently, Robert Jay Lifton has argued that our culture pushes us to develop "protean selves" in order to adapt to the constantly expanding and shifting demands of contemporary life. Emphasizing the diversity of the selves we can become, he tends to be optimistic about the opportunities this offers, unlike Kenneth Gergen who notes pessimistically that we are saturated by emerging technologies that inundate us with information and experience: "The saturated self becomes no self at all," he laments. Thomas de Zengotita, a contributing editor at *Harper's*, noting how thoroughly experience is mediated in an age of mass communication, has trenchantly pointed out that the net result of these trends is that we possess "flattered selves," reflecting the fact that our culture conspires to tell us how important we are, how we deserve ever more choices, more goods, more services. The psychologist Philip Cushman, noting many of the same historical developments behind the construction of the modern self, asserts that it has become "empty."[6]

THE SELF AND THE NEW UNCONSCIOUS

The self falls short as a concept adequate to encompass the complexity and diversity of unconscious experience, the multiplicity and distribution of the new unconscious. First, it implies a high degree of separation and isolation among selves. Its emphasis on possession highlights the fact that each self is not only different and distinct, the possessor of its own objects, but also disconnected from other selves. Second, the concept of the self does not adequately reflect the continuous malleability that is a feature of interpersonal and social life. Too great a capacity to vary in the face of external pressures is generally considered a weakness, a sign of the self's lack of integrity. Yet without flexibility and adaptation the self is incapacitated in dealing with contemporary life. Finally, the self implies an idealization and valorization of its distinctiveness. Unique selves deserve and demand respect, and that puts them in an essential competition with other selves for the finite allotment of status our society offers.

Let me begin with the isolation of selves, their separateness from each other. Our sense of a unique self, usually taken for granted, appears to be legitimated by two basic, undeniable facts: we each inhabit our own bodies, clearly demarcated from other bodies, and our thoughts are secluded in our own impenetrable minds, known only to us. Even when our bodies are augmented by technology, we each have a skin that marks off our personal territory. Similarly, no one can read our minds—at least not consistently. Our dreams may bear uncanny resemblances to the dreams of others, but they are still *our* dreams, weaving together images and associations in our own particular ways.

Walter Freeman has observed that our brains wipe away the original data upon which our experience of the world is based, leaving us with our individual constructions of meaning, our perceptions. He calls this the "solipsistic gulf" because our individual minds, left with only the meanings we have derived from our experience, cannot directly compare the data on which our perceptions are based with the data underlying the perceptions of others. As a result, the basic information that could link our experience with the experience of others must be recovered or surmised. To ourselves, each in our own perceptual worlds, we appear isolated and alone.[7]

But, as we have seen, the unconscious is not confined to individual minds; it pervades our entire world. To be sure, the neurons that activate it are in our bodies and our brains, and the raw data of experience may be unavailable once they have been processed into perceptions, but the meaning of the signals that are sent and received, the implications and effects of our perceptions and actions are not simply located "inside" our minds, in the "depths," as Freud and others initially conceived it. We are profoundly networked, and the patterns that govern the sense we make of our perceptual data are not constructed by ourselves alone. It follows that "we" too, every "I," must also be more broadly conceived, extending beyond the boundaries of the self as we have usually understood it. Our minds, our capacity to think and understand, as well as our ability to act—these are all widely diffused and distributed. The center we have taken for granted does not hold; the circumference is impossible to find.

As members of our culture we struggle to overcome our sense of isolation and loneliness, often oblivious to the many ways in which we are already interconnected. As we saw in the last chapter, the assumptions embedded in our common language and myths bind us together, causing us to implement ends collectively, often without awareness of the choices we are making and the alternatives we are neglecting. Our need to belong, moreover, drives us to collaborate and collude with each other in a myriad of ways.

In short, the nutriments for self are collectively mobilized and socially organized. Though we try to develop and assert our distinctive qualities and abilities, our defining features, our increasingly interdependent and interconnected world requires a better understanding of who is being connected to whom—and how the links occur.

A second problem with the concept of self is that it can tell us little about our adaptability and our malleability, our capacity to be different in relation to different others. If we believe that the key thing about us is the boundary that marks us off from others, each of us a discrete container, we also come to think of others as fixed within their boundaries. We may believe we can move our boundary, incorporating others as part of ourselves, or we may appropriate the objects we feel are essential to our well-being. This is the strategy essentially proposed by James's definition of the self. In adversity, on the other hand, we may shrink the boundary to reduce the risk of further loss. But the self that does that is essentially static in that it is reactive and not dynamic. Thus conceived, the self, at best, can be somewhat like an amoeba.[8]

But the modern world demands an extraordinary amount of radical adaptation. Few can maintain entirely consistent selves, given our history of mass migrations; the deracination underlying immigration and assimilation; the reality as well as the idealization of social mobility; the creation and destruction of huge amounts of wealth; the increasing prevalence of divorce, intermarriage, and other challenges to stable family identities; and the rise of alternative lifestyles. We can try to accommodate to such alterations in the self by speaking of our "other selves" or "parts of self," but in so doing we undermine the integrity of the concept. We may get our point across, but a self that can be so radically altered no longer has a meaningful boundary.

In addition to the major social and political events that challenge the stability and consistency of selves, there are more subtle shifts in our sense of who we know ourselves to be. In our look at the dynamics of unconscious belonging, we noted how group members jockey to have their identities recognized and accepted as a precondition for their being able to join and fully engage in the group's work. But as that recognition is not always provided, identities often have to change in order for members to belong, sometimes in minor ways, sometimes radically. It is a feature of modern work life that those who work in large organizations usually occupy more than one role, and constantly move among them. Sometimes they are leaders, sometimes observers, sometimes charged with particular tasks, sometimes representatives of other groups, sometimes visitors. Each role draws upon different qualities and abilities, different memories and skills. Under these conditions, some thrive, but it is not unusual for others to become disoriented or confused.

We have a host of conceptions to label the pathological conditions that arise from social pressures combined with a weak sense of self. If a person is too willing to become what others expect, he is considered to have a "false self." Erik Erikson wrote about "identity diffusion," Eric Fromm about the "marketing personality," others about the "as if" personality, while the *Diagnostic and Statistical Manual of Mental Disorders*, fourth edition (DSM-IV) offers us several varieties of "sociopathy." These terms are helpful in describing extreme and disabling conditions. But their very existence speaks to a new cultural landscape in which adaptability and malleability are increasingly required of us all. We have not adequately chartered this gray territory between normal, necessary adaptation and the troubled, disabling adaptations that many resort to, though we may note when the boundary has been crossed. The concept of self does not come to our aid in those circumstances.

The third limitation to the concept of self has to do with its implicit valorization. It is not a neutral term, as it evokes assessment and judgment. A society of selves is essentially a zero-sum game. The achievements of one detract from the accomplishments of another. But, in reality, the achievements of one do not negate those of another. Not only can more than one person achieve comparable ends, but also the totality of achievements and possessions, in a time of expansion and prosperity, can grow. In our culture, however, one person's achievement is seen to detract from the luster or importance of another's. The second person to reach a goal is less valued than the first, and the more common or frequent any achievement becomes, the less credit it receives. The accomplishment may not be less, objectively speaking, but the increase in the benefit to the individual making the achievement lessens. There is not an unlimited amount of glory to pass around.

It is no accident that in our culture *self-esteem* and *self-assurance* are hyphenated terms, taking their place alongside a number of terms that bear witness to the continual demand on the self to excel: *self-respect*, *self-importance*, *self-regard*, *self-confidence*, *self-worth*, and so forth. We also speak of having "faith in oneself," "taking pride in oneself," and "congratulating ourselves" for our successes. The popularity of the concept of self-actualization reminds us of the need to develop our potentials, not merely enjoy them. To be sure, we acknowledge that too much pride can lead to vanity or arrogance. Such signs of egotism betray an underlying insecurity, we often think, a lack of certainty about the validity of our self-achievements. The self carries a value, but the value is never assured. The search for affirmation, in our culture, can never rest.

Yet the self shares in our culture's privileging of consciousness. Retreating to a private world of its own creation, free from the pressures for outside recognition, or merely able to enjoy the luxury of its own thoughts and memories, the self can expand its boundaries. It can draw on our vast cultural memory of poems and novels, symphonies and philosophical texts, pop songs, films, and TV shows, imbuing them with personal meaning and value. The space is infinite and soothing, enriching but also consoling. Here the self can feel truly special and privileged.

Consciousness presides over this inner realm, offering the additional pleasure to the self of feeling in control of its thoughts, able to range over time at will. But the unconscious is here too, offering associations and recollections, unexpected insights and thoughts. The inner world of the self can offer seductive boosts to self-esteem.

I am far from suggesting that we stop using the concept of the self, even if we could. It meant something to us as children to discover "ourselves," and it still means something to believe that we have distinct "selves." We still have to demarcate the boundaries between and among ourselves and to keep track of our possessions, what is "yours," "mine," and "ours." And, in our culture, it implies many things that we have come to take for granted about our lives: the need to feel a certain self-respect, for example, and to expect if not demand respect from others; the importance of becoming "somebody" and taking our places in the world; an obligation to look into ourselves, to know ourselves; the need to accept ourselves for what we are. Someone has to own the collection of things we are, and defend it while, of course, adding to it.

CHARACTERS, PERSONALITIES, INDIVIDUALS, AND EGOS

In addition to "selves," traditional usage offers us "characters," "personalities," "souls," "individuals," "figures," and "identities," to which psychoanalysis has added "egos." This profusion of overlapping concepts may compound conceptual ambiguity, but there are useful distinctions to make among this welter of concepts.[9] My aim here is to clarify the concepts that will be useful to our expanded appreciation of the new unconscious.

If "self" implies objects and qualities contained inside a boundary, "character" implies an "I" defined by prominent and enduring characteristics. We say that someone with strong moral traits has "character." We also say that someone who has distinctive and defining features is a "character," someone you can pick out in the middle of a crowd. At one extreme, a character can become a caricature, or one of a set of characters in a play. In all cases, however, a character has outline and definition, a set of objective, distinguishing features that enable quick recognition. Wilhelm Reich took this aspect of character and developed it into a theory of character analysis, emphasizing how such inflexible features can become a form of body armor. The aim of his analysis was to develop a more active set of strategies to undermine its distinctive rigidity.[10]

Objects more than subjects, characters are seldom used to refer to oneself. Similarly, "figures" have objectivity but also prominence, assuming historical or social significance. Often larger than life, figures loom; they are looked up to. We gaze across historical time at their standing in particular contexts. Closer to home, we may more simply see them standing out from their milieu. They can become figureheads, when their recognizable features are detached from their real actions, or simply familiar objects that have prominence, if we do not sense a real human being within.

In today's culture, it may be said that celebrities are the figures that capture our attention and, sometimes, our envy. They are the ones who have succeeded in detaching themselves from the anonymous crowd, the background against which most of us fade from sight. Their photographs are plastered all over the media, their foibles reported. But the price of celebrity is that, unlike historical or cultural figures, they do not represent anything but themselves. Emptied of meaning, their fate is a two-dimensional, ephemeral, and sometimes frenetic fame.

An "individual" is similarly set apart from the crowd, but without the clear defining features of a "character" or the prominence of a "figure" within a specific milieu. More of a political or social concept, an individual has rights, and is valued for the autonomy and freedom a true individual is seen to possess. Individuals assert their independence, requiring a certain forcefulness that may stem from being members of a class of individuals in which their individuality has been submerged or is threatened by conformist pressures. We occasionally refer to "faceless individuals," emphasizing the indirect impact on society of their being undeveloped or undifferentiated. But when an individual emerges as someone in his own right, he or she becomes eligible to join the polity of individuals who have the integrity each to take a stand and, together, compose an active and robust society. Our idea of democracy depends on the capacity of individuals to develop a certain degree of autonomy and forcefulness.

A relative newcomer to this collection of signifiers, "personality" implies a person with a distinctive set of qualities or characteristics, conferring interest and value. In the common mind, personalities are colorful, realized, attractive. Socially successful or, at least, appealing, a personality can be thought of as the public face of a successful self, the visible embodiment of the inner qualities of someone fully realized.

"Personality" has also become something of a quasi-scientific term. Psychologists employing personality theories assess subjects in terms of their traits, not necessarily the attributes that are alluring to others but attributes that can be defined and evaluated, that together comprise the distinctive profile of a person. The Myers-Briggs instrument, for example, is based on such an objectified view of personality. Such personalities can be compared with others and matched with jobs and other external demands. Personalities can be measured to see how they fit in with others or fit with objective expectations or requirements.

Along somewhat similar lines, personality "disorders" refer to a range of intractable psychiatric conditions in which certain pathological traits stand out in the functioning of the person, overshadowing and coloring other behaviors. As concept, personality disorder functions as the negative side of personality, referring to commanding qualities commonly viewed as unattractive or disabling.

The concept of personality leads us in two directions. It links to "person," obviously, from which it derives. "Person" has a long history and a complex set of meanings, making it particularly valuable in describing the contemporary dilemmas of the "I." It needs a closer look, and I will turn to that in the next chapter. As a term with scientific implications, *personality* can also be linked with *ego*, Freud's term for the person functioning as an agent. Ego has vied for scientific status, but in a very different way, emphasizing agency and action rather than static qualities or traits.

From the start, Freud appears to have been wary of any traditional concept of self. As he sought to theorize the layered and conflicted person he was beginning to uncover, he avoided terms that had traditional implications. He preferred the familiar and ambiguous "I," (*Ich* in German) slightly objectified as *das Ich*, "the I." Subsequently, his translators and many of his followers employed the Latin term *ego*, appearing more scientific and objective, and increasingly over the years the ego was reified and established as a major constituent of psychoanalytic theory.[11]

It is beyond the scope of this book to acknowledge all the efforts that have gone into elaborating our culture's varied signifiers for the "I." In this chapter and the next, more simply, my ambition is to propose, in effect, a reshuffling of those concepts that will be more adequate to the discoveries of the new unconscious. I aim to pull together a few "folk concepts" derived from our language and common usage,[12] as conceptual tools that should prove useful to practitioners who are struggling to find more adequate ways of working with what we are learning about the unconscious.

Four

PERSONS, IDENTITIES, AND ROLES

■

Who is the "I" that seems to sit at the center of our worlds? Is it merely a linguistic trick, a habit of speech we have come to invest with substantial existence? Perhaps the very notion that there is a coherent entity that sits behind our eyes, that moves our limbs, thinks our thoughts, and utters our sentences is nothing but a fiction. A number of philosophers have arrived at this same, very disconcerting conclusion, from David Hume, who thought the subject was a mere bundle of perceptions, to Friedrich Nietzsche, who thought that there was no doer behind our doing. The postmodern emphasis on how language constitutes experience has given new life to this question of what exactly is this "I."

The very idea of the unconscious challenges the unity or coherence of the subject. The multiple ways in which the world impinges on us inevitably elicits a multiplicity of responses. Though our unconscious systems do work together, as do our organs, our image of ourselves as unitary directors of our actions is something of an illusion.

All the terms we have examined so far capture only a part of the truth. We have discussed the self's shortcomings as a signifier, reflecting as it does the ideals and assumptions of an historical era that is in the process of dissolving. It is difficult to say what will take its place. What concept could describe the subject as a node, for example, in a network of infinitely ramifying links, or a pulse in a field of energy?

Here I offer three terms that are useful in that they provide a supple array of interrelated concepts to describe this complexity: *person*, *identity*, and *role*. These are not essentialist concepts, referring to the way in which the "I" actually breaks down into component parts. They are terms derived from everyday language that offer the opportunity to make some discriminations among the determinants of our behavior. They also help us to avoid some of the more obvious pitfalls of assuming consistency and unity.

Person is the more comprehensive term. Like *self*, it refers to all the personal endowments that belong to a specific human being, but it suggests action more than acquisition, agency more than ownership. It also implies a social presence, a need to be engaged and realized in an interpersonal setting, and it carries the important implication of legal and moral accountability.

Identity refers to the multiple but consistent, durable constructions developed by persons in response to stable interpersonal and social circumstances. As the term implies, identity is what makes it possible for a person to be identified, recognized by himself and others, though each person constructs several identities. One can shift identities, as circumstances demand, but identities cannot easily be discarded or altered. That is, having been constructed to endure and be resilient, identities cannot easily be cast aside.

Role, the most limited concept here, typically preexists a person's engagement with it. Roles are relatively easily assumed, and they are frequently changed. They are based on particular tasks to be addressed, as a result of which they are context dependent, and usually link up with other roles and tasks that are required to complete them. They make demands upon persons—and upon identities—to respond actively and adapt.

These concepts are interrelated: roles, for example, tend to be quite objective, detachable from specific persons, but they require persons to activate and realize them; in turn, persons are often profoundly influenced and changed by the roles they assume in ways that link with the particular identities those roles activate. An identity can often develop out of an important and persistent role, becoming the particular way a person adapts to making it his own.

This triad of signifiers illustrates how impossible it is to grasp the "I" as a whole, as a coherent and integrated set of features. The I, being a part of a larger social field, varies significantly according to its context and its relationships with other I's. It is not fixed and invariant. But the I also contains contradictory qualities: while it has duration and consistency, enough to keep it from being hopelessly disoriented and confused, it is also shifting and elusive. Changing and adaptable, it is nevertheless not infinitely malleable.

PERSON

Our word *person* has two sources. One is from the theater, where it designates each individual member of the *dramatis personae* who enact the story of a play. The other is from law, where it identifies the one who is responsible and accountable for actions and events. Each set of meanings expands upon and simultaneously limits the other.

Originally derived from a character in a play, a "persona," or mask, the concept of the person has assumed a meaning closer to the actor, the one who assumes a mask. A person has come to mean something like the one who is within and behind his roles, not the character that is the role itself. Pliable in being able to assume different roles, a person, like an actor, nonetheless has a certain consistency and possesses recognizable features that set him apart from other actors. We are always aware that a given performance is this person's version of the character, as we are aware that so-and-so is playing Hamlet in his distinctive way. As a result, from the vantage point of this theatrical metaphor, just as a person can embrace a part in a play, a person can also distance himself from any part he assumes: "Yes, I said that. But that was because of the role I was playing."

A person, then, separate from his roles, nonetheless requires roles to realize himself, to be complete. Moreover, he must join other persons in complementary roles to enact a story or drama. Persons do not exist in isolation. There is an implicit audience, as well, that observes and witnesses the performance, conferring legitimacy on the way in which the story is being enacted. The person, as a result, is a profoundly social concept. It is a version of "I" that is fully realized only on a public stage.

At the same time, the concept of person suggests depth. A person is not fully captured by his roles. Like an actor, he is limited in the roles he is suited for, and he re-creates even those that fit him like a glove, enacting them in his own particular manner. A person performs in the public realm, but he has a personal life, a life of secrets, obscure memories, unknown impulses, and undisclosed thoughts. We might go so far as to say that traditional notions of the unconscious refer to this aspect of the person, though a person may consciously choose to maintain his privacy. Moreover, no matter how curious or eager we may be to penetrate that space, we acknowledge the person's right to privacy and our own limitations in being able to grasp what is there.

In the other source of the word, a person is accountable for his actions and thus is the unit of legal responsibility. The eighteenth-century English philosopher John Locke stressed this aspect of the person in conceptualizing a social contract as the foundation of society. We can be citizens only if we are seen as choosing to join in with others, and that act of joining simultaneously defines our agency and makes us accountable for what we do.[1]

Should a person succeed in impersonating another, for example, borrowing the other's identifiable traits and characteristic manners, even to the point of deceiving others, he is liable as the person he was—the person he is—for the harm he does. Similarly, should a person suffering from a dissociative disorder assume multiple personalities, he is still liable for his actions. The courts may excuse him from the consequences of his actions by reason of insanity, but in the eyes of other persons, again, he is the one who did what he did. Like a chameleon, a person can change his colors, but in the eyes of the law, and in the view of other persons, a person bears inalienable obligations.

Thus there is a constant pressure on a person to pull himself together, to be aware of his actions in order to be accountable for them to others, after the fact if not before. A person knows he is responsible, even if he does not feel that he initiated his actions, and this dimension of being a person compels a certain level of integration, no matter how disparate and contradictory the impulses to act may be.

The other side of this legal and moral issue is that a person also has rights. At some point, a child grows up to become a person in the eyes of the law. He becomes eligible to vote and to obtain a driver's license, at which point he is expected to follow the rules. This dimension of the person is most clearly revealed in the fact that in our legal system corporations have been granted the status of persons. They have standing that confers on them privileges that, in turn, create obligations to act, to obey, and, ultimately, if necessary, to submit to punishment should they violate the law. If a self has opportunities to add to or enhance its store of qualities, a person has responsibilities.

This dimension of the person loosens him from the obligation to occupy or maintain any traditional role. He is a free, albeit responsible, agent. Not bound to any particular ensemble or company, he does not have to enact any specific drama. A creature of the modern world, he enjoys mobility and choice. But this is not the freedom of the self to amass possessions and qualities. It is the freedom to choose roles, to engage ensembles within which to perform. It is the freedom to act, to join, to be responsible, not the freedom to become merely a unique collection of traits.

Our culture's most striking representation of what it means to be a person occurs in the last act of *Hamlet*, when the prince appears suddenly at Ophelia's funeral. Having weathered his confusion and indecisiveness, his rage and his lust, his contending feelings toward his parents, his fears of betrayal, as well as the King's actual plot against his life, he is prepared to assume his place in the world. He proclaims,

"This is I, Hamlet the Dane," boldly asserting the right to speak the "I" he now feels himself to be. But this assertion comes in the face of understanding that he is acting in the midst of forces and events he only dimly apprehends and cannot control. A few moments later, facing the duel with Ophelia's brother, Laertes, that he clearly knows may end his life, he speaks in some of the most moving and eloquent lines of the play:

> We defy augury. There is a special providence in the fall of a spar-
> row. If it be now, 'tis not to come; if it be not to come, it will be now;
> if it be not now, yet it will come. The readiness is all. Since no man,
> of aught he leave, knows aught, what is't to leave betimes? Let be.[2]

Hamlet's assumption of personhood is not an act of will, nor is it an inevitable act of fate. It comes as a recognition of who he is, an acceptance of what it means to be a person. We act responsibly because, finally, we have no alternative.

ROLE

In clarifying the meaning of *person* as it arose out of its theatrical origins of *persona*, or mask, I stressed the distinction between person and role, highlighting the flexibility and freedom of the person in assuming and discarding roles, much as an actor plays different parts in a drama. But there is much more to say about roles.

The word *role* derives from the medieval French term for script, *rolle*, referring to the document from which an actor read his part in a play. From this origin it has been generalized to refer to the particular social occupation of a person, and it links with other means that have been developed to distinguish a person from any particular role he may occupy. Thus a person in the role of a policeman or soldier will not only have a script, in the sense of a set of implicit guidelines or rules that instruct him how to act, he will sometimes actually wear a uniform, a costume of sorts, and he will look for the cues that indicate when he should appear to enact his part, such as a robbery, a riot, or a war, and subsequently the changing conditions that terminate the relevance of his role.

Gradually, however, *role* took on a second meaning of "function," and began to be used without any reference to persons. Thus we speak of the role of education in a democracy or the role of scientific research in industry. It is not difficult to see how this meaning of *role* evolved, given the historical developments over the past several hundred years that depersonalized work, dismantling traditional crafts and guilds, while transforming labor into a commodity that was increasingly broken up into more and more efficient units. Today, as a result, *role* has often come closer to mean something like "job," as in "My role (job) in this committee is to keep the minutes," or "My job (role) is to teach you how to read." (Interestingly, as *role* has moved to approximate "job," in some settings "job" has become even further detached from the person who occupies it when it is used to approximate "task," as in the expression "to get the job done.") To be sure, not all roles have been so thoroughly instrumentalized. We still retain such traditional roles as "mother" or "father," roles that are more difficult to break down into simple job descriptions.

As persons we are on a boundary between the personal realm, where we grappled with our infantile origins, preparing ourselves for adulthood and work, and our social existence, where we assess the opportunities and demands of life in the world and prepare to assume roles. In our roles, we have definition and purpose, particular opportunities to accomplish tasks, to be useful, and to be seen. To play again for a moment with the theatrical implications of these terms, as persons we can be actors who are off-stage or in the wings, living with our families, seeing our friends, reminiscing, planning our careers, enjoying the fruits of our success or recouping our missteps, rethinking our next moves. In our roles we are on stage, at work, joined with others in expectations and obligations. We must perform. But, as the theatrical derivations of both terms suggests, the role must suit the person, and the person must possess the aptitudes and qualities required for the role. The connections are neither arbitrary nor given.

This lends "role" something of an inner and outer dimension. We can think of it as objective in the sense of being externally constructed as well as detachable from persons. As we will see in the next chapter, organizations can be conceived of as complex systems of roles designed to fit together so that their interlocking functions enable the system to accomplish its mission. At the same time, the role does not really come into existence until a person assumes it. Occupied, embodied, the role enables work to get done and it allows the person to be effective and competent, to realize his potential, to assume a position among other persons in other roles. Roles are essential to human fulfillment, but they can also be constructed and defined in self-defeating ways, aimed at inconsistent ends, reflecting fantasies or unrealistic hopes. They can also be dehumanizing and destructive, like jobs in factories producing noxious chemicals or roles as interrogators in prison camps.

In its outer dimension, a role is merely an account of a function, a job description. Embodied, however, we can see that roles possess potentials for consciousness in the persons who assume them, as well as potentials for evoking unconscious aspects of the persons. Someone assuming the role of teacher, for example, can develop in herself the authority required to keep order in the classroom, or the fear of being too strict and punishing, or can discover unexpected pleasure in scholarship or, perhaps, hitherto dormant obsessive traits. Being in a role can allow many unknown potentials to unfold.

Amos, for example, the distracted businessman referred to in the previous chapters, worked as a business analyst. In that role he had specific expectations to fulfill, gathering data about the performance of firms he was assigned to monitor, looking at market trends, writing reports for traders and investors as well as advising the bank for which he worked on potential financial deals. Despite his insecurities and spotty training, the role helped him to understand and acquire the competencies he needed, and over time he became good at it, impressing the senior officers at the bank with his skills. It was an uphill battle in which he had to overcome self-doubts about his technical abilities but also learn to manage his innumerable interactions with others in the bank, those who, in their roles, depended on his skills.

In assuming this role, Amos was helped by many aspects of his person: his intelligence, including an impressive ability to work with numbers, a good memory for complex data, an eagerness to please, and a strong desire for financial success stemming from the embarrassment he recalled as a child in a marginal family. Other aspects of his person presented difficulties to overcome: his resistance to being controlled by others, his poor self-regulation, leading to poor work habits, and a general sloppiness and disregard for the perceptions of others. To some degree, he was able to disguise the effects of his resistance to being controlled and his poor work habits because he had the capacity to improvise on demand. But he knew that those conflicts between his person and the demands of his role compromised his success, which, in turn, fed his underlying insecurity about being able to succeed. Interestingly, his sloppiness and disregard for social conventions got him into more trouble than his other difficulties with his role, as he developed a reputation at the bank as something of an oddball who made others uncomfortable, an eccentric who did not fit into its culture.

Accepted as relevant and embraced without resistance, "role" can have an educative and developmental function, encouraging its occupant to learn required skills. It can tap into unknown abilities as well as unconscious fears. Through our roles, we each encounter socially constructed demands upon us that can help us to adapt or, as with Amos, lead us to resistance and conflict.

IDENTITY

On a continuum of our three concepts, *identity* falls in the middle. *Person*, at one end, refers to the unique human entity, separate and

distinct from any particular role. *Role*, at the other end of the continuum, is distinct and separate from any particular person; a role can
be occupied by many different persons. Roles can primarily be thought
of as objective; concrete, fixed, defined, they can be crafted, reshaped,
duplicated, and even eliminated. "Identity" fits between these extremes, arising from the interaction and integration of the personal
and the interpersonal and historical context. It is a particular form the
person comes to assume as he interacts with his environment.

Historically, identities have been linked to the concept of individuals who need some form of identity in order to be distinguished from
others in society. This is the outside dimension, reflected in the fact
that, in the modern state, it is common for all individuals to have
identity cards of some sort, ID's that distinguish one individual from
another, a practice that easily lends itself to deception. In this sense,
identities can be assumed, and discarded, and changed. In this digital age, reduced to numbers and codes, they can also be stolen.

The outside dimension of identity also includes such givens as
gender, race, and ethnic origin, recognizable features that are, largely,
originally conferred by birth but assimilated in various ways over time
by different persons in different ways. Such aspects of identity nicely
illustrate the boundary between outside and inside. A girl normally
accepts being a girl with the physical features that accompany being
a girl, just as a boy accepts being a boy, an African American accepts being black, and so forth. But that is just the beginning of forging an identity. What kind of a girl will she be? Like her mother? A
tomboy, perhaps? A flirt? Studious? Prim? Will she compete with
boys? Will she try to seduce them? Does she aspire to a career? We
might infer that these questions are being posed to her, but in reality
the answers are assembled over time in response to a myriad of factors that no doubt include the attitudes of her parents, the perceptions
of others in her immediate environment, her native abilities, the accidents of experience, cultural beliefs, and other influences for which
it would be difficult to make a comprehensive account.[3]

It is through such experiences that the inside dimension of identity is forged into its distinctive shape. Being constructed over time, an identity adheres to a person, offering some clarity and consistency about who the person is. But, more importantly, it offers the person who possesses it both guidance and a degree of flexibility in adapting to various situations. A person will inevitably have several complex and authentic identities, as a professional, as a member of an organization, as a parent, as a man or a woman, as a source of influential ideas, and so on. There are limits to the identities each person can assume, just as there are limits to the characters an actor can impersonate. An identity is an authentic "I," but a particular "I" that has been fashioned out of particular elements of the person for particular reasons within more or less enduring circumstances.

In the context of his difficult childhood, for example, Amos had formed an identity as an outsider, someone excluded from normal participation in the lives of others, an identity that shaded into that of a loser in more despairing moments, someone destined to fail in his efforts to be accepted by others. His formative experiences can be seen as almost leading inexorably to this identity: his parents' neglect of him as a child, their own outsider status as former hippies, the absence of other adults who might have provided him with guidance, and frequent moves throughout his childhood.

Certainly he had a part in constructing his identity: his poorly controlled temper and his difficulty regulating his appetite and managing himself contributed to his identity as an outsider and loser. While he felt trapped in this identity, he also helped in creating it, choosing idiosyncratic activities and engaging in actions he knew to be bizarre because, defiantly, that was how he felt. He dismissed conventional ideas, and was arrogant and careless in his dress. His disregard for conventional appearances at the bank and his odd behavior were actions stemming from this identity that compromised his ability to fit into its culture and, as a result, his ability to work easily with others and successfully fill his role.

When Amos discovered in early adolescence that he was gay, he had little difficulty embracing it because it cemented his difference from others. Gays are born that way, he firmly believed. And if it made them different, or odd, that was a form of destiny. Being an outsider, then, was not his fault. Being gay became part of his identity, and proof of his outsider status in society, but also gave him insider status among a subgroup of gay males, a group that would accept him, he might have hoped, and among whom he would not be seen as a loser.

For Amos, his role was his job, work to do, expectations to fulfill. Some of those expectations were formally stated and consciously known, having to do with crunching numbers, forecasting trends, and advising investors. Other expectations were more informal: expectations of suitability to the culture, requirements of propriety and style in an institution whose success depended not only on performance but also on creating an image of sobriety and order that would lead clients to trust it.

Amos's identity as an outsider, on the other hand, was internal, not easily visible to others, constructed by him as a response to his situation in life and his abilities. It was a way of being that provided guidance and order. If you asked him about the specific qualities of his identity, he would say that it was who he was. This might be expressed as a rueful admission, or an angry and defiant confession, since he consciously hated being an outsider. His identity did not appear to him as something he chose, like his role, even though he had forged it over time out of the elements of his person and his life experience. It felt more like his fate.

In Chapter Two, we saw that the assertion and preservation of individual identity is a key element in the unconscious dimensions of group life. We also saw how powerful were the motives engaged in protecting self-esteem, the unconscious "security operations," in Sullivan's term, employed to keep the "self system" intact. Here we can now see that identities are specific ways of being in relation to others, constructed by persons to provide consistency and reliability in their interactions with particular sectors of their interpersonal environment.[4] Inevitably, then, Amos tended to stick to his identity, following its dictates, even though in many respects it was painful and restrictive. It told him who he was in ways that helped him to avoid even more painful disappointments and failures. Much time and therapeutic effort went into trying to alter it, even more so after it became clear to him that it stood in the way of his success at the bank.

Throughout, Amos longed to assume the complementary identity of "friend" as something of an antidote to being an outsider, and he was often attracted to friends who were quirky and odd, able to share in and understand his outsider identity. He worked assiduously at it being a friend, though often at cross-purposes because he did not know much about friendship, except from outside, as it looked to be a part of the lives of others. In his efforts, he embraced the role of friend, we might say, taking on friendship as if it were a job, with objective requirements and informal expectations. He made dates with others for dinner or the movies, he did favors and asked favors in return, he planned trips with others, but he was always haunted by fears that he could not success-fully carry it off: he would demand too much, give too much, seem too needy or desperate, show his impatience or his loneliness. Not know-ing how to be a friend, he tried to play the part, though assailed by doubts about his ability to succeed. Drained by the effort, he continuously fell back into the more securely established identity of outsider, haunted by the threatened identity of loser, retreating into solitary activities such as playing music, accumulating and watching videos, learning lan-guages, supplemented by acts of anonymous sex. He got better at friend-ship over time, and gradually came to believe that he really did have friends. Eventually, after much effort, he could feel that his successes attenuated and eroded his outsider identity.

Another identity evolved as a result of his successful work in ana-lyzing business trends. He found colleagues who had confidence in his ability, asked his opinions, and appreciated his contributions to deals they worked on together. Younger men in his firm, feeling en-couraged and helped by him, frequently sought him out, and continued to do so after they left the firm to work elsewhere. Amos eventually came to have confidence he possessed the skills and talents his work required and that he could transfer those abilities from one job to another. He received raises and promotions, and even when he encountered setbacks they did not cause him to believe he was a failure. He was hampered by his fear of being controlled, as we saw in Chapter One, but while that limited his success, it did not prevent it. In effect, over time, Amos was able to transform a role as business analyst into an identity as a successful analyst. At the start, he had not aspired to establish that identity, though he certainly did try to succeed at his job and build financial security for himself.

Eventually, Amos was able to ameliorate some of the more painful aspects of his outsider identity. There was always some ambiguity about the friends he made in business, so that he remained uneasy about what he could ask for or expect from them in return. For safety's sake, he tended to curb his requests for help out of fear that his friends would not respond as he might wish, and he was frequently overly generous with information and gifts he provided in order to earn their friendship. Nonetheless, his successes in cultivating business relationships helped him to feel less apart.

Amos was also a brother and a son. He visited his sister and mother several times a year as well as inviting them to visit him. He provided essential financial support, though he worried frequently about being overwhelmed by their needs. Increasingly, the identity of a gay man became important. He monitored the news about the movement to authorize gay marriage and avidly followed the reception of movies with gay themes. He joined a gay outdoors club and attended a gay support group. While linked to his outsider identity, this became a way in which he could cultivate a social life and approach the longed-for identity of friend.

WORKING WITH ROLES

This section focuses on the possibilities for helping those who experience conflict and difficulty in their work roles. A common term used

to describe such work is *coaching*, though, as is true of any burgeoning practice, coaching takes many forms and labors under a number
of misconceptions.[5] My chief point here is that one can use the same
conceptual system of person, identity, and role in approaching this
work. Psychotherapy starts from the other end of the continuum with
its focus on the person, so to speak, but working with roles can be
equally complex, inclusive, and rewarding.[6]

Vico came to me for help with a new job he had just been offered
as a senior manager in the sales department of a large advertising firm.
Intelligent, ambitious, handsome, energetic, a graduate of an elite prep
school and an Ivy League university, possessing an advanced degree
in accounting, he reported being frequently disparaged for shortcomings he had difficulty grasping, with accusations that often felt unfair. He wanted to understand why he had such problems working
with others; above all, he wanted to succeed. Having been involved
in a failed technology start-up a few years before, recently married
with a second baby on the way, he felt he was at a critical turning
point in his career.

A large man with a powerful voice who often spoke quickly and
loudly, he strung together ideas that were sometimes difficult to follow but that ultimately made sense. He wondered if others were jealous of him or if they saw defects and shortcomings that he himself
suspected he had. He knew he was sometimes careless, and impatient with details, and he feared that he was deficient in the analytic
skills required to parse complex contracts. On the other hand, he was
warm, encouraging of others, a team player as well as a quick and
creative thinker who could put together varied ideas in new ways.
To himself it appeared that he cut others a good deal of slack. Why
could not others cut him slack as well, he wondered, rather than harping on his typos and minor oversights?

As we went over a number of incidents at work that had led to
complaints, several issues emerged. In the work role of team leader,
he sought to be inspiring by setting an example of hard work and fresh
thinking, but he often ended up making some of his subordinates

anxious and disgruntled. Many actually did thrive under him and appreciated his stimulating and appreciative leadership, but others felt insecure and confused. Vico saw himself as generous with praise, engaged in problem solving, and willing to give subordinates leeway in how they were to carry out their responsibilities. What we came to appreciate, though, was that some of his subordinates left his meetings unsure of what they were supposed to do. Afterward, they sometimes could not recall clearly the specifics of what they had been delegated to do, and groused among themselves over his disorganized manner. Not surprisingly, these comments reached his superiors, allowing them to conclude that he was difficult to work for.

Moreover, his impatience with detail, his carelessness in checking typos and numbers in financial tables, led his bosses to be mistrustful. Their harping on these minor failings may have seemed unfair, but it jibed with the complaints that were coming up from the ranks about his disorganization. In addition, as we came to see, these shortcomings mattered more, and stood out more, in the context of a large bureaucratic organization that valued precision, consistency, and detailed coordination. To be sure, the agency was desperately in need of creative thinking in the upper levels of management, and top executives repeatedly spoke about the need to encourage it, but the well-established culture of the agency was based on the careful following of established procedures. Vico ran afoul of those norms. That, in turn, made him vulnerable in the infighting among managers for recognition and promotion. As in many such organizations, what defined success, finally, was maintaining the values and norms of the culture and appearing to superiors to simultaneously fit in and to show promise. Deviations were discouraged if not punished, even when they offered greater possibilities for success in the long-term.

Once we began to understand these issues, it came to seem obvious that Vico had to slow down in order to be more successful in filling his managerial role: he needed to repeat the conclusions reached at the end of a meeting, carefully parcel out assignments, and check his emails and reports for errors. In that way, he could fill the expectations of his role more successfully. He was able to do that to some extent, but then it became apparent that he ran into considerable inner resistance. He tapped into a level of rage about not being seen as the person he was, not appreciated for his sincere efforts to bring out the best in others, and being forced to curb his energy. His identity was at stake, and he did not want to change, to confine himself to be someone he was not.

As we explored his family background, we began to understand more precisely what that was. He had grown up in a prosperous Armenian family, but with a dark hidden life. His father was a prominent, hard-working lawyer. His mother was a beautiful but narcissistic woman who not only battled with his father constantly but who took out her frustration and rage on Vico, his three younger brothers, and his sister. Vico recalled innumerable instances of being verbally and physically abused by her, sometimes in ways that narrowly avoided serious injury. When his mother calmed down, she would explain bitterly that he deserved the punishment he got—and more—for inciting her. At times, she praised his gifts, but just as frequently would disparage and mock him for complaining, for taking his father's side, or for having failed to gain a better grade in school. Her moods were unpredictable. His father, on the other hand, worked long hours and was frequently absent. Ill-tempered and impatient at home, he frequently disparaged what he took to be his sons' laziness and entitlement. On occasion, he could be kind and interested, but for the most part he turned over the responsibility for raising his sons to their mother and seldom intervened.

Vico coped with this difficult home environment by trying to be the peacemaker, a hopeless task given his mother's narcissistic rage and his father's contempt. The effort, however, did provide the rudiments for an identity we could call the "good son," an identity that he could experience with each parent separately at times but one he could assume more consistently with teachers he sought out for recognition in school. He learned to be sympathetic, sensitive and helpful, resourceful and not easily discouraged, as well as creative and smart. Underlying this identity, I came to believe, was a degree of separation anxiety that was a product of his insecure attachment to his mother. That impelled him to keep on trying to make the best of it and, as an adult, maintain relationships with both his parents as his siblings separated and moved further away.

He also developed an identity as a lover, finding many girlfriends and sexual partners with whom he established intimate and empathic relationships. Often seeking out older women who suffered from similar insecurities, he became special in their lives through his uncanny ability to sense their moods and fulfill their sexual desires. No doubt this identity was based on a displacement of his own desires for intimacy with his difficult and sexually frustrated and provocative mother, but it also offered an affirmation of his potency, his attractiveness and charm, as well as providing some of the comfort and closeness lacking in his early childhood.

These two identities, as a good son and as a lover, guided Vico as he negotiated his way in the world. Older men, responding to the good son, often appreciated his interest and loyalty, taking him under their wing; on the other hand, they were also often able to sense the urgency of his need for them and exploit him in ways that were bewildering and hurtful to him. Similarly, though he was successful in establishing relationships with women, the women often came to want more from him than he was willing to give. Frustrated, they became demanding and manipulative. Both identities helped him make connections with others, but both frequently led to his feeling disparaged and exploited.

His third important identity, the heroic leader, also had its origins in his early childhood. As a young boy he identified with superheroes, and later with Napoleon. As he learned more history, Winston Churchill became a kind of model. He was drawn to their narratives of struggle, exile, or disappointment, and eventual success. This identity gave expression to Vico's own narcissism, but also to the ambition and talents that he needed to believe in and keep alive throughout the dark days of his childhood. Grandiose, his heroes nonetheless offered him hope as well as instruction in the patience and tolerance for frustration he needed when he felt blocked or unappreciated. He read biographies of his model heroes carefully, searching for lessons, and he frequently looked for parallels with his own life. His model heroes populated his dreams as well.

The identity of the heroic leader alternated with the identity of the good son, helping Vico to feel that, even as the good son was doomed to failure in his mission of preserving the family, he could envision ultimate success and vindication for himself. The heroic leader also offered Vico distance from the petty squabbles and setbacks, energizing him for renewed efforts. Thus, while the identities of good son and lover often backfired, causing him to feel disparaged and exploited in ways that uncannily replicated his childhood relationship with his parents, he could retreat to the identity of the heroic leader and keep alive his belief in himself.

From the perspective of these identities, it is easier to see how giving advice to Vico to slow down was futile: slowing down would negate his heroic identity. He could not submit and fit in, though he might need to lie low for a while. What he needed was a strategy for ultimate success. Being a manager was part of his exile and preparation for greatness. It was not his destiny.

Our analysis of the good son was particularly helpful in clearing up the recurrent problems he experienced with a succession of mentors. He could see how his eagerness to put them in the role of the appreciative father both blinded him to their indifference to the complementary role he hoped to play, and offered them the opportunity to exploit him with excessive demands and, at times, contempt. He was often no better at reading his mentors than he had been in reading the capacity of his parents to appreciate him as a child.

This deeper analysis of Vico's difficulties in his work role did not emerge in ten sessions, and *coaching* would have been a woefully inadequate term to describe our work. We veered and zigzagged across his life, his other roles as husband and father, his dreams and his perceptions of me and others. Yet the primary focus was always on his work, and our effort remained throughout helping him to become a more effective manager, to get his career back on track.

My work with Victor, a commodities trader, had a similar focus. Victor came to me after losing several million dollars on the trading floor of the Mercantile Exchange, a spectacular feat but easy to accomplish when markets undergo dramatic, sudden shifts. Huge amounts of money are routinely made and lost, but Victor's losing streak had gone on too long and had put him in an extremely precarious position.

Working with Victor helped me to understand the unique combination of traits and skills required of a trader: an ability to make instantaneous and continual assessments to arrive at snap decisions, which requires an intuitive mathematical mind; a focused attention in the midst of extraordinary distractions; and a taste for competition. I subsequently learned that many traders had attention deficit disorders, conditions problematic in normal life but well suited to the frenzied activity of the trading floor where events kept pace with their hyperactive minds.

In his role as trader, Victor was exceptionally talented, but clearly something had gone wrong. We quickly learned several useful things. Since Victor depended so much on his mind's ability to focus and calculate, we could see that he needed to guard against impairments to his concentration. Hangovers, lack of sleep, and anxiety were enemies. Along similar lines, he needed to be free to discern the trends of the market. Competition with other traders as well as his setting of financial goals for himself inevitably backfired. Impatience, rivalry, and stubbornness interfered with the acuity required to adapt to unexpected shifts.

Victor had little difficulty understanding this. As an experienced and successful trader, he knew how it worked. My role in these discussions was simply to codify this knowledge, put it into clear language, and then find out why it was that these simple and clear rules were not working for him. Fascinating as it was for me to learn the psychological principles behind successful trading, Victor's problems lay elsewhere.

The oldest of four sons, Victor had had a contentious relationship with his parents. His father, a professor at a prestigious Ivy League university, was distant and formal, while his mother seemed preoccupied with her status as the wife of a tenured faculty member. A key event in his childhood was the family's move from a somewhat ramshackle neighborhood with a varied population, a place they could afford at the beginning of his father's academic career, to a more affluent neighborhood they felt was more suitable to an established member of the faculty. That move separated Victor from the many friends with whom he had played sports and hung out after school, many of whom were black and working class. He went back to his old neighborhood repeatedly to be with his friends, but the move marked a dramatic shift in his relationship with his family. Henceforth he actively tried to separate himself from what he took to be his parents' pretentiousness and detachment from real life, objecting to their lack of interest in who he really was and what he really valued. Graduating from high school, Victor went on to college but soon dropped out. He got involved with drugs and alcohol, and lived with a former barmaid with whom he had an illegitimate child.

Victor had developed the identity of a rebel against his parents' values, a rebel and a daredevil who lived on the edge, courting danger in ways that, it appeared to him, his parents never had. But this was a confusing time for him. He did not fully grasp what drove his actions. He could not accept his parents' goals and values, and no viable alternative presented itself to the life he found himself embracing. Eventually, he got back into college, graduated, and moved to New York, where he found a job at the Mercantile Exchange. The exchange appealed to him, in part, because it was a place of unpretentious, self-made men, crudely and openly competitive. It also provided opportunities to flirt with danger. Ability alone seemed to matter, and he found that he possessed the ability to make significant money.

Success gradually impelled him into a new world of affluence. He married a beautiful, European-born wife, had two children, and moved into a lavish apartment, trying to settle down, though obviously feeling some discomfort with the trappings of his success. He would invite fellow traders over to drink beer with him on the terrace of his new apartment, while making fun of his establishment neighbors. Clearly he was at odds with the life he found himself living, pulled in different directions. The mix of money, European culture, crude competition, and family did not harmonize, to the point where, I came to think as I spoke with Victor about these developments, he felt compelled to sabotage his success. A series of big losses forced him to sell the apartment. Continuing losses forced him to scramble with debt and unpaid taxes. He was in trouble, but he had managed to cancel what had been, in effect, a repetition of his childhood move away from his old working-class neighborhood, affirming an identity as a rebel who would rather flirt with danger than settle for a life that felt stifling and false. His losses restored excitement to his life. They provided him with a temporary focus on survival, but they did not suggest an alternative set of goals, a new definition of success.

It took some time for this to be clarified, and more time for some answers to emerge. Victor's trading gradually improved. His self-destructive tendencies did not change easily; having been integrated into his identity as a rebel and daredevil, they took many forms, abetted by the ease with which he could be distracted and his tendency to be impulsive. Nonetheless, he eventually paid his debts and back taxes. He separated from his wife, and began to think more directly about the kind of life he actually wanted to lead. That, in turn, began to produce some reflection on to what use to put his earnings. The bits of his life gradually began to look as if they could coalesce.

For both Vico and Victor, our work on their roles took us, inevitably, into issues of identity because that was where any effort to change ran up against significant resistance. If roles are constructed in accord with external pressures and defined in terms of function, the key question for helping the role-holder becomes how to mobilize skills and the inner resources necessary to succeed in each role. Does the person have the native talents and skills to do what is required, and does he have the motivation to carry it through?

Traders, as we have seen, need to be gifted with mathematical skills, a capacity for concentration, and a taste for rough-and-tumble competition. Moreover, Victor's identity allowed him to find the milieu of the trading floor congenial and welcoming. The problem he faced—and still faces—is how to integrate his various interests and values into a coherent life so that his taste for taking risks does not bring about self-destruction. It is a matter of balancing a complex mix of identifications and interests so that success does not force him to be untrue to himself. In short, he has to modify his identity so that it is compatible with success.

In Vico's case, the requirements of his identities as a good son and heroic leader made his role at work difficult for him. He was too willing to please, too willing to overextend himself, too generous and gullible to succeed in a culture that valued conformity and reliability over creativity and drive. For Vico, finally, the solution was to find a more suitable job and congenial environment. He needed a new role.

Perhaps the most important lesson of these examples is how identities can work against roles, compromising a person's ability to succeed at work. Amos had a very difficult time overcoming his identity as an outsider in applying himself to the role of business analyst. Unconsciously resisting the control of the authorities at work, he was struggling to maintain the safety of the familiar identity of someone who did not fit in. Similarly, Vico's identity as a good son compromised his ability to be an effective manager at his firm. Though some of his difficulty was rooted in the impulsivity of his "person," his identity blinded him to the motives of others; he could not see how they exploited his persistent efforts to reconcile differences and resolve conflicts. In Victor's case, the identity of rebel, which gave zest to his work as a trader, undermined his ability to enjoy his success. To avoid emulating the lives of his parents, he plunged himself into debt.

In such cases, the work of the therapist or coach is to realign the links between identity and role; one or the other has to be modified. Once Victor became aware of the danger his identity as a rebel posed to his economic stability, he was able to begin to construct a new sense of what success might mean for him, a new identity in which money and social status did not mean what he believed it did for his parents. We could say that in Vico's case, a better grasp of his identity held out the promise of finding a role that could more fully mobilize his enthusiasm and skills. Amos, over time, built a substantially new identity as a financial analyst.

This helps us to see that the person who is able to find a role, supported and enhanced by his identity, is blessed. We can also see that the ability to construct an identity in alignment with the givens of a person and the demands of a role is a strong basis for successful work.

It is crucial to bear in mind that all these factors are constantly shifting. Roles change as systems are reorganized and as persons in related roles take them up in new ways. Roles can be de-authorized, undermined, even abolished. Identities can be slowly reconstructed, but they also can shift or be transformed. Amos's identity as an outsider was vulnerable to collapsing into that of a loser. Vico's identity as a heroic leader did not articulate easily with that of the good son; similarly, it often did not jibe with the identity of lover. The sudden discontinuities were troubling and disorganizing. "Persons," of course, are the more stable entities in this constellation, but even they change over time. Aging, illness, wars, economic reversals, and natural disasters change persons. Marriage, births, divorce, and the death of parents or of children lead to radical changes in identities as well as persons.

SOME CONCLUSIONS

A role can be thought of without a particular person to occupy it. In this sense, roles are durable, outlasting their inhabitants, though a role cannot function without a person to embody it. It is through identities that one becomes an actor on the social stage, but roles are the means of accomplishment, the vehicle through which one joins others in addressing tasks. It is possible to think of a person without a role, but in our interconnected world it is increasingly difficult to imagine. A person without a role suffers from, in Milan Kundera's memorable words, "the unbearable lightness of being." Adrift in an alien world that has stripped him of the ability to be embodied in work, he appears to himself to float.

Any particular "I" reflects an overlapping complexity. We are inevitably at a loss to say what part of this complexity is being expressed at any given moment. We usually know the person uttering the "I" or enacting its intentions, but we will not know the hidden personal meaning or motivation of the utterance, even as the person himself may not know it. We are more likely to know the role, though the intent or strategy it arises from may be obscure to us. We are less likely to be conscious of the identity mobilized in the role or the identities being obscured by it, though we will inevitably have some sense of them. We are even less likely to know how they contend with each other and with the identities of others. An "I" is manifest, and all we know is that a response is called for.

A concluding word about roles: As we have seen, roles are designed in such a way that different persons can occupy them. Usually, they are not tailored to individual persons, though different persons can sometimes alter them to suit their unique talents. In the final analysis, though, the justification for altering the role comes from the fact that the change is more efficient or effective in achieving the goals implicit in its design, not because it is more congenial to the person.

Organizations can be seen as structures built of roles, offering similar demands and constraints. They are inevitably infiltrated with irrationality and contradiction, but because of their stress on objectivity and task, and on the capacity of persons to be interchangeable in roles, they almost attain a kind of permanence. Roles survive persons. For this reason, it appears that organizations are able to strive for an immortality denied to persons. In the next chapter, we will see how this appearance of transcendence profoundly affects our relationships to organizations and to each other in organizations.

Five

ORGANIZATIONAL LIFE

■

THE NEW CONTEXT

Our world is a densely packed, overlapping mosaic of organizations, creating deeply ingrained expectations of predictability and order. Today, we anticipate wages will be paid as expected, dividends as promised, loans repaid as agreed. Trains and planes should leave on time. Products and supplies should be reordered and replaced as needed, deliveries made, promises kept. New social trends will be monitored, new regulations put forth. Corruption and fraud should be prosecuted. Police will continuously patrol our streets, while firemen are on call to cope with emergencies. Should these expectations not be met, we tend to be outraged and turn to the courts and elected officials for redress; sometimes we organize protests and political action groups. When, inevitably, disaster strikes in the form of earthquakes, storms, epidemics, and wars, we turn to organizations for help with the disruption of our lives and, eventually, the restoration of our familiar worlds. If those organizations fail to act effectively, we call for task forces to investigate and report.

Over the past several hundred years, vast upheavals of political and economic revolutions, wars, and mass migrations gradually dissolved the traditional social orders that once provided stability to our lives. Speculators, adventurers, inventors, explorers, and entrepreneurs, working behind the cutting edge of change, transformed historical dislocations into sources of wealth and power for themselves as well as jobs for workers and streams of income for shareholders. This was far from smoothly or equitably done, but it slowly brought about today's complex social landscape of organizations.

To be sure, our world is plagued by injustice and inequality. Not everyone profits from or enjoys these networks that promise stability. The poor, the unemployed, and the displaced still live on the margins. But this expectation of order has become our norm of civilized life. Even the failures of society are measured against a standard that, in the past, did not exist.

This does not mean that the world as a whole is actually more secure than it was two hundred years ago. Innumerable local conflicts, genocidal campaigns, terrorist plots, epidemics, new diseases, and environmental disasters still afflict us. But the locus of our insecurity has shifted. By and large, we think of the threats as coming from outside, elsewhere: from nature, the realm outside our world of carefully drawn boundaries, or from the disorganized Third World, not the First. Within the last century, at least in the West, we have come to turn to our corporations, partnerships, and conglomerates; our local, state, and federal governments; our associations, unions, agencies, leagues, societies, cooperatives, and guilds—while we strive to build coalitions, federations, and syndicates to coordinate their activities. When unexpected trouble strikes, we create new government departments, task forces, and special units to assess the problem and develop new procedures and regulations. We have come to believe that organization is what lends stability and order to our world.

This is far from an unmixed blessing. The dream of organization in the twentieth century produced the nightmare of totalitarianism. The Third Reich and Communist regimes killed millions, applying our capacity for mass production to death camps and gulags. The massive wars we endured in the twentieth century were based on our new ability to create powerful structures of command and control, while leading to the invention and manufacture of weapons of unprecedented destruction.

Less immediately threatening are the myriad ways in which mass production and world trade, while lowering prices and increasing the distribution of goods, have often degraded their quality. Our homes, often stocked with unneeded and obsolete products, are less solidly built. Well-meaning city planners have brought new slums into existence, while social planners have unintentionally disrupted existing family and community bonds. Fruits and vegetables, available now from sources around the world, can be standardized, but also tasteless.

Social critics have noted with alarm how the space of human relationships has become increasingly structured, monitored, mediated. As a result of living in a world so thoroughly planned, dependency is encouraged, while spontaneity and originality seem more and more difficult to achieve, and authenticity and honesty harder to preserve.[1] Expecting planning and order, we are unprepared to act ourselves, to take initiative when it is needed. The unconscious, driven by the need to adapt, to help us survive, inevitably pushes us to fit in and conform to this new reality, unless ambivalence causes us to equivocate or conflict causes us to rebel.

Those who work in business are surrounded by intricate arrays of suppliers and distributors, law and accounting firms, advertising agencies, PR experts, lobbyists, recruiters, consultants, government agencies, and unions. Not-for-profits are likewise woven into organizational networks, whether as partners or allies, or as monitors of other organizations; in addition, they must interact with foundations, funding agencies, and regulators. The self-employed belong to professional associations, societies, and support groups. As citizens, we belong to political parties, community and block associations, chambers of commerce or rotary clubs, and myriad other groups that promote local goals. As taxpayers, we support and rely upon the organizations of government to police our streets, collect our garbage, put out fires, and supply water and other essentials. In addition to public schools, we are serviced by an immense network of private schools, colleges, and universities. We belong to alumni groups, veteran associations, lobbying organizations that promote environmental, human rights or other interests that concern us. We join book clubs, co-ops, choruses, and groups that travel together, dance together, and clean up their communities together. We are team members in sports we play, and the leagues they form. We become "friends" or "members" of the cultural institutions we enjoy.

To a remarkable degree, the rise of organizations parallels and shadows the invisible, continuous work of consciousness. As we saw in Chapter One, our brains work ceaselessly to construct a world we can rely upon, one that organizes our perceptions and responses to provide coherence and predictability. While our brains edit out discontinuities so that the world appears seamless and consistent, the world through its organizations also works perpetually to renew itself and impose order. Our organizations tell us what we need to know and how to act. They foster our sense of agency, our belief that we are responding to events. Within their organizations, executives and managers, not just presidents and CEO's, are prone to believing that they really are in charge of events.

This should not be surprising as organizations are, after all, human constructions. Since we continuously make and remake them, they will inevitably reflect who we are and how we think. Like our minds, they will always lag behind events, reflecting our understanding of how things were and of how we expect them to be. They will struggle unsuccessfully to incorporate new information, inevitably tending to reject and discard the new—if it does not sound silent alarms, rousing themselves to repel or disconfirm what does not fit.

This is how the mind works, too, but it also reflects a profound historical development, the increasing rationalization of the world. In the spirit of the Enlightenment, organizations became our way of extending the sway of reason over human affairs and our control over nature. New conventions and traditions were developed, but over time they became more flexible and adaptive. Over the long run, they offered the promise of progress, the expectation that more wealth will be generated, more leisure created, while poverty and diseases are gradually ameliorated. This was, at least, the hope of reason.

But there are also some crucial differences between minds and organizations. Organizations are slowly and laboriously constructed;

unlike minds, they do not function automatically. As a result there is room within organizations for persons with critical or oppositional identities to detect the inconsistencies in conventional thought, or for those in competitive or analytic roles to see through what look like smooth, impenetrable arguments. The ubiquitous presence of markets in our society fosters and normalizes such aggressive scrutiny; the clash of competition produces more critical awareness, and that, in turn, produces new organizations for new purposes.

Moreover, organizations are far more prone to deceptions. While we have come to expect a world of order, and have come to rely upon it, we are frequently let down. Indeed, our expectations can make it easier for us to be misled. Our tendency to edit out disparities and discrepancies from perception is all too easily exploited by those who use the procedures of organizations as facades to hide plots and obscure injustice.

Another difference: failures of adaptation to new social and natural developments will eventually be highlighted. Task forces will be set in motion to find out what went wrong. Heads will roll. Individual minds tend to be more forgiving of their failures if not altogether oblivious of them.

Early theorists of organizations emphasized the value of these rational and orderly developments. Max Weber, countering Marx's analysis of the increasingly destructive cycles of capitalism, noted the stabilizing effects of bureaucracy. The new discipline of sociology brought structure to our understanding of society. As industrial organizations came to dominate our economy, the field of management studies was developed, largely to help increase productivity. Charles Taylor, founder of "scientific management," analyzed the sequence and speed of production, while Elton Mayo studied the motivation of workers in his famous Hawthorne experiments at Western Electric. Henry Ford's assembly lines brought huge economies of scale, while Alfred Sloan, chairman of GM, pioneered the development of industrial organizations characterized by vertical and horizontal integration. Organizations, it came to be thought, advance the project of enlightenment, and consciousness is an indispensable element in their design and management.

But consciousness, as we have seen, is a small fraction of our mental activity. Organizations, too, are profoundly infiltrated with unconscious processes. Individual minds hold on to their familiar patterns and convictions, even if they consciously comply with new procedures and agree that changes must be made. People do not easily give up what feels familiar and safe, and they tenaciously protect their self-esteem. Groups, moreover, forge unconscious agreements to preserve the identities of their members, and set imperceptible limits to their thinking while sabotaging ideas that do not conform. They self-organize in ways that cannot be predicted or controlled. Each organization has its unique history and set of myths that limit and shape current thinking. Departments will be motivated by unconscious enmities toward other departments. Management may come to seem oppressive, an enemy.

Organizations could never entirely live up to their promise of rationality, hard as management tried. Hidden conflict, irrational behavior, and defenses against anxiety have become inextricably woven into their fabric. Indeed, the very expectations we have developed about the orderliness and predictability of organizations create the space for procedures and rules that are not primarily in the service of an organization's ostensible goals but serve, rather, to promote security and comfort for those, housed inside, who find refuge in familiarity and control. On the other hand, organizations cannot renounce their striving for predictability and order. The structures we build for ourselves, whether houses or committees, factories or institutions, have to be reliable and conform to common expectations. And they have to produce results. This tension is a fact of organizational life.

Recently, however, this whole structure has been called into question. The new conventional wisdom among management experts is that the world is changing so rapidly that organizations need to become more adaptive in order to survive. Decision making must be accelerated and decentralized, with authority extended to the frontiers. Stability has come to be viewed as an obstacle to change, predictability as a liability. Organizations are now under pressure to become nimble, flexible, relentlessly innovative.

Certainly for major corporations there is much truth to this. A number of significant forces have brought about sweeping changes in our economic landscape. First, the rapid pace of technological development, especially in the realm of information and communication, has disrupted old assumptions. Multibillion-dollar corporations that did not exist twenty years ago have been built on the basis of new products and markets. Second, economic competition is now waged on a global scale, requiring both the scope and diversity of multinational corporations. Meanwhile, China and India are emerging as new world powers.[2] Third, we have entered into a new unstable phase in the evolution of capitalism, "investor capitalism," in which the price of shares has eclipsed all other indicators of success, including profitability, employment, and market share. Economies, which once relied on the market to raise funds, are now continuously tied to the market; through pension plans, savings accounts, mortgages, endowments and loans, we have all become dependent on our investments increasing in value. As a result, reliable products, high employment, market share—traditional earmarks of success—are becoming less and less relevant.[3] In the background lurk other threats to the status quo such as the aging population and the threat of global warming.

Perhaps the stability and economic security we took for granted, especially in the post–World War II era, guaranteed by our massive corporations and equally massive governments, was an interlude. Corporations can no longer deliver the predictability and security we came to expect of them. Our changing expectations have had a significant ripple effect throughout society. Government is pulling back from commitments to health care and retirement benefits, modifying if not dismantling the social safety nets that supplemented the security that organizations once offered.

Initially corporations focused on downsizing and outsourcing to become leaner and more aggressive. Productivity was the focus. Now it appears that, efficiency of production and service delivery having reached a limit, management experts need different ideas to cope with these continuing new pressures. Much interest has been expressed in "culture change," helping members of organizations become more active and assertive, less dependent. More recently, learning has become a focus of attention. Peter Senge has written about the "learning organization," encouraging the belief that continuous learning and openness to new ideas can provide the new products and strategies corporations now require. Charles Handy, following Peter Drucker's reflections on our world of discontinuous change, stressed the need for "upside-down thinking."[4] The interest in coaching that we noted in Chapter Four is a function of these efforts to galvanize management, as is the proliferation of institutes of leadership.

On a less rational level, troubled corporations engage in the search for "saviors," CEO's who have track records of turning their organizations around. Despite little evidence that those reputations are deserved, as it takes time and substantial collective effort to bring about significant change, boards of directors are under pressure to come up with solutions that will satisfy their shareholders and investment analysts so that the price of their shares will rise.[5] Along similar lines, there has been an extraordinary increase in the salaries and stock options offered to senior management. The justification is that their contributions were indispensable to their corporation's success, yet there is scant correlation between success and compensation.

Clearly this has introduced a profound insecurity into the world of major corporations, the ones that generate headlines and a major share of stock revenues. But most businesses, by far, are still family owned and run. The vast majority of organizations are small, and new ones are continually created to serve new needs. We still seek to build, rebuild, or repair the systems that will help us to address the problems and opportunities we face.

To be sure, the world has come to feel considerably less secure in recent years. We work harder, vacation less. Savings are declining, health costs increasing, as insurance benefits are curtailed. The gap between the rich and the poor is growing. As a result, as worry and stress increase, we search for distractions and palliatives. Fundamentalist religious beliefs are on the increase; the use of medications to counter depression and anxiety rises; tensions between social groups escalate. We know from past experience how easily such conditions of insecurity and deprivation can be exploited. As people seek scapegoats to blame and opportunities to restore some sense of control over events, however illusory, large-scale movements of repression and persecution can thrive.

More immediately, however, these conditions have stimulated interest in the organizational unconscious. The pressure to be more adaptive and responsive to change is breaking down some conventional barriers to thought. New ideas are welcome—at least they seem worth a try. More attention is being paid to ingrained resistances to new information and change. Some of this new thinking is in the service of increasing productivity and profits, some for the sake of increasing personal satisfaction and fulfillment. These are not always mutually exclusive goals, as the ability to work successfully increases human satisfaction. But it is happening, and will continue.

This chapter presents an array of examples that illustrate how an understanding of the unconscious helps those working with organizations. It is a collection of cases, not a systematic overview, because the field is too complex and varied to offer that degree of conceptual clarity to practitioners—at least at this stage. Not only are organizations themselves varied, reflecting their deep ties to their purposes, but also the problems they face are constantly changing. As I will argue again in Chapter Seven, what is required by this complexity are eyes that are trained to see and tools that work, not overarching theories that pull it all together. Standardized approaches will not suffice.

This chapter will be a mosaic, then, reflecting the mosaic of organizations in our lives. It will also describe some approaches that have proved useful. It will also describe some of the conceptual tools that are needed, in the contexts of their use. That should help to give a

fuller picture of what is being accomplished, without creating a misleading impression of comprehensiveness or certainty. This is a field
under construction, and it may well always be that way.

GROUPS IN FLIGHT

The smallest unit of organization is the group or team, and the cockpit crew of a modern airliner is a good example of a tightly constructed
work group. Each crew member has a carefully defined role, closely
articulated with every other role in order to accomplish the task of a
safe flight. Economy dictates efficiency, a minimum number of members with little overlapping responsibility; safety mandates clarity.
At least, this is how it is supposed to function.

In her examination of the training of cockpit crews, Amy Frayer,
an educator and a pilot herself, has been able to pinpoint how two
unconscious factors can easily infiltrate such a tight system: group
process can distract crew members from their primary task of keeping their plane on course, and feelings of intimidation in the face of
authority can prevent crew members from speaking up, even when
faced with disaster. Reconstructions of crashes that could easily have
been avoided make her case compelling.[6]

The crash of Eastern Airlines flight 401 in the Florida Everglades
in 1972 illustrates how an internal problem distracted a highly experienced crew. A recording of the conversation in the cockpit revealed
that the crew had become preoccupied with a malfunctioning landing gear light. Uncertain if the light indicated a defect in the landing
gear or was itself just broken, the flight engineer engaged the whole
crew in his dilemma. It became the focus of their attention, as they
tried other ways of checking on the problem. To be sure, it was not
an insignificant matter: had the landing gear been defective, there was
no way the plane could have averted a crash landing. But as the crew
became engaged with a problem that was the specific responsibility
of the engineer, there was a breakdown in the system of roles, as a
result of which the primary task of the team as a whole was gradu-

ally abandoned. At the last minute, the pilot realized that the plane was dangerously low, but it was too late to avert a crash that killed all on board.

This is a good example of a form of "groupthink" or "basic assumption" behavior, in which a group unconsciously and inadvertently constructs an alternate focus that screens out the primary reason for its existence.[7] We all have had such experiences, usually with a less disastrous outcome: a committee will meet, become focused on a procedural detail, and, at some point, someone will wonder, "What are we here for"; or an athletic team practicing its plays will become preoccupied with its internal competition and lose sight of its goal. In each case, we could say the group became too cohesive, too preoccupied with its own internal dynamics to hold in mind the external reality that its primary mission required it to address. In the case of the Eastern flight crew, several factors probably combined to cause the group to become distracted: the engineer's need for technical and, perhaps, emotional support, the internal locus of the problem (was it the light or the landing gear), the pilot's too great confidence in the automatic flight systems. As always, other factors contributed to bring about the disaster: the failure of the air traffic controllers to notice or to question the plane's loss of altitude and, perhaps, inadequate training in using automated flight controls. But whatever the specific factors, the group did what groups do, easily and often: it lost sight of external reality.

Six years later, United Flight 173 ran out of fuel while preparing to land in Portland, Oregon. In this case, the focus of the distraction was the same, but the dynamics were different: the pilot's preoccupation with a potential landing gear problem led him to neglect the fact that, while he was arranging for a possible crash landing, the plane was running out of fuel. In this case, both the engineer and co-pilot repeatedly warned him about the declining level of fuel in the tanks, but, as the information did not register with the pilot, they gave up their attempts and kept to business as usual—until, one by one, the engines sputtered and stopped. Here, a major factor was clearly the intimidating force of the pilot's authority, no doubt reinforced by his authoritarian behavior. But it had to be the case that the acquiescence of the cockpit crew, staying at their posts even as they were facing certain catastrophe, reflected a collective denial of reality. The crew was intimidated by the pilot's authority, but they each also turned away from the fact that they too would inevitably die as a result of his preoccupation.

The task force investigating the Portland crash, taking into account the intimidating power of authority, recommended assertiveness training for crew members, but more may be required to avert future disasters. For teams to work effectively, particularly under difficult circumstances, team members need to be trained to understand the complexities of team life and its capacity to distract their attention unconsciously from reality, without their knowing it. As these examples illustrate, it is important to maintain roles and their coordination; the failure to do that led to the Everglades crash. At the same time, each member has to bear in mind that there is a larger purpose to their ensemble; a crew member cannot abdicate his responsibility for the performance of other crew members. All group members share responsibility for the group's effectiveness.

Balancing responsibilities is an essential, if difficult, requirement for the success of group efforts. It is difficult to hold to one's role and its responsibilities, especially when unconscious pressures arise. Faced with insidious inclinations to conform as well as avoid confrontation with authority—pressures outlined in Chapter Two—group members may inadvertently subvert their work. There is no simple solution to this problem apart from a greater awareness of the danger and an understanding of the need to speak up and intervene, the solution Frayer proposed as a part of training for cockpit teams.

LEADING AND FOLLOWING

We tend to think that leaders have inherent talents for leadership— or that they lack them.[8] But as the examples we just looked at suggest, leadership is actually a complex relationship between leaders and followers. A leader has specific obligations, but he is the first among equals, not an unquestionable authority. The pilot may lead the cockpit crew, but he also has to work with them.

Another example, from an academic institution, should make this interdependence clear. I had never met the dean whose departure triggered the events my colleague and I were called in to help the faculty cope with, but by all the accounts he was a remarkable man and his achievements had been extraordinary.[9] The faculty and the acting dean sought consultation because, in the aftermath of his resignation, the school was paralyzed. The record of his achievements was truly impressive. In just a few years he had significantly increased the school's endowment, including the establishment of several chairs that allowed for the recruiting of nationally prominent scholars. He had instituted a number of exciting new programs and linked the academic resources of the school with pressing needs of the local community. In the process he was able to link a number of important local institutions to the school, providing more local support and backing than the school had ever enjoyed previously. Finally, as a result of these and other advances, the national standing of the school was dramatically improved. Indeed, the school turned the corner, eliminating the risk it had faced of being disbanded by the university's administration, whose support had always been shaky.

But now the faculty was paralyzed. Several national searches for senior faculty positions had ended in failure and acrimony. Faculty in-fighting made it impossible for new courses to be approved. Confidential faculty discussions were leaked to the student newspaper, prompting bitter public accusations and counteraccusations. Everyone agreed about the dean's record of achievement, and yet it could not be denied that in some way the paralysis and bitterness was also a legacy of his leadership. What had happened to bring this about?

The former dean more than willingly agreed to be interviewed by us over the phone, as part of our plan to speak individually with all senior faculty members. My experience of interacting with him confirmed his engaging leadership qualities; he himself was eager to understand how he might have contributed to bringing about this distressing state of affairs. But as we assembled the information we gleaned from our interviews, two things gradually began to emerge. One was that the dean, by his own admission, loved to concentrate on the new projects that represented for him the future of the school, and he focused his attention on those bright and energetic members of the faculty and staff who came up with new initiatives and projects. Those he encouraged and supported. The others, he left alone.

Or so it seemed. Actually, as we probed more, it came to seem that he actually avoided confrontations with the more conservative, traditional faculty members or those whom he came to view as unproductive or uncommitted. One example of this: a faculty search committee was established to find a senior person to fill an endowed chair. He realized early on that the committee, in his view, was not paying sufficient attention to affirmative-action guidelines the school had established, but he put off speaking his mind until the committee had almost completed its work. At the point when the committee was about to submit its short list containing the name of not one woman or person of color, he felt he had no choice but to suspend the committee, an action that deeply wounded the committee chair and angered the other members who had invested considerable energy and time in its efforts.

Likewise, he had repeatedly passed over requests for promotion from some faculty members whom he perceived as unproductive, but he did not speak with them about it. In reviewing these incidents with him, one could sense his strong aversion to people he felt were self-indulgent and lazy, qualities quite the opposite from those he sought out and rewarded in others. Perhaps he feared expressing his contempt were he to talk with them more openly, but it does seem as if they picked up on his contempt for them nonetheless. And, of course, they were the ones who leaked inside information to the newspaper and spread rumors of the school's internal troubles after he left, undermining his efforts to bolster the reputation of the school in the university.

The result of these actions over several years was that tensions within the faculty were exacerbated. In effect, he chose—though it certainly was not a fully conscious choice—to lead part of the faculty, not the whole. The part he neglected and into which he projected and perhaps allowed others to project feelings of incompetence, lack of commitment, and backwardness, found its opportunity to retaliate and vent its envy and rage upon his departure.[10]

But there was another dynamic factor that contributed to this backlash. In fact, had the problem been simply neglecting one segment of the faculty, the school might well have found the means to surmount these divisive forces. Those the dean disparaged were generally not widely admired; their complaints might have been discounted. The second issue was, I believe, the unconscious dependency the dean had fostered during the period of his energetic and highly successful leadership. Forging powerful alliances with outsiders as well as the administration, which vigorously backed his efforts to transform the school, bringing in new money, he became something of a savior. Many people paired with him in initiating new projects. I think it is fair to say that many people loved him—just as others came to hate him. So when he left, it was as if the school was bereft: it lost a person that many felt, unconsciously, they could not do without.

The people mobilized by the dean were highly intelligent and capable, not prone to relying on others to get things done. But it seemed that their relationships were virtually entirely with the dean. Much revitalization and transformation had occurred under the dean's leadership, but a new sense of group identity had failed to coalesce. The institution that had changed under his leadership was based less on new sets of relationships among the faculty than on relationships with him. When he left, then, it was as if the linchpin was removed, and no other structures of group relationship had come into existence to support the institution in his absence.

The dean failed to attend to group dynamics. But we also have to take into account the fact that the kind of organization he led was particularly resistant to change. Academic institutions are exceptionally vulnerable to this kind of disarray and acrimony because there can be little incentive to individuals to pull together as a group. Tenure, which is permanent job security, and the tradition of academic freedom promote the notion that each classroom is a separate fiefdom under the control of an individual professor. At the same time, the enormous divide between the work of administration, on the one hand, and the work of teaching, on the other, promotes a kind of institutional helplessness on the part of instructors—if not, at the other extreme, a Machiavellian, almost sociopathic competence. In such a setting, instructors themselves resist the notion of collective responsibility. They tend to assume that the administration is "up to no good," has "sold out," lacks serious scholarly purpose, and so forth. Evidence points to the dean's having inherited exactly such a polarized situation. Previous administrations had fostered such virulent projections across the administration–faculty divide, rendering the faculty even less able to experience itself—much less think of itself—as a cohesive entity, as a whole.

Thus, there may not have been a way to bring the faculty together. Perhaps there was little choice but to form individual alliances with ambitious younger faculty members, as the dean did, in order to expedite change. Nevertheless, as a result, two opposing groups were gradually brought into existence. It was inevitable that they would fight, and that the advantage would be on the side of the excluded, the group that had a common set of grievances as well as securely entrenched positions. The newer group had only relationships with the dean, not with one another, and, bereft of his leadership, were unprepared for the backlash when it came. Had the dean stayed longer, had he prepared his cadres for the battles he might have foreseen, had he grasped the need for them to establish bonds with each other as well as with himself, had be been more aware of his behavior toward the more senior faculty members, or less inattentive to the impact of his behavior on them, the outcome might have been different.

The dean's strategy here echoes that of contemporary corporate leaders who, like him, are hired with a mandate for change but have far more authority to hire and fire. Looking to shake up their organizations, their first priority is often to dispose of the old executives, frequently seen as encumbered by tradition and old assumptions, and to replace them with a team of new followers bringing fresh ideas and innovative methods. Indeed, this approach has often been characterized as a kind of "war" against the established organization.[11] Such strategies are often effective in bringing about dramatic change quickly, but not without a cost that is usually paid out of sight.

Jack Welch has famously observed that loyalty has no place in the modern corporation, meaning that one has continually to prove one's value in order to keep one's position. There is a point to that in the sense that an organization is not a family; one has to work for the right to belong. But it is an incomplete truth. Welch himself demanded loyalty from his followers as he set about to fight the entrenched corporate culture of GE, and he rewarded them handsomely.

More importantly, loyalty has to do with reliability and trust. It is a fundamental part of human relationships that, neglected or abused, leads to resentment and fear. Denied or disclaimed, it will lead an underground life. Without claims on others, persons will inevitably feel alone, insecure, anxious. And as a result, they will collude unconsciously to create defenses that distort work relationships, and that may threaten both their ability to collaborate with coworkers, and their ability to advance their projects.

EMBATTLED GROUPS

An organizational chart displays the hierarchy of positions in a system, who reports to whom. But consistent with our cultural bias toward individuals, it neglects the fact that each position in the chart actually represents a leadership role, a role that has a particular function to fulfill within the group. More than anything else, an organization is an assemblage of groups whose coordination makes it possible for the organization to accomplish its mission. Groups do the work of organizations best by working together.

Bureaucracy is the term we usually use to describe a structure of integrated groups, each with its carefully designed function. But indispensable as bureaucracy is to modern organizations, it is frequently denigrated or derided; "bureaucracy" has come to describe systems that are slow moving, inefficient, and obstructive. This, too, points to our cultural bias in favor of individuals. We tend to view individual persons as trapped by bureaucracy, thwarted, hamstrung. We do not see bureaucracy as providing opportunities for persons to thrive in roles. This bias often undermines those who speak up for the essential aspects of bureaucracy. As we just saw, leaders often end up fighting their bureaucracies, waging war in order to make their organizations more responsive and efficient. On the other hand, this attitude toward bureaucracy is often more than a bias. All too often, bureaucracies do become obstructive and inefficient. All too often their purpose becomes the provision of security—not the accomplishment of work.

Larry Hirschhorn worked with a bank that was trying to adapt to rapidly changing market conditions and described the difficulties of engaging its bureaucracy in the struggle.[12] Deregulation and the rise of competition from other financial organizations had led the bank's management to realize that, to survive, it had to diversify its offerings to its traditional customers. It concluded that it had to be more active on its front line, its point of contact with customers. Tellers, formerly required simply to be careful and accurate in providing routine services, now were going to be trained to be more active in promoting and selling the bank's other services. In effect, they were being transformed from functionaries to part of the bank's sales and marketing forces.

The senior managers, not being naive, knew this would entail a culture shift. Employees who, in the past, had been exposed to relatively little risk while ensconced in a system that provided precise expectations and stable routines, were now required to take the initiative with customers. That meant that they would have to use their judgment more, try harder to engage customers and, as a result, in-

evitably run a greater risk of failure. The senior managers set up training courses to help tellers make the shift in their roles. To monitor
progress in this change, the managers set up a tracking system requiring tellers to record what their customers' initial requests were
as well as what services they ended up purchasing. Hirschhorn was
hired as a consultant to see how it was working.

Not surprisingly, there was considerable resistance. Tellers re-
sented the extra work and the increased insecurity of their newly
defined roles; they also complained about the implicit devaluing of
their traditional customer services. Often they failed to fill out the
forms. Management, angered in turn by their failure to comply with
the new rules, accused the tellers of sabotage and, even, the theft of
services. What seemed like a fairly traditional labor–management
conflict escalated into a battle in which each side projected destructive motives onto the other: the tellers saw management as aloof and
punitive, while management saw the tellers as lazy and dishonest.
The irony was that an initiative designed to generate a new culture of
commitment ended up creating a new culture of blame and punishment. Reflecting on this situation, Hirschhorn noted that management
"could not force workers to feel more responsible. Such feelings had
to emerge through a complex combination of incentive, negotiation,
and daily collaboration."[13]

To be successful, Hirschhorn saw, such a process would require
management itself to be more engaged and, hence, also more willing
to be at risk for failure. Management, in short, needed to engage more
fully with the tellers on the transformation of their responsibilities,
meeting with them, acknowledging the new stress they were exposed
to, or listening to their gripes. But to do so would have meant facing
the same risks they were asking the tellers to assume. And encased
in the same hierarchical bureaucracy, the managers were just as reluctant as the tellers to give up the security their traditional roles had
provided. Hirschhorn noted, for example, that in a meeting of branch
managers, called to report on the progress of the new program, the
branch managers were almost uniformly silent. In their own way,

paralleling the resistance of the tellers in simply not filling out the required forms, they were subverting the program by disengaging from the opportunity to learn what might be done to make it work. Moreover, Hirschhorn noted, not a single vice president attended the meeting, yet another form of disengagement—and yet another sign of how management acted as if it could conduct business as usual while expecting a radical transformation of responsibilities on lower levels.

This example demonstrates how bureaucracy earned its reputation as inefficient and obstructionist. While a bureaucratic structure allows for clarity of roles and responsibilities, it also lends itself easily to defensive rigidity. Knowing what your job is makes it easier to say, on the other hand, "But that's *not* my job," and turn away. It also lends itself to abuses both up and down the hierarchy. Typically, as in this example, risk gets assigned downward. An executive who recoils from a task can assign it to someone who reports to him. Power and authority, on the other hand, increases the higher up one is, so that those lower down must gain approval from on high for any request that is not routine.

This provides an ideal set of circumstances for "social defenses," a set of psychological mechanisms designed to minimize the anxiety of risk, to arise.[14] Those lower down in the hierarchy tend to project all power and authority upward, so that only those at the top are seen as capable of really getting anything accomplished. This spares them from the risk of trying and failing, but it also has the effect of making them feel weak and helpless. On the other hand, those at the top, receiving those projections, feel an enhanced sense of power and effectiveness while being able to project weakness and incompetence downward. That projection, in turn, reinforces the feelings of helplessness in those below. Not only does this risk disabling the efforts of workers needed to carry out the work of the organization, it also encourages those on top to believe that they know more than they do or are more competent than they really are. That false sense of security and potency easily leads to carelessness and poor judgment.

This is the psychological system that Hirschhorn detected at the bank. The senior managers thought they could dismantle and reconstruct their traditional system of roles without paying attention to the ways in which social defenses had infiltrated that system. The tellers sabotaged the new arrangement because their sense of psychological security was threatened, and they did that without overt or conscious communication, just as they had constructed their original system of defenses without knowing why or how they did it. Just like defenses constructed by persons, social defenses are strongest when they are unconscious and when the psychological threats that they are designed to cope with never reach consciousness.

The second error of management was in failing to think of the whole system: they believed they could dismantle the intertwined systems of work roles and defenses piecemeal. Had they been more thorough or more thoughtful and included themselves in the restructuring, they might have helped the tellers to find alternate defenses in linking up with management as well as a greater capacity to tolerate the new insecurities they were being asked to assume. Instead, receiving management's increasingly hostile projections, they had virtually no option but to fight back passively and indirectly, the only way that those who have been rendered weak and helpless know how to fight.

AMBIGUOUS TASKS

In looking at the dynamics of the cockpit crew, we saw how easily small groups are seduced away from their work. This is true for teams, committees, hospital units, small departments, boards, and other groups. The need for cohesiveness and coordination, always present, can become dominant and obscure awareness of the external world and the task of the group.

In the complex interplay between leaders and followers, the effectiveness of leaders depends on not only the support but also the critical judgment of followers—a point we saw illustrated not only in the cockpit crew but also in the relations between the dean and his faculty.

The dean's "successful" leadership came at the price of his shutting out a significant portion of his constituents, who, instead of following his initiatives, stood on the sidelines until they saw the opportunity to retaliate.

Hirschhorn's work with the bureaucracy of the bank took us to another level of complexity in illustrating how easily conflicts between groups can emerge within organizations. Groups are all too willing to coalesce around an enemy; finding external dangers not only allows group members to come together with renewed urgency but also to ignore their own internal differences, if not actually project them onto the external threat. There is a temporary sense of solidarity in identifying an enemy that group members can combat together.

Conflict is endemic in organizations. In a sense, it is normal. As the goals of an organization require the coordination of an array of departments and groups, each subsystem will compete for resources with virtually every other subsystem; each will inevitably put a higher priority on its own function. A well-known example of this is the tension between the sales and manufacturing divisions of a corporation: sales, being close to customers, will want the company to produce what customers want, what it can sell, while manufacturing will want to make what is reliable, what it can safely deliver. Both are legitimate desires, both essential to the firm's success, but as each task is lodged in different subsystems, each subsystem may try to gain an advantage over the others.

A successful organization does not strive to eliminate conflicts but to modulate and balance them: it provides forums for competition to be played out and negotiated. Elliott Jacques, recognizing this tension and the anxiety it produces, noted that all organizations are paranoiagenic.[15] That is, one part of an organization will find enemies in another, and plan counterstrategies. Detecting plots in each other, all can feel persecuted by management.

Yet another source of destructive conflict in organizations warrants our attention. Some conflicts stem from ambiguity about an organization's mission or competition over its purpose. Of course, some ambiguity is inescapable, as different persons in different roles, enacting different identities, will have subtly competing versions of what the organization is in business to accomplish, especially today, when organizational missions are subject to modification if not drastic change under the constant pressure of changing technologies and markets. But in the absence of consciously stated agreement, employees may truly believe that they are working for different organizations, toward different ends, even if under the same roof. These disparate visions can lead to sometimes heated conflict.

A poignant example of this was described by Eric Miller and George Gwynne in their work with a home for incurably ill patients in the United Kingdom.[16] After interviewing staff and patients at the facility as well as observing how they functioned, it became clear that there were two competing concepts of the purpose of the home. One, what the authors called the "warehousing" concept, was that the home existed to provide a safe and secure container for patients in order to prolong their lives. Under this concept, risks were discouraged, such as excursions or unnecessary socializing, and order was maintained with respect to patient care; baths, meals, bedtimes, and visits to the toilet were carefully supervised. In some cases, patients were routinely given suppositories to ensure regular bowel movements. The competing concept, the "horticultural" model, aimed to develop the unfulfilled capacities of patients, to help them grow and achieve maximum satisfaction. Toward this end, there were fewer rules; patients had their own rooms, were free to come and go as they pleased, and could have visitors at any time or go on excursions, so long as they made their own arrangements. They were encouraged to use wheelchairs and actively engage in hobbies and crafts.

The warehousing model, emphasizing order, easily provided social defenses for the staff. It allowed them to maintain a safer psychological distance by keeping them securely in control of patient's behavior and by focusing on their physical care. Their anxiety about the suffering and distress of patients, their frustration in coping with them, and their disgust at their bodily functions were all effectively minimized.

On the other hand, the way that the social defense system and the task system overlapped provided opportunities for abuse. Patients could easily be kept waiting or reasonable requests denied, simply because the staff did not wish to be inconvenienced. The authors cite an example of a patient who was denied the use of his own record player, even though there was a room available, because it would have required extra work for them; when he persisted with his request, he was transferred to a psychiatric hospital.

The horticultural model seems infinitely more human, but it was not without its own social defenses. Focusing on the growth and fulfillment of the patients allowed the staff to minimize and deny the realities of physical decline and death. It promoted the fantasy of rehabilitation even in the face of overwhelming evidence of diminishing ability. In some cases, it actually discouraged patients from asking for the help they needed. Failing to grow, in this system, could be experienced as a threat to the optimism and faith that sustained the staff.

What, then, was the real task of the institution: to prolong the lives of its inmates or to provide them with as much fulfillment as possible? Clearly both are worthy and relevant goals. The inmates deserved the respect and encouragement provided by the horticultural model, and yet they also needed the protection and care of the warehousing model. But each goal was in potential competition with the other. Armed with conviction about their particular goal, staff members could deplore and denigrate the motives of those who thought otherwise.

Miller and Gwynne proposed an encompassing conception of the mission of the institution: to help inmates manage the transition from their "social death," their withdrawal from playing useful roles in society, to their "physical death." Such a concept seeks to transform conflicts about institutional purpose into problems and dilemmas about what to do in any given circumstance. But it depends on our capacity to accept painful realities and face difficult choices.

This is an example of how conflict in organizations can be managed by surfacing and resolving unconscious assumptions and facing uncomfortable facts. But it means introducing an element of complexity into daily operations, as well as managing perpetual conflict. The new integrated purpose that Miller and Gwynne proposed would allow for more sophisticated recognition of the tensions in the work of the institution and require more active management to stay on top of it.

There are many organizations that have two or even three competing missions, where such conflicts are a constant threat. Prisons do a notoriously poor job of balancing the competing priorities of punishing criminals and keeping them off the streets while attempting to rehabilitate them. Universities try to balance the competing tasks of providing an education for students and supporting research. They often argue that the two tasks can come together effectively: faculty members who do significant research will know their fields better and be able to teach more accurately. This may work in graduate education, to some degree, but the pressure on faculty members to integrate the dual roles of research (or scholarly publication) and teaching (particularly undergraduate teaching) often creates significant internal stress. University hospitals add a third task to this ensemble; in addition to fostering research and training new physicians, they must provide patient care. At times it is true that exceptional treatments can be offered under these circumstances, but the patient does not always come first in such a system, unless he is lucky enough to have an interesting disease or needs a new cutting-edge technology that is under development.

These complex tensions easily go underground and produce conflict, the real meaning of which is often obscure to those who find themselves embattled. Only a system that is committed to exposing its conflicts and contradictions, the better to manage them, is likely to do a better job.

STITCHING IT BACK TOGETHER AGAIN

The "immortality" of organizations is based on the fact that individual job holders can be replaced, work flows reconstructed. But it is only through the persons in those roles and the relationships between those persons that the roles function at all. There are times when the scale of disruption is overwhelming.

On the morning of September 11, 2001, there were eighty-three employees in the office of Sandler O'Neill, an investment services firm in the south tower of the World Trade Center, plus two consultants and two visitors. Of the total of 171 employees who worked for the firm, 149 usually worked in that building. Twenty-four witnessed the events from the concourse or nearby; forty-two were not at work. Seventeen exited the building safely after the airplane crashed into it. Twenty-two people worked in satellite locations throughout the country.[17]

The human impact was extraordinary. Sixty-six employees were killed, 39 percent of the total in the firm, as were the two consultants and two visitors. Of the fifty-five men and eleven women killed, forty-six were married, five were engaged to be married, and fifteen were single. There are thirty-six families with children who lost a parent, seventy-three of them children under the age of 18. An additional eleven spouses were left as widows or widowers. Nine partners out of thirty-one perished, including two of the three partners who ran the firm as part of the executive committee. Twenty-five members of the firm's twenty-eight-member New York equities group, including the founding and managing partner, also perished.

The next day, in a crowded midtown office, the one surviving member of the firm's executive committee interviewed a team from a consulting firm, Triad, that had been asked to help. According to Marc Maltz, the Triad partner who managed the project, the meeting started off with typical Wall Street bravado:

> The senior partner, Jimmy Dunne, was purposefully intimidating. "So, tell me something," he challenged, "tell me what you would say to one of my people who just lost his two best friends in the world, his mentor, his closest colleagues? How can you possibly help this person?" The inquiry was a bit longer, more direct and peppered with anger. My partner began to respond. The man in charge, Jimmy, shot back looking for the "bottom line." I interrupted my partner and offered,

"May I ask a question? We are talking about *you* aren't we? Are you the person who has lost his two best friends and mentor? Aren't we talking about Herman and Chris?" Dunne said yes, with tears emerging. He asked again, though in a more engaged tone, how we could possibly help.

Triad was hired the following morning, and quickly devised a three-pronged strategy. As Maltz's response to Dunne made clear, their thinking was informed by understanding the need to look below the surface, to grasp not only what could not be said but also what could not be directly understood at the time by those going through it.

First, they put together a program for the families of the victims, consisting of a mix of family treatments offered by clinicians working for Triad and local referrals. Second, they developed a therapeutic program for the surviving members of the firm, consisting of a twenty-four-hour hotline, on-site counseling, plus a mix of longer-term individual and group therapies. The third prong was consultation with management, to help reconstruct the firm.

In both therapeutic programs, for families and for employees, the clinicians quickly found, as did many who responded to other traumatic events, that they needed to be active in seeking out and offering their services to the victims of these events. It was not just that those victims were numbed by what had happened, incapacitated from seeking the help they needed; they tended to withdraw from the world that had just proven itself to be profoundly treacherous. Their ties to the firm were immensely helpful, as a result. For bereaved families, the network of relationships that existed among them allowed for communication about unexpressed needs for help and access to families that sought to isolate themselves. For individual employees, the firm provided innumerable informal occasions for impromptu counseling to take place. Maltz reported, in fact, that the outer corridor of their temporary office space became known as Triad's "clinical office."

Their work roles and the work relationships of the survivors needed to be reconstructed. It was important that the therapy they received came through the firm, via its consultants, so that they could experience the firm as a sustaining presence. It was not just that the firm needed to get them back to work so it could resume functioning—which it did. It was also the case that most of them needed to reestablish their sense of their capacity to work, as well, in order to experience the support their work roles could provide: the sense of knowing their competencies, of understanding their relationship with others at work, and regaining a sense of the future.[18]

In this respect, the configuration of the therapy groups was also important. At first, the groups were organized around members with comparable experiences, such as those who had escaped the building, those who witnessed events from the concourse, and so forth. Eventually the groups were restructured around their work roles in the firm; it was important for them to move from the role of a traumatized victim to the role of engaged employee. To be sure, some threw themselves into work as a kind of distraction, a manic defense to attempt to blot out overwhelming and devastating memories. The clinicians needed to be extremely sensitive to those defenses, while gradually helping to reconnect them to the more suitable and long-range defensive adaptations provided by work roles.

The third prong of Triad's strategy, consultation with management, was needed because the firm's management structure was decimated, requiring a significant infusion of thought and reflection. A first priority was help in thinking about the tasks of mourning and the provision of support services for survivors. Triad provided advice about dealing with the press, coping with the offers of outsiders to help, and planning for the various memorial services it soon became apparent were needed. At the same time, the surviving member of the executive committee needed help in thinking about how to reconstitute the firm's management structure and rebuild the firm's departments, while dealing with the immense psychological pressures they were under.

This work with the executive committee was divided into three parts. First, as the executives worked feverishly to rebuild the firm, they needed to be reminded of the grief and fear that they were coping with as well, stresses that they themselves might find little room for acknowledging otherwise but that, unacknowledged, could sap their ability to work effectively. All three members of the reconstituted executive committee had to be helped to find the balance between grief and mourning, the work and the worry associated with getting the firm back in operation, and the additional tasks required by the disaster itself. One member of the new committee, Fred Price, who had been visiting a client when the towers came down, took up the work of managing the interface between the families and the police and medical examiner's office. The new chief operating officer (COO) of the firm, he also became intimately involved in all of the details regarding recovery of remains, including how each identification was made, what body part was discovered where, the financial and emotional needs of the families, the state of each child, and so on. The psychological stress of such a job can only be imagined.

Dunne, an avid golfer who at forty-five had been considering retirement, gradually became the public face of the firm. In the beginning, propelled by his strong sense of identification with the partners he had lost, one of whom had been his closest friend since age twelve, he tirelessly tried to implement what he believed they would have done. The consultants helped him to broaden his role. First, an exceptional amount of emotional leadership was required, given the stresses on the firm from the catastrophe. People needed help in acknowledging their losses, in grieving, as well as in dealing with their insecurities and fears. It was by no means a foregone conclusion that the firm would survive, or that the leadership had the determination to pull it off, much less a realistic assessment of what they were up against. Second, Dunne had to get out in front of the firm in its relationship with other firms. This was not only a departure from the usual leadership demands within a financial services firm, but it was not something that came easily to Dunne. In retrospect, he said that it had taken him a long time to grasp that need.

After a time, moreover, Dunne needed to relinquish his identifications with the two partners he had lost and his commitment to work on their behalf. The process of grieving had to run its course, but also, as the firm was rebuilt, developing new business and acquiring new employees, it inevitably changed. The consultants helped him with these transitions, as well as helping him to reestablish his own ties with his family and children, neglected under the pressure of rebuilding the firm.

The second focus of work with the executive committee had to do with helping the executives think about preserving the firm's unique culture of relationships as they brought new managers into it. As the firm had grown over the years, friends and family members of employees and also of clients had been recruited, and this web of relationships had become a distinguishing feature of the firm's culture. Business was frequently conducted within this informal network, on the golf course, at recreational outings, and on vacations. The distress of the losses the firm suffered in the attack was amplified by this web of relationships. The losses were multiple and intertwined. At the same time, the shared grief united employees and inspired their determination to work on behalf of lost colleagues and their families who now needed the firm, more than ever, to succeed.

Now, as they desperately sought replacements, they ran the risk of endangering the unique culture they had built. At the same time, they needed to be able to adapt and change. Marc Maltz reported an interesting manifestation of this pressure. Every morning he dreaded going to their new office space, and yet every evening he found it difficult to tear himself away. It was difficult, at times unbearable, to face the immensity of what had been lost and what needed to be rebuilt. Yet, once there, it was both compelling and enmeshing. For him, this was valuable information about what others must be feeling who joined the firm. It was not just another job; newcomers needed help in managing the intense and conflicting pressures to which they were subject.

A third task for which management needed Triad's help was providing assistance to individual departments that were struggling to reestablish links with clients, to rebuild procedures and records that had been disrupted or lost, and to integrate new employees, all the while coping with the anxieties of grief and loss, not to mention the traumatic memories associated with their work.

As Triad worked with individual members of the firm, it soon became apparent that new employees hired to replace those lost needed to be integrated into the firm. There were a number of conflicts stemming from the simple fact that the newcomers brought with them their own assumptions about how to do their jobs, assumptions often at variance from the firm's traditional practices. Bringing in one or two new employees at a time affords everyone opportunities for acculturation and integration. But on this scale, inevitably, there were clashes from the start.

Familiar with the dynamic of intergroup conflict, the consultants worked both sides. The group of newcomers to the firm felt the extraordinary opportunity of so much to do, so many vacant spots to fill, along with a corresponding sense of guilt, often buried, about the fact that these great opportunities stemmed from the tragic misfortune of others. The surviving employees of the firm, on the other hand, had considerable difficulty assimilating the newcomers, who could not fully understand what the others had been through, and who certainly had no idea of what place those they were replacing held in the minds of the survivors. These differences were difficult enough and led to considerable tension as the members of each group increasingly recoiled from the others, finding among themselves common grounds of resentment: the newcomers resenting the suspicion and reserve toward them on the part of survivors, the survivors resenting the lack of understanding and sympathy of the newcomers.

Added to these resentments were projections from each group onto the other. The survivors disowned and projected onto the newcomers their own fears about being able to carry on, given the stress they were subject to, and the sense of rivalry they felt with those who, in many cases, had worked for competitive firms a few months before. It came to seem that these were thoughts and feeling the newcomers had about them. This sense of having enemies in their midst enhanced the solidarity of the survivors, but hardly made it easier to accept the help the newcomers had to offer and find ways of working together. On the other hand, the guilt of the newcomers for profiting from the suffering and loss of others, projected onto the survivors, was often experienced by the newcomers as accusatory feelings of the survivors toward them. Group work was extremely useful in integrating these two groups, which were essential to the functioning of the firm, moderating if not entirely preventing the eruption of conflict.

This is only a brief and perhaps schematic account of developments that took place over more than a year. The work of consultation is now concluded, though the work of therapy to cope with ineradicable traumatic memories will go on and on, in many cases, I suspect, throughout the lives of those affected.

In spite of the devastating losses, however, the firm has managed not only to survive, but to thrive. Two months after the attack, the firm became profitable again; no deals or clients were lost. By May 2002 (eight months after the collapse of the towers), revenue and profitability recovered to pre–9/11 levels, and they continued to trend upward, while Wall Street as a whole was experiencing a severe decline in activity and profits. The firm was able to develop a new business underwriting an annualized $23 billion in initial public offerings, and a second new business in preferred stocks. Moreover, all this was achieved as the firm rebuilt its primary business and a new facility, into which they moved four months after the attack, reconstructed their records, hired replacements, and attended funerals. The financial results were achieved while providing generous care, salary, bonus, and benefits to the families of the deceased.

It is a remarkable story. To make this happen, a number of elements came together: a surviving managing partner who was determined to keep the firm going, and had significant charismatic presence; and much good will toward the firm on Wall Street, increased substantially by a determination not to let the terrorists succeed in their project. Moreover, the many close relationships and family connections with employees and clients were a source of strength. But these elements were pulled together by a team of consultants that had a sophisticated grasp of the unconscious and its workings on many levels.[19]

Jimmy Dunne increasingly referred to Marc Maltz as his "head doctor," which Maltz took to have two complementary meanings. In the first meaning, he was the "doctor" who helped him sort out his personal tangle of thoughts and feelings, the better to manage his immensely challenging role. An MBA, neither a psychologist or psychiatrist, Maltz had the intuitive sense and background of experience with the unconscious that enabled him to see below the surface in this sensitive work. The second meaning, Maltz thought, was that he was the "head" of his firm, Triad, that was functioning as a doctor to Dunne's firm. Taken together, the phrase implied not only that the two men had paired effectively, but also that the two firms had paired as well. As a result, both patients were doing well.

CONCLUDING THOUGHTS

Working with the unconscious is not just about fixing problems, though that may be a primary focus. Each one of the examples we have looked at suggests how useful it could be to integrate an understanding of unconscious process into the daily operations of organizations.

The training of cockpit teams, for example, as Frayer suggests, could lead to more supple forms of collaboration. If team members understood better the complexities of their roles, and potential for projection and collusion, they could ask for help from each other more confidently, and they could engage more routinely in reflective evaluations of their performance. They could be more effective and relaxed— and we all could fly more safely.

If we all understood better the subtle and often hidden interplay between leaders and followers, we could have more realistic expectations of each other. We could be better prepared to see how certain roles pull particular projections. The delegation of tasks could take place with more realistic, more negotiated outcomes and a lessened risk of acrimony and scapegoating. Leaders could have a more objective grasp of the teams they have to build and manage. That, in turn, could allow us to be more supportive and effective in the work we do together.

Bureaucracy, which can lead to such frustration and inefficiency, could be rendered more effective if illuminated from inside. The dual tasks of providing security and accomplishing objectives—always present in organizations—could be balanced if we accepted the need for both. Then we might see them more clearly and distinguish them more sharply.

In complex organizations with multiple purposes, the inherent conflicts could be anticipated and modulated. Rituals and strategies for reconciling differences can be developed. We might be able to spot virulent projections before they got out of hand. We might reduce casualties in the workplace and limit burnout.

This may sound somewhat utopian, and to some degree it is, though I have seen such strategies put in place. As we saw in Chapter One, consciousness lags behind events. It does not prevent us from making mistakes, but it can allow for the possibility of noticing them more quickly and altering course before disaster strikes. However, we can transfer learning from one setting to another. It is not only a utopian wish to develop a greater awareness of the role that unconscious factors play in organizations. Many people have the talent and sensitivity. More importantly, eyes can be trained to see, ears to hear. We can learn what to look for, and we can hold on to the traces of unconscious processes that we detect before they disappear from our minds.

Six

PSYCHOTHERAPY TODAY

The history of psychotherapy is brief, but the pace of its development has been extraordinary. Before Freud, who is generally credited with offering the first credible form of psychotherapy, there was
Anton Mesmer and mesmerism, with its belief in the power of animal magnetism. Throughout the nineteenth century, a handful of
others treated the contradictory and self-defeating behaviors of the
mentally ill with electrical stimulation, baths, rest cures, and exhor-
tation. Before that, there were asylums and prisons, along with a
mélange of spiritualistic and religious efforts.[1]

Today, there are over four hundred distinct psychotherapies. In the
United States, more than 100,000 well-trained and fully qualified
practitioners, and perhaps as many as 250,000 all told, offer psychotherapeutic services of one kind or another. And the demand is growing. According to a recent survey conducted by the National Institute
for Mental Health, more than half of the U.S. population will develop
a mental illness at some point in their lives, while 40 percent of those
afflicted seek help. If the market is viewed from the perspective of
promoting health, that is, if mental health is viewed as a matter of
"flourishing," not the absence of illness, then recent studies suggest
that 80 percent of the population could use assistance. There is considerable controversy about drawing the line between illness and
normal need for support and guidance, but, at the very least, the figures testify to an extraordinary expansion of awareness of psychological distress and an increase in the demand for help, along with
the recognition that many do not get the help they need. The new
mental health industry struggles to define and to keep up with the
demand.[2]

Surprisingly, the word *unconscious* rarely appears outside the literature of psychoanalysis or its various psychotherapeutic derivatives, which are often referred to as "psychoanalytic psychotherapy." Partly, this is because its existence is sometimes taken for granted. Our culture increasingly accepts it as a fact of life, no longer viewing it as the domain of conflict and dread. Moreover, the research into cognitive and emotional processing that we examined in Chapter One is being widely incorporated into current thinking, helping more and more practitioners to account for the way that deeply embedded patterns of behavior can be so difficult to change.

But while the existence of the unconscious no longer needs to be proven, the absence of explicit reference to it has much to do with the fact that it has been so strongly associated with psychoanalysis. Much of the contemporary psychotherapy landscape has been defined in opposition to psychoanalysis, challenging the assumptions it made and the hegemony it once enjoyed. As a result, referring to the unconscious explicitly today, for some, would be like granting a competitive advantage to a movement that many still hope will fade away.

In fact, though, today's vast and burgeoning psychotherapy industry is rediscovering, reformulating, and repackaging the unconscious. This should not be surprising, as psychotherapy is centered on understanding the complexities of human behavior, and yet it presents a bewildering array of choices. How should those seeking therapy attempt to determine what treatment makes the most sense for them? What questions should they ask?

It can be bewildering to professionals as well. There is a widely acknowledged deficit in outcome studies, the kinds of data that might help discriminate what kind of treatment is best for which specific disorder. Little evidence is available about the number or frequency of sessions required to be effective. Moreover, not much is known about what factors lead to success, though some studies strongly suggest that the most important factor may be the patient himself. Other studies suggest that it is the quality of the relationship with the therapist that matters most.

Psychotherapy does appear to work. Even if particular approaches cannot be distinguished as more effective than others, the evidence is growing that psychotherapy is useful. This may suggest that the confusion of choices facing the consumer does not matter, in the end. The prospective patient will be helped if he finds someone he trusts.

Meanwhile, as the old rivalries persist, the focus in psychotherapy is shifting from schools of thought to treatment problems, and with that shift there is a new eclecticism, a new movement toward integration and synthesis. More and more, what matters is what works. As Jack Gorman put it recently in *The New Psychiatry*: "In the Old Psychiatry, each clinician learned a set of techniques from one school of thought and insisted on applying them to all comers. In the New Psychiatry clinicians may still feel more comfortable with the tools of one school, but they readily admit when they don't have the right skill for a particular patient."[3]

This optimistic vision may still be more of an ideal than a reality, but it does describe a real trend. The willingness to "readily admit" one's limitations is not universal, but it is reinforced by pressure from insurance companies monitoring treatments and dissatisfied clients threatening malpractice suits, as the emphasis shifts to patients and the problems they face. That shift is aided by an increasingly competitive and varied professional work force. Psychotherapy, once the province of neurologists and psychiatrists, is now routinely offered by psychologists, social workers, pastoral counselors, nurses, and others, as the economic pressures affecting the entire health care industry are forcing economies and consolidations. It is fast becoming a different ballgame.

Now, despite the proliferation of psychotherapies, it is generally agreed that they fall into three major types: psychodynamic, behavioral, and psychopharmacological. The psychodynamic therapies, largely those that have arisen out of psychoanalysis, tend to focus on motivation and meaning, helping patients understand what drives them to act or feel as they do. The behavioral therapies focus on the patient's actions, what they do that is harmful or self-defeating, and they seek to alter those behaviors. Psychopharmacological treatments intervene into the nervous systems of patients directly, altering chemical imbalances with drugs. Some consensus is emerging that certain mental disorders are best suited to particular types of treatment. Moreover, often, some combinations are seen as most helpful. Thus, schizophrenia, which can benefit from some behavioral management, is helped most by drugs that directly eliminate or attenuate hallucinations and calm hyperagitated states. Obsessive-compulsive disorder (OCD) can be helped by some medications but often yields best to approaches that deal directly with the repetitive and seemingly automatic behaviors themselves. But knowledge of how to treat specific mental health disorders is in its infancy, and clinicians are still learning about what works best under what circumstances and for whom.

My goal here is to ferret out the roles that the unconscious is now seen to play throughout the field. Psychopharmacology is not discussed here because its role is direct intervention into the wetware of our nervous system; distinguishing the conscious and unconscious realms of learning, as a result, becomes less relevant. Dynamic psychotherapy is discussed because that is where the unconscious gets the most overt recognition and attention from practitioners. But the realm of the cognitive and behavioral therapies is where the story gets most interesting and complex, and that is where I will begin.

FROM BEHAVIOR TO COGNITION AND BEYOND

Behaviorism arose in the beginning of the twentieth century as a challenge to any form of psychological thought that was not "scientific" in the strictest sense of the term. Its giant figures focused only on what could be objectively observed, verified, and replicated. Its founder, John Watson, for example, rejected any form of evidence that came from the conscious reporting of subjects. He was profoundly influenced by Pavlov's work modifying reflexes in experimental subjects, such as the dogs he trained to salivate at the sound of a bell. As Watson wrote in his 1913 manifesto aimed at the new profession of psychology, "Psychology as the behaviorist views it is a purely objective branch of natural science. Its theoretical goal is the prediction and control of behavior. Introspection forms no essential part of its methods."[4] This stood in dramatic contrast to the work of Freud, who just four years before Watson's manifesto had been invited to lecture in America, where he was warmly received by William James, the unquestioned dean of American psychologists at the time. Watson was clearly throwing down the gauntlet, rejecting the lax methodology of the "talking cure" as well as the speculations about unconscious impulses that animated Freud. Watson and, later, B. F. Skinner thought of the mind as an impenetrable "black box," the contents of which could not be directly known. For them, only behavior that could be observed and measured counted as the basis for science.

The purity of the science they espoused did not, at first, have much practical value. Behavioral conditioning had few applications in the years before World War II. Occasionally it was used to modify the disorderly behavior of children; several treatments were developed, including a promising one for bed-wetting ("enuresis," in the professional literature). Not until the 1950s was the concept of behavior therapy developed by Hans Eysenck and his associates at Maudsley Hospital in London. But once established there, it took off. Additional applications of behavioral conditioning developed throughout the world. In South Africa, Joseph Wolpe developed a form of "systematic desensitization," applying Pavlovian principles to human problems such as phobias. In the United States, Skinner published his highly influential book, *Science and Human Behavior*, and demonstrated the value of operant conditioning in managing the disruptive behavior of severely mentally ill patients.

The militant fervor that characterized Watson and Skinner at the start of their scientific research became a feature of behavioral therapy. Eysenck, at first, attacked the whole enterprise of psychotherapy itself, challenging the evidence of its effectiveness. After he established behavior therapy, however, the focus of his attack narrowed to psychoanalysis. As a disciple of his wrote, "Hans went gleefully into battle. If behavior therapy based on theory was to dominate, then Freudians had to be demoted and psychiatrists put in their proper place. If his personality theory was to rise, others had to fall."[5]

To be sure, this doctrinaire stance was more than equally matched by psychoanalysts themselves, entrenched in departments of psychiatry at British and American medical schools, scornful of what they saw as the superficial and transient cures of the behaviorists. But inevitably, this polarizing stance infected the behaviorists themselves, as it had the psychoanalysts. Any compromises were severely criticized, and attempts were made to proscribe any variations not based on strict scientific principles. When Arnold Lazarus introduced his multimodal approach to behavior therapy in the 1970s, for example, advocating the introduction of techniques from other schools, Wolpe accused him of destroying the purity of behavior therapy, and Eysenck removed him from the editorial board of *Behavior Research and Therapy*.[6]

But behavior therapy did inevitably change and broaden. As psychologists became interested in studying cognition, the black box of the mind gradually became less opaque, and the value of directly addressing the thoughts and perceptions of patients became more and more apparent. In the 1960s, Albert Ellis, a former psychoanalyst, developed rational emotive therapy (RET) as a means of more actively engaging patients' irrational ideas. Aaron Beck, also originally a psychoanalyst, in the 1970s developed cognitive approaches to depression, helping patients alter the patterns of thinking that led them into repetitive depressive episodes and often kept them there.

Ellis, Beck, and others who spearheaded the development of cognitive therapy identified themselves with the behaviorists. Having abandoned psychoanalysis, they sought a professional affiliation congenial to their new beliefs as well as some place to present their findings. At first the behaviorists pushed back, unwilling to compromise on their scientific emphasis on objectively measurable data. Michael Mahoney, who in 1974 published his highly influential book, *Cognition and Behavior Modification*, in order to help bridge the gap, felt threatened by his behaviorist colleagues; moreover, there was a strong push to ban cognitive presentations from conferences of the Association for the Advancement of Behavior Therapy (AABT). The cognitivists, for their part, considered setting up their own organization, but eventually decided to stick it out with the behaviorists.[7]

Over time, that decision was vindicated. The field has come to be known as cognitive behavioral therapy (CBT), and it has blossomed into an array of diverse treatments for many different disorders. Pure forms of behaviorism are now difficult to find. Some historians of behaviorism have characterized its development as a shift from an experimental model to a pragmatic model. This coincides with the decline of logical positivist modes of thought in science, and the erosion of what has been called "ideological" behaviorism, with its insistence on rigid and no longer convincing objectivist standards of evidence. But it also reflects the success of the behaviorists as clinicians and the growing acceptance of their work with clients in the mental health community. The more opportunities they have had to demonstrate their effectiveness, the more flexible they have become in finding new ways to be effective. Moreover, CBT practitioners have come to recognize that they are not just scientists dealing with experimental subjects; the communication they establish with clients impacts their success.[8]

With this expanded focus on cognition, not only have windows been opened into the "black box" of the mind, but also the unconscious has become more directly relevant. As we saw in Chapter One, the bulk of cognitive processes are automatic, not under conscious control. The existence of the cognitive unconscious means that any effort to change human behavior inevitably encounters entrenched patterns of thought, beliefs, or schemas that are hidden and unknown. This simply cannot be avoided, though it may not need to be acknowledged for change to occur. In 1984, two prominent CBT researchers, recognizing this dimension of cognition, published *The Unconscious Reconsidered*, a collection of papers reflecting this renewed interest in entrenched cognition. In 1990, G. Terence Wilson, co-editor of the annual *Review of Behavior Therapy* for many years, noted the growing importance "of these largely unconscious, affective processes or structures to cognitive and behavioral interventions."[9]

On a practical level, CBT is increasingly developing strategies for exploring the unconscious. A striking example is provided by Arnold Lazarus's use of the empty-chair technique developed by Fritz Perls as a part of Gestalt therapy. In Lazarus's adaptation, the patient engages in a dialogue with an empty chair, which often stands for a significant lost figure, such as a deceased parent; he then changes places and responds as he imagines the person he was addressing might respond. This way of accessing the buried emotions of unfinished business in personal relationships has proven remarkably effective, as the patients discover how much more they knew about the thoughts and feelings of the persons they have lost than they were aware of knowing. Clearly, it is based on a form of insight, though it is more spontaneous than reflective. Lazarus calls his approach "technical eclecticism," justifying it on the grounds that using a technique does not imply agreeing with its underlying theory. A number of others have endorsed this approach.[10]

Practitioners of CBT also pay increasing attention to unconscious factors in their relationships with clients, something that early on they had neglected. Over time they learned the importance of clarifying clients' expectations while providing reassurance. In practical terms, they were working to establish the clinician as a nonthreatening authority in order to reduce anxiety and overcome resistance. Psychoanalysts have always seen these issues as part of transference, the re-creation of past relationships in the present. But *transference* is a term that would ring dissonant bells for behaviorists, making it difficult to conduct reasoned discussions. As Lazarus concluded twenty years ago, "Basically integration or rapprochement is impossible when a person speaks and understands only Chinese and another converses only in Greek."[11]

Lazarus's comment about language suggests the possibility that, in addition to an increasingly pragmatic overlap between the two fields, some form of theoretical integration can occur. Drew Westen, one of the few researchers familiar with both theoretical languages, believes such examples of transference can be understood in terms of "mood-dependent memory" and "schema-related affect," both significant constructs in cognitive psychology. Jeremy Safran and Z. V. Segal have looked at the client relationship in terms of John Bowlby's "attachment theory," an approach to understanding early parent relationships that originally grew out of psychoanalysis but that has come to have an independent standing among researchers on infancy.[12]

Now CBT is moving into a new phase, what Stephen Hayes calls "the third wave," characterized as being "sensitive to the context and functions of psychological phenomena, not just their form." This third phase is marked by a new openness to ideas as well as a pragmatic search for more effective methods. It stems from an increasing recognition among CBT practitioners that, as one group of researchers put it, cognitive therapy "has failed to achieve its intended impact."[13]

Hayes stresses the importance of "mindfulness." In his approach, clients must first come to accept the conflicts they want therapy to resolve in order to be aware of the essential information that is embedded in those conflicts. If clients can learn to tolerate their anxiety, giving up the search for immediate relief, therapists can devise more informed and effective treatments. But this requires the behavioral therapist to depart somewhat from his traditional emphasis on symptom relief.

Such "radical additions to behavior therapy," as Hayes puts it, essentially bring back to behaviorism the introspection that Watson rejected, and suggest the kind of attitude of openness to conflict that psychoanalysts have often suggested as a prerequisite to psychological exploration of the unconscious. Hayes calls his form of therapy acceptance and commitment therapy (ACT).

Other practitioners have developed approaches that stress the unique opportunities provided by focusing on the therapist–client relationship. Those who have developed functional analytic therapy (FAT), for example, argue that capturing and identifying the problematic behavior of the client *in vivo*, as it occurs in the relationship with the therapist, provides a powerful reinforcement for its extinction. They refer to those key incidents as therapist–client relationship learning opportunities (TCRLOs). As if to illustrate how far they have come from the ideological battles of the past, they note, somewhat warily, "FAP may at times appear more like psychoanalysis than standard behavior therapy. It rarely appears strictly behavioral in form, though it rests on solid behavioral foundations, and all interventions can be viewed through the lens of modern behavioral therapy."

Marsha Linehan, another practitioner in this "third wave," calls her approach dialectical behavior therapy (DBT), employing the term *dialectical* to describe the importance of holding together the contradictory attitudes of accepting conflict, on the one hand, and needing resolution or change, on the other. DBT practitioners also stress the importance of mindfulness in maintaining this tension. As Linehan and her colleagues recently put it, "It is a way of living awake, with one's eyes wide open." They note parallels with Eastern contemplative practices, echoing similar interests in meditation on the part of a number of psychoanalysts. Maintaining the space of expectation and reflection, refraining from premature action, allows for the emergence of associations and thoughts into awareness.[14]

These therapies—DBT, FAP, ACT—are just some of the new approaches emerging out of mainstream CBT. They are not only challenging the old ideological positions of the behaviorists, continuing to open up the "black box" of the mind to useful introspection, they are also challenging the conviction that the cognitivists brought to their behavioral colleagues thirty or so years ago that cognition could not be ignored because it mediated behavior. Clearly, most CBT practitioners believe in the power of thought to influence human action, and they work effectively to uncover and change the thinking of clients. But they are also discovering how much of cognition is buried in the unconscious and how resistant to change it can be. In short, they are discovering the cognitive unconscious, and devising strategies to work with it. Joining with clients in order to engage with them in the uncovering process, they offer new promise of change.

SHORT-TERM DYNAMIC TREATMENTS

At virtually the same time that behavior therapy took off, interest surged in short-term psychodynamic methods, promising relief in ten to twenty-five sessions. The first International Symposium on Short-Term Dynamic Psychotherapy was held in 1975. The third symposium, two years later, attracted over a thousand participants.[15] Very quickly it became apparent that there was no single organizational umbrella adequate to cover this burgeoning interest and the myriad techniques it gave rise to.

The hope of compressing their lengthy explorations of unconscious processes had been expressed by psychoanalysts for a long time, though efforts to find appropriate methods tended to be marginal and tentative. Directly after World War I, Freud expressed the idea of "alloying the pure gold of psychoanalysis with the copper of direct suggestion." That was his formula for extending the exploration of the unconscious to those unable to afford lengthy treatments, implying that psychoanalysts could push the process along because they had a grasp of what was likely to be uncovered. Other psychoanalysts took up the challenge of trying to access the unconscious without the drawn-out procedures of free association and reverie, notably Sandor Ferenczi and Otto Rank, but they risked the charge of alloying the "pure gold" of psychoanalysis with "dross"—as Freud's metaphor came to be remembered. The growing orthodoxy of the psychoanalytic establishment meant that any experimental variation of standard technique increasingly came to be viewed as suspect if not deviant.

It was not until after World War II that Franz Alexander and Theodore French, in Chicago, directly challenged psychoanalytic orthodoxy with their book *Psychoanalytic Therapy*.[16] Advocating active methods, including the use of "corrective emotional experiences" to disconfirm patients neurotic expectations, they argued strongly for flexible, active, and shorter approaches, and provoked an outburst of criticism from the psychoanalytic establishment for their "radical" departures. Their book is frequently cited as the culmination of the first generation of short-term work, the generation that labored under a cloud of skepticism and official disapproval. It was also generally agreed to have been the major antecedent for the surge of interest that finally emerged in the 1960s and 1970s. By then, psychoanalysis was in retreat—certainly in medical schools. Those outside the psychoanalytic establishment were increasingly open to techniques that would expand treatment options. There was also pressure from the competitive behavioral and cognitive treatments that academic psychologists were developing, and the research evidence they were rapidly accumulating for their effectiveness.

Other factors led to increasing interest in short-term work. Because the data were easier to gather and the controls easier to maintain, shorter treatments lent themselves more readily to research. Also, shorter treatments appealed to the public. Many prospective patients, most of whom tend to be ambivalent about entering psychotherapy, to begin with, if not actually reluctant to undertake prolonged treatments of uncertain duration, turned out to be more likely to commit to it, and stick it out, if it was presented as a matter of twelve or even twenty-five weeks.

Then, as the demand for psychotherapy grew, there was the growing appeal of cheaper methods. The federal Health Maintenance Organization (HMO) Act of 1973 applied pressure to lessen costs by shortening treatments. Employers trying to reduce the expense of employee benefits, insurance companies trying to protect profits, and consumers seeking to balance their budgets all joined in the effort. The accumulating evidence of research gave them a means to legitimize their decisions and extend the control of managed care companies over the field.

This second generation generated the enthusiasm and captured the limelight at the first three International Symposiums on short-term treatments in the 1970s.[17] In the 1980s and 1990s, a third generation, largely based in medical schools and departments of psychology, built upon this work.[18] These approaches reflected more recent developments in psychoanalytic theory and practice, relational theories, social constructivism, self psychology, and so forth.[19] Third-generation approaches are also heavily research oriented, and many include manuals that specify how the therapies are to be conducted. Several other approaches represent modifications and extensions of second-generation models. By and large, new approaches have proliferated and have been modified as new researchers joined in the efforts of the pioneers.

All these forms of brief dynamic therapy have in common the conviction, derived from psychoanalysis, that the beliefs and patterns of behavior underlying dysfunctional and self-defeating behavior are buried in the unconscious. They differ in that, being ti.ne limited, they require a specific target toward which the therapy is directed and an active stance by the therapist.[20] Practitioners tend to insist on these features, arguing that if one is going to be more active, one must know what to go after. Conversely, knowing what you are seeking to find, you can be more aggressive in searching for it. A corollary to these guiding principles is the importance of initiating treatment with a clear diagnosis.

Given the pressure of time and the need for the therapist's more active engagement, short-term dynamic approaches tend to focus more on interpersonal issues in the "here and now," but they all inevitably encounter old patterns of relationship. Deeply ingrained and habitual, those patterns are often difficult for patients to see, but one of the most effective tools the therapist has is the ability to point to issues as they appear, *in vivo*, before the patient's eyes.

The techniques may be new and promising, but the underlying assumptions about the person and the mind, usually extracted from the complex theoretical background of psychoanalysis, tend to be consistent with the findings of the "new unconscious" we examined in Chapter One. That is, the established patterns of the emotional and cognitive unconscious, usually the product of early adaptations to family life, are laid bare. Family and cultural myths reflected in unconscious language patterns and dreams are addressed, as are the relationship strategies designed to protect self-esteem and preserve identity. All the unconscious issues that are relevant to long-term psychodynamic treatments are equally relevant and available in the short-term.

Recently, considerable differences of opinion have emerged about what constitutes "short-term." Originally, the concept of brief or short-term therapy developed in the context of traditional psychoanalysis, and simply pointed to a time-limit on treatment that had normally lasted for years. With more experience and acceptance, short-term dynamic psychotherapists have come to be concerned with the meaning and rationale for the description "short-term." This is all the more important as it could easily come to mean merely what insurance companies are prepared to pay for, what has been wryly referred to as the "survival of the shortest."

Hanna Levenson, working with a method developed by Hans Strupp at Vanderbilt, refers to being "time attentive," developing a "time-limited attitude" that strives to be "cost-effective." Michael Hoyt writes that the focus should be on making the most of each session; his motto is "Get to it."[21] The underlying dilemma is that, except in treatments that are designed to highlight issues of loss, the therapist can seldom know in advance what will emerge in the process and how long it will take. An openness to renegotiating time limits has become more standard among practitioners, and even insurance companies have shown that they can be somewhat flexible.

Perhaps the most extreme example of efficiency is what has come to be known as single session therapy (SST). This ultra-brief method, reported anecdotally by many noted therapists over the years, usually arises by chance, and often catches even the therapist by surprise. On the other hand, single sessions are the most common form of treatment as many patients drop out after one meeting. Even if they stay the course, their insurance companies will usually pay for only a limited number of sessions, a number based less on patients' need than on their package of benefits. A related problem is that most therapists have not been trained to work short-term, and are not inclined to choose such an approach, if they have a choice. Patients may like short-term treatments, but most therapists still view them as second best, too short to do much good.

Twenty years ago, a survey found that 91 percent of psychodynamically oriented therapists favored long-term treatments. Since then, exposure to training in short-term methods has not increased for psychologists or psychiatrists. Other surveys have revealed that many therapists are conflicted, forced to conduct brief treatments for economic or administrative reasons but are untrained in them and unconvinced of their potential effectiveness. Short-term treatments are still the most common, *de facto*, but practitioners tend not to be adequately prepared with the skills needed to make them work.[22]

PSYCHOTHERAPY INTEGRATION

There have always been a few therapists interested in crossing the boundaries of different schools, but in the last thirty years, a movement for psychotherapy integration has developed. Arnold Lazarus, the behavior therapist we noted earlier in this chapter, advocated "technical eclecticism," the use of compatible techniques from different schools without regard to their original theoretical rationales. He sought methods that worked, caring less about consistency or, even, theoretical integration. While he succeeded in his aim of developing useful therapeutic strategies, he paid a price by being marginalized by his behavioral colleagues.

Today, integration is far more common. It has even become something of an ideal. We saw that Jack Gorman framed it as an aspect of contemporary practice in *The New Psychiatry*, even if traditions of training and professional development make it difficult to implement. The profession of psychotherapy is still largely carved up into distinct territories, and while the penalties for crossing theoretical boundaries are far less severe than they once were, there often are no incentives even if there are opportunities.

Paul Wachtel, one of the key figures in this movement, described himself in the beginning as a skeptic, setting out to learn about behavior therapy in order to debunk it. Trained as a psychoanalyst, he began by believing behavioral approaches were "foolish, superficial, and possibly even immoral." Realizing, on the other hand, that he did not know enough about it in operation to write a credible paper proving his points, he called Gerald Davidson who ran the training program in behavior therapy at the Stony Brook campus of the State University of New York, in order to observe his work first hand. Davidson describes being extremely impressed by Wachtel's careful observations and thoughtful questions. More important, Wachtel, impressed by what he observed in Davidson's clinic, was stimulated in the development of his own thinking. He did not change his views as much as expand his thinking. As he wrote in his preface to the book that eventually came out of his observations, "Instead of slaying the philistines I have embraced them."[23]

Wachtel's approach to integration is theoretical and conceptual. Unlike Lazarus, he was less interested in techniques that might work in concert than in finding underlying theoretical compatibilities or new theoretical formulations to unite seemingly incompatible points of view. As we saw earlier, behavioral therapy has evolved significantly since Wachtel started out, and now encompasses both unconscious cognition and the repetition of old relationship patterns.

In 1983, the Society for the Exploration of Psychotherapy Integration (SEPI) was founded. As Wachtel has explained, SEPI's somewhat clumsy title was chosen because it emphasized exploration without claiming that integration is even likely or feasible; it is seen as a distant goal, an ideal. Moreover, it was sure to take many forms on several different levels. The idea for the society was to gather together those who wanted to engage in that exploration and were unlikely to find support within their own professional associations.

The society has proven to be a very broad organization. In addition to those, like Lazarus, who search for compatible techniques and those, like Wachtel, who look to develop theoretical bridges, it includes many who search for common factors in successful but different therapies. Members are bound together by their commitment to research. In that sense, Wachtel's original experience of trying to validate his prejudices against behavior therapy points to a common ideological base: as a psychologist working in an academic setting, he was obliged to find the evidence. On the other hand, members' commitment to investigation and research ensures that any progress SEPI makes toward its goals will be slow, methodical, and evolutionary.[24]

For the same reason, SEPI provides something of a haven for the "new unconscious." Just as psychoanalysts or dynamically oriented psychotherapists cannot dismiss behavioral treatments as superficial or temporary palliatives when the evidence shows otherwise, so those for whom psychoanalysis has become a discredited belief system cannot ignore that people's unconscious schemas shape current behavior or that their relationships replicate the patterns of past relationships.

Earlier in this chapter, we saw that the "third wave" of CBT has already moved in this same direction. Centered in large university departments, this is also a research-based movement, committed to finding evidence. Several third-wave CBT researchers have joined up with SEPI to present their findings.

RADICAL THERAPIES

The same 1960s and 1970s that saw the growth of cognitive-behavioral approaches and the development of short-term dynamic methods also saw an explosion of more unconventional techniques. The time was more adventurous, consumers more credulous. It did not seem to matter that these techniques did not have much evidence to back up their claims. Some of these older and more radical approaches are still around. I call these therapies "radical," but not because they seem "far out," departing from conventional expectations, though they have often been characterized as "New Age," and lumped together with therapies designed to channel spirits, discover past lives, or recover memories of abduction by aliens.[25] Rather, they are radical in the sense that they seek to get directly at the unconscious roots of patients' problems. Like surgery aimed at diseased tissue, these therapies target what they see as the basic problem from which patients are suffering, the underlying cause, promising cures without the tedious intervention of consciousness. Patients undergoing such radical psychotherapies, as a result, tend to believe they can be cured of their mental distress without expanding or changing their sense of who they are. The radical therapies promise to be efficient and quick, but they also promise to bypass issues of self-esteem or identity.

Many of the early radical therapies were essentially cathartic, aimed at accessing and discharging long-pent-up emotions. Perhaps the best known of these is Arthur Janov's primal therapy, in which patients are encouraged to get in touch with their repressed primal emotions of pain and rage, thought to be derived from very early traumatic experiences, including birth. Janov has claimed that primal therapy is the only therapy needed in the treatment of many disorders such as anxiety, depression, and addiction because those disorders derive from earlier traumas. Once patients can recall past events and get in touch with the traumatic pain the events have caused, the belief is that patients' more superficial fears, inhibitions, and conflicts will be swept away. They will be reconnected with themselves.

Janov's first book, *The Primal Scream*, was published in 1970 and sold over a million copies. He went on to found the Primal Center for training and research in Los Angeles, publishing eleven more books, most recently *Primal Healing* in 2006. The concept has inspired many followers, some of whom have modified Janov's ideas, many of whom have been captivated by its underlying logic. It influenced the development of "rebirthing" treatments, for example, and had an impact on the development of encounter groups. The notion of a fundamental, underlying cause for unhappiness and suffering has a deep appeal, and can kindle a fervent conviction among those who believe they have come to experience it directly themselves.

Janov insists that his methods are essentially scientific and warns about the dangers of poorly trained persons using this approach. He and his colleagues at the Primal Center report that they are continually evaluating and refining their techniques and searching out new ways of helping patients to access the depths of their unconscious pain. They no longer stress the importance of screaming.

Critics have noted the danger of arousing such powerful emotions, and there is considerable controversy over the basic idea that the encouragement and stimulation of catharsis produces a reduction of symptoms. The discharge of emotion can be useful as a therapeutic goal. But its use with trauma victims has been questioned. The search to get in touch with memories of the traumatic incident can often lead to what trauma experts call "re-traumatization," a renewal and intensification of the original trauma itself. Moreover, it is far from certain that the search for primal pain and its release is universally helpful. On the other hand, it is hard to dispute the testimony of patients who are convinced that they have been helped.[26]

Apart from spinoffs of Janov's work, there are other therapies that focus on the body and aim for a similar release of repressed or deeply embedded emotion. Bioenergetic analysis, for example, founded by Alexander Lowen and John Perrakis, seeks to discern ways in which the flow of energy is blocked in the body and can be freed. Many others who focus therapeutic attention on the body have developed other means of unleashing that energy.

Wilhelm Reich, a psychoanalyst who was the inspiration for much of this work, was convinced by Freud's early emphasis on the link between the repression of sexual energy or libido and neurotic symptoms. He went on to develop a groundbreaking and still influential theory that "character armor," the particular ways in which energy is blocked or channeled in the body, is the foundation of personality, and that therapy needed to be directed at the entire character structure, not just neurotic symptoms, in order to bring about meaningful change.

Reich became a radical psychotherapist—and a discredited psychoanalyst—when he developed the belief that this energy flowed through the universe in a form he called "orgone." Therapy then became, for him, a means of increasing and accumulating orgone. It appeared to many of his colleagues that he went off the deep end when he built orgone "accumulators" in which he believed patients could increase their exposure to orgone. A charismatic figure, he even persuaded Einstein to give it a try, but after World War II the Food and Drug Administration successfully prosecuted him for mail fraud, and he died in jail shortly afterward.[27] Today there are many forms of body therapy, many tracing themselves to Reich's early innovations. But the theories and practices of body therapy while proliferating, have also tended to become less radical than Reich's.[28]

There is another set of radical ideas that focuses on the nervous system, the software of the body, so to speak, not the wetware of tissues. The aim of these therapies is to intervene directly into the information stored in the brain or the learned neural patterns for processing experience. Hypnosis was Freud's original "royal road" to the unconscious, his first means of gaining direct access to repressed memories. Hypnotism went out of fashion among psychoanalysts, but it never fully disappeared as a treatment, and many kept experimenting with its intriguingly mysterious effectiveness in influencing behavior, diminishing anxiety, and relieving pain.

To promote its use as a clinical tool, Milton H. Erikson founded the American Society for Clinical Hypnosis in 1957. By all accounts an extraordinary and uncanny clinician, Erikson came to believe, like many contemporary neurobiologists encountered in Chapter One, that the unconscious was always present and could be accessed directly. Hypnotism was just one of his more explicit means for reaching it, one that easily could be taught if used in a nondirective and nonthreatening manner. Always seeking to find ways of connecting with his patient's unconscious, Erikson had the knack of inducing connections through simple, unobtrusive means.

As Jay Haley wrote in *Uncommon Therapy*, the book that brought wide attention to Erikson's work, Erikson would often seek to create mild states of confusion in his patients, catching them off guard or confounding their expectations by encouraging them to exaggerate their symptoms or "improve" them in ways he might suggest. An uncommunicative young woman, for example, might be urged to be completely silent, or a verbally abusive man encouraged to expand his vocabulary of curses. It seems, in short, as if he had a kind of intuitive genius for undermining set behaviors. In his clinical work he continually sought to destabilize consciousness and make contact with the underlying unconscious.[29]

Erikson's work inspired John Grindler and Richard Bandler to develop neuro-linguistic programming in 1973. Intrigued by Erikson's abilities to reach patients on unconscious levels—an ability they also saw in Virginia Satir's work with families and Fritz Perls' work in his gestalt groups—they set out to capture the unique features of these exceptionally gifted clinicians by modeling their language and behavior. Working with Gregory Bateson, who in turn had been influenced by Alfred Korzybski's concept of unconscious mental maps, Grindler and Bandler believed that behavior was guided and shaped by such maps and could be altered if the maps were changed in interaction with therapists. They developed a "toolbox" of methods derived from the gifted clinicians they observed, an eclectic array that included many of Erikson's strategies for distracting conscious attention, instilling confusion, and overloading perception in order to bring about behavioral change.

Neuro-linguistic programming (NLP) was highly influential in its beginning years. It attracted many patients as well as practitioners for training. It was also used by coaches in their work with business executives, no doubt because of its scientific sounding image and rationale. But Grindler and Bandler fell out with each other. Their methodology lost credibility as new techniques were embraced haphazardly. Increasingly, critics noted that there was little if any empirical evidence to back up practitioners' claims of effectiveness. As we have seen, the idea of unconscious learning and adaptation is born out by current research, but the concept of mental maps is not. NLP has been called "neuromythology," and the author of an authoritative handbook on hypnotism noted that Grindler and Bandler's techniques were "a much adulterated, and at times fanciful, version" of Erikson's work.[30] NLP fell on hard times.

In some respects it has been superseded by a new technique known as eye movement desensitization and reprocessing (EMDR), offering a similar promise of direct contact with the unconscious. In 1987, psychologist Francine Shapiro discovered on a walk through a park that the anxiety associated with painful memories seemed to fade as she moved her eyes rapidly back and forth. She experimented with others to see if her experience held true, and became convinced that she had found a means to intervene directly in the nervous system, changing the way in which the information of past experience is stored. EMDR holds out the possibility, as she puts it (emphasis hers), "*of direct, nonintrusive, physiological engagement with the stored pathological elements.*"[31] The memories, in other words, can be cleansed of the disturbing emotions that are associated with them.

This theory, rooted in the idea that the mind functions as a computer, does not fit with what we have learned about the cognitive and emotional unconscious. Moreover, it seems unlikely that the cognitive learning from experience can be detached so neatly from emotional learning that discrete systems in the brain can be so simply manipulated. On the other hand, there is much we do not know about how old learning is extinguished or how it is supplanted by new learning. Shapiro's theorizing may be thin and her model shaky, but she does acknowledge that her information processing concepts are hypothetical models. The strength of her technique lies in the results it appears to have produced. We may not know how or why it works, but there is substantial evidence that it does help people get over many of the crippling effects of anxiety in posttraumatic disorders.

Moreover, EMDR has become immensely popular, particularly as a treatment for trauma. The American Psychiatric Association has endorsed it in its practice guidelines for the treatment for posttraumatic stress disorder, and both the Department of Veterans Affairs and the Department of Defense have formally recommended it. In addition, a number of highly credible experts recommend it and use it as a clinical tool. On the other hand, EMDR continues to be criticized on a variety of grounds: the lack of statistical validity of its outcomes, its theoretical vagueness, and the absence of a clear definition of trauma.[32]

It is too early to tell if these radical therapies actually work in consistent and reliable ways, but it is clear that most of the explanations offered are inadequate. More research and experience will help our understanding. Given the pressures of the marketplace for effective and less costly methods, new radical therapies will probably emerge. But it is fair to say of most of these approaches that, even if they do work, they tend to leave their beneficiaries in the dark about how or why. Whether patients are subject to manipulation by Eriksonian sleights of hand or converted by myths of primal pain, they can end up feeling better while not knowing what has happened to them. The therapist ends up as a kind of miracle worker, and the patient, feeling relieved, can be uncertain of what, if anything, he has learned about himself.

As we saw in our examination of consciousness in Chapter One, consciousness does not play a key role in initiating behavior, but it can play a significant role in correcting our behavior and planning new initiatives. Without an understanding of what has been corrected or why it needed to be corrected, we may be hampered in sustaining change.

SYSTEMIC THERAPIES: FAMILY AND GROUP

If the radical therapies aim to get at the root causes of psychopathology in the afflicted persons, systemic therapies point in the other direction—to the interpersonal environments within which problems occur. Family therapy originated in the 1950s when a number of therapists, trying to address such traditionally intractable problems as schizophrenia and juvenile delinquency, began to think of the family as the essential unit of treatment. Influenced by the field theory of Kurt Lewin, the systems thinking of Ludwig von Bertalanffy, and Gregory Bateson's work on communication, family therapists looked outside psychoanalysis for new conceptions of mental processes that went beyond the boundaries of the individual.

Their success in reframing the issues led to a corresponding shift in focus from the cognitive and emotional unconscious in the individual to dynamics of the family system. They began to work with patterns of communication in families that implied some of the other domains of the unconscious we identified in Chapter Two: the unconscious influence of myths and metaphors within a family, sometimes over several generations; unconscious strivings for self-esteem that enlist the support of other family members; and the unconscious need to belong that pervades all groups, including families. Broadening their theoretical framework to include such dynamic issues, family therapists quickly developed different strategies for intervention.

Family therapists have tended to pay more attention to the shifting dimensions of the person that we addressed in Chapter Four. Role has emerged as a key concept, as they question the constellation of roles that family members assume. Often beginning with close attention to the role of the "identified patient," the person whose disruptive behavior or pain has brought the family into treatment, they seek to find the underlying roles that led to the assignment of that status. Moreover, they have been animated by the conviction that roles are changeable and negotiated. Given the overarching impact of the system of relationships, they tend to see persons as more malleable and adaptable than do those who work singly with patients.

A recent review of the field identified ten distinct types of family therapy,[33] but a key unifying concept in family work is the idea that families establish powerful homeostatic patterns of interlocking roles, highlighting the role of the "patient" with the presenting problem. Some "strategic" family therapists set about to destabilize those systems, forcing families to free patients from their roles and allow them to constitute themselves in new ways. Others try to analyze family structures and negotiate changes through conscious and deliberate interventions. But family therapists tend to agree that roles can change, identities established in families can shift, and dysfunctional personalities can be transformed by altering the contexts in which they function. Family therapists have entered into domains of interaction seldom seen by most therapists who work with individuals.

Similarly, group therapies tend to be more inclusive of the larger world and better able to reflect the potential diversity of roles and identities contained in the person. Originally popular for pragmatic reasons—they were cost-effective and efficient in disseminating information to patients—they have now become extremely widespread for other reasons. The original pragmatic advantages still hold, but groups are now seen as useful in stimulating a wide range of unconscious reactions because of the variety of relationships they contain. They also provide useful feedback from group members about interpersonal behavior, and they can offer support over time for members who are trying to change.

The range of therapy groups is immense and confusing. One senior practitioner reported on an informal survey he conducted: "The 111 senior clinicians who responded to the questionnaire furnished nearly 50 unique orientations and approximately 200 different names."[34] And this did not look at more specific factors such as whether the group was time-limited or open-ended, focused on any one particular clinical issue, was restricted to a given population, or was led by one leader or two. Moreover, many groups are self-organizing around specific issues or interests, often working without leaders. Alcoholics Anonymous has become something of a model for how groups can spontaneously organize themselves and maintain a useful focus on serious issues.

Almost by necessity, groups are open systems; they have a more or less permeable boundary, a purpose, and inevitable pressures for some degree of homeostasis.[35] In the public sector, psychiatric hospitals, addiction centers, prisons, and so forth, membership in groups is frequently mandated; the focus is constant but the population is constantly shifting. In the private sector, groups tend to be collections of diverse individuals, which means, in practice, that they contain random assortments of interpersonal problems. The group therapist divides his time among them, more or less fairly or in response to the urgent needs of particular members. An exception to this is systems-centered therapy developed by Yvonne Agazarian.

One of Agazarian's innovations was to conceptualize that the basic building blocks of groups are subgroups—not individual members. To be sure, in joining groups, individual persons have issues they hope to clarify or resolve, but once they join a group they inevitably enter into a process of subgrouping that continuously structures and restructures the group. A group member with an issue—whether it is a response to another member, an anxious or hopeless state of mind, an obsessive preoccupation, difficulty in joining the work of the group at any given moment—is asked to find the subgroup composed of others who share that issue. As the subgroup forms, the issue becomes decentered from the particular person who introduced it, explored as an aspect of the system within which it has arisen. The exploration of similarities within subgroups inevitably leads to greater understanding about the issue and greater clarity about its meaning for the system. Inevitably that also leads to further differentiation, as members of the subgroup begin to discriminate different aspects of the issue that connects them. Gradually, then, subgroups re-form around the newly emergent differences, and the identification of new issues leads to the formation of new subgroups, as the system moves on.

The group process is dialectical. Problems are not solved, dealt with, or disposed of, but rather transformed as a by-product of the system's continuing process of adaptation. Along the way, personal meanings become less relevant to the group process. Subgrouping moves the issue away from personal exploration or individual historical meaning, as the person has moved on from being self-centered to system centered.

Agazarian's approach, thus, shifts the locus of therapy away from the particular forms that the person has assumed in his interactions with others, the roles and identities that he experiences as defining his personal relations. Through its focus on how malleable and adaptable we are, we can see ourselves as continuously shifting parts of the systems we inhabit.

Agazarian writes about a moment in the early development of her thinking when she suddenly saw that our culture promotes the belief that we are the center of the world: "I then hypothesized that this unconscious pathogenic belief is acted out, in both individual and group therapy, by treating the patient as if he or she is the center of the world and that the patient is thus unconsciously encouraged to take things personally."[36] System-centered thinking turned out to be her way out of this dilemma.

CONCLUSION

Once clients make a connection with a therapist who is helpful, who does not make them feel worse or ashamed of having the problems they have, they tend to stay. Despite the economic pressures that promote short-term treatment and the demand for research into psychotherapy outcomes, individuals usually get the help they need in random and accidental ways. Moreover, if they can afford it, they tend to hang on. And therapists, for their part, often hang on, too. They may research a problem that has arisen in their practice or seek out supervision from a more experienced clinician, but there is a strong tendency for therapy relationships to persist.

Not much attention has been paid to this tendency. To be sure, there is always some value to be found in continuing to talk, participants tend to believe, and some benefit in postponing the final break. In a world of constantly shifting pressures and uncertainties, of frequent moves and dislocations, this may be serving another purpose. Today, more and more families are scattered far and wide or broken up by divorce. Parents know less and less about what their children are facing; as they age they become preoccupied with their own communities, and less available to provide advice to others. Superiors at work have less time to guide subordinates. Moreover, they change jobs more frequently than they used to, or they shift roles in their organization. Friendships are not easy to maintain in an increasingly competitive and pressured world. As a result, the advice and counsel that used to be more readily available in standard social relationships is increasingly hard to find.

Once the acute and focused work of psychotherapy has been concluded, therapists sometimes slip into the role of advisor or consultant, filling a need that is not met elsewhere. Or patients come back, intermittently, to "touch base," for a "refresher," or just an occasional talk. There are no statistics on this, and not much reporting about it. But it makes sense that therapy bends itself to this need, providing connection in a fragmented world. Intimacy and warmth are not for sale, but once they have been found it makes a kind of sense to hold on to them.

Seven

THINKING IN A POST-PROFESSIONAL WORLD

■

Over the past 150 years, the professions gradually became the guardians of society's specialized knowledge. They were entrusted with the responsibility for developing that knowledge and the skills to use it, for setting standards, and for monitoring the ethical behavior of practitioners. But today the professions bear little resemblance to what we once took for granted they had to be. In many cases, the terms, the concepts, and the old professional organizations persist—the identities live on in the minds of practitioners and clients—but the familiar substance is gone.[1]

How does the new unconscious affect those who work with their minds, who market their services as specialists in professional knowledge? The question has two parts. First, how do knowledge and skills need to be reconceived to make them compatible with what we are learning about the new unconscious, and how does it alter our traditional understanding of knowledge? Second, how can traditional "knowledge workers" offer their services to others in reliable and effective ways? The first question is about how the new unconscious alters the nature of what we know and how we know it. The second is about the social arrangements and delivery systems required to apply that knowledge to problems and needs.

At the beginning of this book, we saw a stunning example of the collapse of a profession. Psychoanalysis, having constructed a rigid set of independent and isolated organizations to protect itself against unwanted change, curtailed the possibility of adaptation to new social conditions and undermined its chances for survival. Other professions have been far more successful in adapting to change. Many, in fact, are booming. But as they found ways to fit into the highly

competitive landscape of investor capitalism and thrive, their organizations and structures have shifted radically. Under intensified social and economic pressure, they have lost much of their distinctive
status and autonomy.

Professionals will probably continue to lose control over the conditions of their work.[2] The immunity from the market they once enjoyed and the monopoly control they exercised have eroded beyond
recognition, in some professions to the point of disappearance. The
term *professional* will continue to be used, but more and more it will
refer to specialized bodies of knowledge and the skills in using them,
less and less to the conditions that were enjoyed by the possessors of
that knowledge in the past. Economies of scale and the management
of costs have become mandatory. New levels of control have been
interposed between practitioners and their clients. As a result, most
professionals no longer control the conditions under which they use
their skills or exercise their judgments.

If we look at the professions of law or engineering, for example,
increasingly we see huge multinational firms recruiting their associates
directly from graduate schools at competitive salaries. The legal structure of these enterprises may still bear some resemblance to the initial
partnerships of origin, but they no longer actually function as those
partnerships did. Those professionals are now, by and large, employees. Physicians, too, are amalgamated into larger systems. Increasingly,
rather than going into private practice, they join group practices, which
frequently evolve into clinics or specialized centers, or they become
employees of outpatient hospital services. The choice for a physician
is to be entrepreneurial, if he can figure out an opportunity that has not
already been exploited, or become a worker in someone else's shop.

Other professions have imploded under these pressures. Auditing
has been computerized and, increasingly, outsourced. Accountants,
in turn, have sought out more lucrative careers as business consultants. In universities, vast increases in enrollments have led to a new
stratification of faculties, with a small number of endowed chairs and
tenured professors at the high end and vast numbers of part-time teach-

ers staffing required courses at the bottom of the scale. These trends are exacerbated where costs are associated with social entitlements, such as workplace benefits and insurance coverage. Nursing has become highly layered, with many functions pushed down into the hands of those requiring less training. Social workers are becoming rank-and-file workers, if not, on the other hand, moving up into management roles in social agencies.

In this new landscape, there are new ambiguities. Are managers professionals? The case has been made that they have specialized knowledge derived from their training in business schools. The MBA degree is a ticket of admission to a new class of jobs. On the other hand, there are few agreed-upon standards or ethical guidelines. Despite their high profile, it is not clear that their knowledge has moved much beyond an intuitive set of practices based on experience or a sequence of fads. Moreover, managers have often been viewed as antithetical to professionals: they interpose themselves between experts and clients, undermining the traditional autonomy of the professional practitioner. Another ambiguity: the term *professional* has now often come to include someone who is paid for services or skills traditionally exercised by amateurs and exercised totally outside the market. Today, for example, we speak of "professional" baseball players and boxers.

This is the social and organizational landscape faced by the knowledge workers of the new unconscious. They cannot take for granted professional standing and independence. And yet, it is obvious that their work requires specialized knowledge and skills of the kind traditionally associated with professions. A high degree of training and supervision will continue to be required. How can quality be ensured and ethical standards maintained? What will attract new practitioners to this work? How will they be trained? How will they be able to extend their knowledge and develop their skills? How will they organize themselves? What kinds of associations will they need to develop to maintain and increase their proficiencies? How will the public be protected?

In the sections that follow, I will look at several areas of work involving the knowledge of the unconscious. Management consulting that is psychodynamic, a relatively new and somewhat unorganized profession, faces a robust future. But it faces the dilemma of learning how to incorporate knowledge and skills relevant to the unconscious dimensions of organizational life with the hard skills of management and finance. Psychotherapy, an established profession aligned with medicine, is undergoing profound changes that are only likely to increase over time. Finally, there are areas of immense potential relevance that enjoy, at this stage, only fledgling development. I will sketch out how these areas might grow to fulfill their promise.

What about the knowledge and skills that the applications of the new unconscious require? Professional structures work when they reflect the particular requirements of the knowledge base they were designed to protect and foster.

APPROXIMATE KNOWLEDGE

As we have seen, the "black box" of the mind is no longer entirely opaque. Science confirms the existence of unconscious processes, and even provides glimpses into its functioning. But what concerns practitioners is practical knowledge of what is unconscious at any given moment, what is going on that shapes behavior but remains a mystery to those in the midst of it. What do people need to know that is unavailable to them? How can they get a grip on what is outside their view? What do they stand a chance of recognizing as valid once it is pointed out to them? Here we are in the land of pervasive ambiguity, of permanent gray.

Such knowledge is always inexact and subject to continual revision. The objects of unconscious knowledge are not only out of sight, but also incapable of definitive verification; the understanding of them is provisional, subject to change. At best the understanding can be "good enough," providing enough basis for actions that, with probing, can provide the basis for still further actions.

This approximate knowledge is elusive and slippery, constantly being constructed, reconstructed, and revised in response to changing circumstances. The very act of trying to know it alters it. Each effort at understanding inevitably reflects what is happening now, what is going on here, with you and me. Being certain, convinced of the truth of what you know, is to be closed off to other possibilities. Moreover, set beliefs will blind you to the impact that your own inquiry is inevitably having upon the thing you are searching to understand. Entirely unlike information on the Internet, knowledge of the unconscious is not waiting to be found. Though it is infinitely complex and dispersed, no search engine will find it. It is analogous to what, in physics, is referred to as the Heisenberg principle. In the realm of the mind, this is tied to our profound capacity for adaptation. The unconscious mind continues to adapt freely, eluding efforts to control it even as we engage it.

Hard work, discipline, and due diligence do not always yield access to what we know unconsciously. We might formulate rules or guidelines or checklists to guide our searches for what we want to find, to remind ourselves of our goals and possible avenues in inquiry, but we have to be prepared to discard them when we get a whiff of the scent we are after, a glint of light on a different hill.

Then there is the danger of finding just exactly what we are looking for, what we are hoping to find. It can be that our intuition was on target, but it can also be that we trick ourselves into seeing what we want to see. Our own unconscious processes will be present throughout our searches, and they will be all too capable of discerning resemblances that are not there, that offer premature resolutions to our inquiries.

A second related characteristic of unconscious knowledge, apart from this fluidity and inexactness, is the fact that it is very much about particulars. The mind moves from perception to perception, object to object. It works by association and links, rather than by generalizations and broad similarities. Proust's taste of the petite madeleine is a case in point. A certain texture, a look, a familiar shade of green, an uncanny thought, a weird association—one detail leads to another and a pattern of connection emerges. Consciousness, on the other hand, searches for common principles. It constructs maps of reality. Such efforts are superimposed upon the rambling networks of association that actually compose mental life. To work with the unconscious requires attention to unique incidents, odd facts, and strange shapes that stand out from their contexts, unexpected qualities that a discerning mind can seize upon as clues to be followed.

This links with another characteristic of knowledge of the unconscious: it emerges from process, not logic. One particular perception or thought leads to another. Associations flow, often across boundaries of groups and persons. One can focus on a problem and do one's best to concentrate, but the object we are searching for will emerge in ways, akin to revelation, that cannot be anticipated. Such revelations, however, are not facts or clear realities so much as hypotheses, in effect, that lead to further searches and inquiries. The pursuit of unconscious knowledge is like following a trail that takes us around a corner where, suddenly, someone else sees what was being sought behind you or off to the side. In retrospect, it can seem to have been in plain sight all along.

These qualities of unconscious knowledge present unusual challenges for practitioners and their relationships with clients. For one thing, professional workers today are increasingly subject to what has become known as the "commodification" of services. That is, the professional services they provide are increasingly viewed as products to be measured against other products. They are broken down into components in order to be analyzed for cost, effectiveness, and consistency. In the language of the market, this is known as "pricing," "value," and "quality control"; the total package is often promoted as a "brand," a reassuring image of reliability. In this world, professionals become providers. Clients become consumers.

Practitioners of unconscious knowledge do not easily fit into this model of service. As we have seen, knowledge of the unconscious is elusive, local, particular, hard to pin down. Outcomes are difficult to predict. A management consultant may be hired to help a senior executive be more effective in his role, but he may find in the course of his researches that perceptions of incompetence are being projected onto the executive, deflecting attention away from a feared boss. Or the unit may be ineffective because of structural factors in the organization, and the executive who has been targeted for help is actually being scapegoated for its failures. A patient comes to a therapist for help with feelings of intolerable guilt toward his father, only to find that he is enraged at the father's persistent competition with him. A child shows behavior problems in school, but it turns out that he is expressing his family's hidden conflicts.

Physicians deal with comparable unknowns, the unpredictable course of a disease or the unexpected discoveries of surgery. Lawyers, however experienced and competent, cannot guarantee the outcome of their cases. But those working with the unconscious face an extra element of uncertainty. For one thing, a surgeon can actually point to the tumor he found. Persuading a client that things are not what they seem, that his preferred targets of blame are not the real source of his problem, can be immensely difficult. Unconscious motives are frequently hedged about with defensive convictions, which are fears that prevent alternative interpretations from being thought or expressed.

For this reason professionals who work with the unconscious need exceptional flexibility in negotiating their contracts with clients. Ideally, they can specify an exploratory or diagnostic phase in which information will be gathered before a course of action is planned. That is still no guarantee of avoiding mistakes or following false leads.

A second strategy to deal with the elusive and unpredictable nature of unconscious knowledge is to build into the process a high degree of collaboration. In therapy, the presence of the therapist not only brings into the room someone better able to tolerate the uncertainty and ambiguity that is distracting and upsetting the client. It also introduces someone who, from past experience with similar issues, is likely to be familiar with the issues the client is grappling to understand. Working with a consultant gives the client opportunities to develop sensitivities and skills that add immeasurably to the process of exploration. The client learns to pay attention in new ways to what was always there, and the process is enhanced.

The client is where most of the data are located. It is not so much that the unconscious needs space in which to emerge, as that the interaction allows the client to shift out of familiar and repetitive patterns of perception and thought, so that what the client knows— without knowing that he knows it—becomes available for conscious thought. In the relationship, the implicit is made explicit. Even in the mere act of talking to another, the client can recognize his own thoughts in a new way and gain a greater understanding that was previously unavailable.

This brings up, in turn, the question of context, the setting in which the process of inquiry is occurring. If either the client or the practitioner is charged with anxiety or pressured to come up with answers to urgent questions, his mind will not be free for the inquiry. Or if the client is feeling, for any reason, unsafe, the unconscious will protect him by closing down and refusing to cooperate. If the reason for the inquiry is ambiguous or if the client has any reason to suspect that the thoughts the inquiry uncovers will be used in any ways other than what he has agreed to, the process is likely to grind to a halt. Practitioners of unconscious knowledge need to pay extraordinarily careful attention to the conditions of their work because safety and trust are indispensable.

This relationship, then, is what allows the process to change as needed in response to new discoveries and changed hypotheses. The client is more likely to agree to a renegotiation because, deeply implicated in the process of discovery, he is better able to grasp the reason for the change. We might say that the authority of the professional here becomes grounded in the trust that client and practitioner have mutually constructed. It is based on experience, earned rather than conferred.

Before that can happen, however, there has to be a certain amount of professional authority that the potential client perceives in the prospective professional practitioner. As we saw in the Introduction, among the reasons for the collapse of psychoanalysis was its reliance on a professional authority that has drastically declined, as it has throughout our society. But some forms of professional authority nonetheless need to be built. Without a reliable framework for professional activity, the public has little to guide it, and practitioners become increasingly dependent on unpredictable currents of publicity and local fads. The robust forms of the past may never be reconstituted, but it is in the interest of new professionals to establish their reliability and competence in the eyes of the public.

This is beyond the scope of what individual practitioners can accomplish. It may not be possible to marshal strong evidence, but so long as there is an obvious need for help and clients actually feel helped, the information about what can be done will need to be disseminated. And some monitoring of unethical or incompetent practices will have to be put in place. Obviously, this is best done by the practitioners themselves, who will know how to recognize and define competence firsthand. Their doing so through their professional associations will also strengthen their standing.

MANAGEMENT CONSULTANTS AND MANAGEMENT TRAINING

Management consulting possesses few features of a traditional profession. Gatekeeping is haphazard, with little direct training available and no certification. There is no agreed upon set of standards for practitioners, no ethical guidelines. And yet, like a traditional profession, it offers specialized knowledge and skills to those who need them.

Moreover, with many different kinds of services offered to address an array of problems, the field is unorganized and difficult to categorize. What links this all together into a "profession" is simply the fact that consultants have knowledge and skills that management can use, and that consultants can be contracted with in order to provide help. While the lack of standards and guidelines is a problem for clients, there is little question that managers need to hire outside experts to cope with the immense array of specialized problems they face, and, often, that is far easier to do than trying to increase their internal capacity. They do not burden organizations with fixed costs, and they can easily be fired or replaced. As outsiders, consultants can often see things that those inside have come to take for granted.

Though only a very small percentage of management consultants are familiar with the unconscious dimensions of organizational life, outlined in Chapter Five, their numbers are growing, and the value of understanding those dimensions is being increasingly recognized. As we saw, there is virtually no organizational problem that is without its unconscious aspects, though this is often not apparent to those who are confused and anxious in the midst of the dilemmas they are trying to resolve. It would be worth our while, briefly, to identify some of the more obvious organizational issues in which the unconscious is implicated, and then look at the wider range of issues where understanding the unconscious could prove to be useful.

The more salient problems have to do with relationships in the workplace and impediments to collaboration. The most salient problem of all may be the eruption of persistent, destructive conflicts within an organization. Often such conflicts are seen as personality issues, as groups unconsciously seek out and blame individuals for problems they find themselves unable to face together. Occasionally, one person is to blame, whether through incompetence or rigid behavior. But blaming individuals has become the preferred diagnostic mode in organizations looking for a quick fix for engrained, systemic problems, while more complex underlying issues are ignored until they recur. Not infrequently it is the talented and exceptional individual— and the one who has difficulty fitting in—who ends up as a casualty in the process.

Related to this problem of internal conflicts are resistances to adaptation and change. Outside consultants who are able to probe beneath the surface of rationalizations and excuses can often help an organization overcome the subtle and indirect ways in which newly designed structures and policies are subverted by those they are meant to benefit. If they are caught up in the organization's web of established relationships and traditions, insiders may not easily perceive such forces and may be at a loss in thinking how to deal with them. Even those who are enacting such resistances directly are often far from aware of the effects of their behavior.

Frequently, restructuring takes the form of downsizing or, as it is sometimes euphemistically phrased, "right-sizing." Here the traditional emphasis has been on the effects on those who are let go, and their need for counseling. But those left behind, the survivors, are often assailed by feelings of guilt or ongoing fears that the ax will eventually be aimed at their jobs—thoughts and feelings that are frequently covered up and neglected. There are related problems having to do with reintegrating the work force in the aftermath of these losses, and ameliorating the demoralization that saps energy and inhibits adjustment.

Groups of managers working together can get help from consultants who understand the ease with which groups slip into "groupthink" or just fail to jell. Advisors in an executive suite can become more effective with outside help, as can boards of directors who meet infrequently but carry immense responsibility, often without much direct knowledge about the organizations over which they preside. Consultants, who may not know much more about the organization than the directors, can help to keep their conversations on track by challenging unwarranted assumptions or inadequately explored decisions.

All these problems can be conceptualized as relationship issues, having to do with the problems encountered by people working together. The vast majority of consultants, however, are hired to solve complex technical problems that management could not be expected to handle on its own: designing and installing information technology systems, conducting sophisticated market analyses, constructing benefit packages for employees, devising public relations strategies, branding, and so forth. This is where the big consulting firms have a distinct advantage, as they can mobilize technical resources and deploy experts quickly and efficiently. But even here knowledge of the unconscious can be a valuable adjunct to their expertise. To begin with, the client's request for help would need to be read accurately for the intervention to succeed, including what is not being said or what is being taken for granted. Moreover, different overlapping or competing systems within the client organization would need to learn to work together, and resistances to change would have to be overcome. Sophisticated observers can ferret out incompatible expectations and assumptions or detect the hidden rivalries and suspicions that undermine projects even before they get underway.

A little-noted development, related to the use of outside consultants, is the development of in-house advisors. A number of firms in highly competitive industries have quietly recruited psychologically sophisticated senior advisors and even psychoanalysts, to be consulted by senior management on a regular basis. Such advisors, understanding systems and familiar with business issues as well as corporate cultures, can play key roles in helping senior management think through complex issues. Moreover, as they come to understand the firm and its culture more intimately, they can help management reflect on itself, unearthing hidden assumptions or conflicts that can impair management's ability to work as a team and think through difficult questions.

It would be a mistake to try to set up a separate profession of psychodynamic consultants, specialists in the organizational unconscious. Attempting to structure it according to the traditional models of training, credentialing, and certification might well prevent the market from helping practitioners locate the variety of needs that demand service. A better strategy would be to disseminate knowledge of the unconscious dimensions of organizational life through the array of existing educational organizations, business schools, schools of public administration, graduate schools of industrial psychology, and so forth. A number of psychoanalysts and other mental health professionals have been recruited into consulting firms or found their way onto the faculties of business schools. Much is known about training skillful practitioners in this work, and journals, conferences, and workshops already exist to develop and extend that knowledge. The building of the requisite professional organizations for practitioners has begun and will inevitably increase, helping them build their knowledge and proficiency.[3]

The first step, however, is getting prospective clients to see the value of this work. Here we run up against the inherent difficulty of helping others to see the importance of what they do not know about or understand. This is particularly true in an age of investor capitalism, when the fastest way to increase stock value is through financial restructurings, mergers and acquisitions, downsizings, breaking up companies, or selling off assets. Building internal strength in a company often does not seem sufficiently rewarding. Making organizations more efficient, productive, and resilient, and less stressful and more satisfying places to work may easily be discounted in the executive suite, as such factors do not necessarily directly increase shareholder value.

The target group most in need of stronger and more manageable organizations are those preparing for leadership roles within them, those working their way up the corporate ladder. They are the ones more likely to appreciate the value of understanding the unconscious in organizations. To be sure, consultants who are engaged in efforts of restructuring or developing new systems are also promising targets, as they encounter directly the complexities and resistances of bringing about change. But it is the executives and managers who most often have the burden of implementing those changes, after the consultants have left, who can best appreciate how messy and convoluted are the real organizations they are trying to lead. As they work to advance their careers, learning about the paradoxes and complexities of leadership and management, torn in different directions, subject to conflicting pressures, they are the ones likely to be more open to what sheds light on the issues they are grappling with.

Most companies today have made it a practice to cultivate and train their future leaders. Many have set up their own in-house schools or colleges for that purpose, though more rely on outside management training courses where 360-degree evaluations (from those above, below, and alongside the subject) and coaches help promising executives assess their leadership styles and plan improvements. Virtually all business schools offer programs in executive education, and such programs are growing as management leaders increasingly ask for and expect to receive such help.

Much of this training is fairly conventional. A substantial portion of the educational budgets of large businesses is devoted to motivational speakers, providing a momentary lift with little lasting impact. Additional intensive courses stress standard approaches to management based on cookbook theories and case studies that are truncated versions of the management courses offered to MBAs. At another extreme are the forms of management training that emerged in the 1960s and 1970s, aiming to help executives become more open and self-disclosing, trusting, and expressive. Those programs were seldom effective because managers found that when they returned to their jobs and were subjected to the familiar, competitive environment of the workplace, without the support of their T-group leaders and fellow trainees, they reverted to old habits. As a result, organizational development and psychological interventions got a bad name, and "touchy-feely" became a term of abuse.

But much of the new management training is radically different, emphasizing actual experience and insight in the context of organizations. Such programs focus on effectiveness, bringing in data from coworkers as well as providing the kind of understanding that a good, psychodynamically oriented coach can provide. Often, in fact, the two go together. A coach using data from coworkers can recommend such intensive immersion for a client, and can also follow up with continuing feedback and support.

Substantial learning is possible when executives have the opportunity to reflect on their own behavior, questioning their assumptions or exploring their deeper motives. If they have been helped to look below the surface of their own behaviors and that of others, if they have been able to see how old assumptions and obscure resistances pervade the systems they manage, they actually stand a chance of improving. They can view the problems they encounter in deeper, more complex ways. And they will remember that there is value to be had from such exploration because they have the opportunity to implement their new insights as soon as they return to their jobs.

Henry Mintzberg, professor of management at McGill University, speaks of a "third generation" of management training, grounded in managers examining their own experience: "In this world of hype, angst, and confusion, people need to stop and take stock. . . . Management development is too important to leave to short, easy, strobe-light courses or longer boot camps." Together with Jonathan Gosling at the Lancaster Business School in the United Kingdom, Mintzberg developed a program that brings managers together to discuss their own experiences, reflecting and learning from each other. Like most people in the field, he does not use terms like *unconscious* or *psychodynamic*. But by focusing on reflection, paying attention to emotional communication, using improvisation and introspection, and gathering hunches and intuitions, they collect information about the unconscious dimensions of work. Moreover, by offering real problems and encouraging the expression of "gut reactions," by working in groups and offering personal exploration, they develop skills at working with the factors that are often hidden from view. Their programs are open-ended and flexible, leaving room for new insights or problems to emerge.[4]

Managers who have learned experientially about the unconscious can be leaders in disseminating such awareness. The primary focus in such training events is improving individual performance. But that also opens windows into understanding the dynamic factors affecting the performance of others, and it allows managers to see how individual unconscious issues can combine and interact to affect groups and larger systems as well.

More sophisticated and self-aware leaders are learning about the complex relations between leaders and followers, and how followers often collude unconsciously to subvert leadership initiatives. Leaders who are trained to be aware of their own layered motivations and hidden assumptions are better prepared to detect such obscure machinations and work to counter them. And they know how to get the help they need by asking questions, consulting with colleagues, or bringing in outsiders in order to grasp the patterns they are caught up in and to act more effectively.

The third generation of management training is gaining support from new approaches to decision making in organizations—what David Snowden calls the third generation in knowledge management. Snowden, former director of IBM's Institute for Knowledge Management, challenges the "universality of three basic assumptions prevalent in organizational decision support and strategy: assumptions of order, of rational choice, and of intent."[5] In other words, those at the cutting edge of managing the flow of information in organizations and thinking about how decisions are made now are working to gain access to the knowledge buried beneath consciousness. They do not refer to the unconscious, preferring to reference theories of narrative as well as complexity and chaos, but what they are talking about clearly overlaps with what we are calling the "new unconscious."

PSYCHOTHERAPISTS

Whatever the future prospects of psychotherapy, its past development as a profession has placed it within the field of medicine. This was neither inevitable nor necessary. But it has shaped its development and constrains its future.

As the sociologist Andrew Abbott pointed out, "The jurisdiction of personal problems was created, split, reattached to other jurisdictions, split in new ways, and reconceptualized a dozen times between 1860 and 1940. Groups associated with it subdivided, joined, then divided along new lines, both ideological and organizational."[6] Neurologists competed with psychiatrists; Christian Scientists competed with evangelicals, electrotherapists with hydrotherapists; psychologists and social workers made concerted efforts to claim specific areas of work. One of the most powerful claims came from the clergy, already deeply engaged as advisors to the laity at crucial junctures in their lives. At stake was the opportunity to get into a rapidly growing business and claim the new social importance it conferred.

In the 1920s and 1930s, the battle was joined by the mental hygiene movement, developed to bring the benefits of scientific thinking to social problems, free from ideological and moralizing judgments. The concept of mental illness promised to take the stigma out of mental suffering, making it a problem, not a failing. But it also provided a boost to the field of medicine as it competed against the clergy to establish jurisdiction over this burgeoning new field.

Powerful critiques have been waged against this medical identity. In 1961, Thomas Szasz attacked the "myth" of mental illness, arguing that psychotherapists are "shackled to the wrong conceptual framework and terminology." And many have continued to protest what is frequently referred to as the "medical model," urging us to refer to "clients" instead of "patients," and "problems in living" instead of "diseases."

The medical concept of disease is actually complex and multifaceted, reducible to no simple physical condition, according to medical doctors who have wrestled with this problem. Indeed, one scholar has plausibly suggested a "sociopolitical definition" of disease, in which a disease is an "undesirable" condition that "it seems on balance . . . physicians (or health professionals in general) and their technologies are more likely to be able to deal with it effectively than any of the alternatives, such as the criminal justice system (treating it as a crime), the church (treating it as a sin), or social work (treating it as a social problem)."[7]

The concept of mental health is misleading for a number of reasons. It introduces the idea of normative functioning into human behavior, replacing traditional morality with a new set of standards about the healthy personality that is constraining but hard to justify on scientific grounds. It also suggests a similarity between organic diseases, treatable by surgery and drugs, and the kinds of difficulties that clients experience. The increasing array of psychotropic medications reinforces that implication, arousing false hopes of palliatives if not actual cures. Moreover, in emulating medical procedures, psychotherapists find themselves often engaged in a collusion of bad faith, searching for a diagnosis that will make a patient eligible for the care he has come to expect, that the therapist thinks he should have, and that employers want their insurance to cover.

Let me take a moment briefly to survey the range of issues, lumped together by Abbott as "personal problems," that are now under the jurisdiction of psychotherapy. Some are entirely about meaning, helping clients through difficult life transitions: the death of a spouse or close friend, divorce or other forms of separation, job loss, illness, and so forth. Though such problems of adjustment may provoke intense anxiety and depression, suggesting the temporary use of medication, by and large these problems are clearly not illnesses that require medical attention. Closely related are family problems: marital disputes, child/parent conflicts, aging parents, and so forth. People need considerable help in understanding and managing these issues or reaching painful decisions. Here the clergy has had a distinct historical advantage. No one would question the relevance of their interest in such matters or the appropriateness of their concern and desire to help.

Expertise in interpreting experience becomes more clearly relevant when working with clients who suffer from self-defeating behaviors: the incapacity to sustain intimate relationships, the failure to pursue their own self-interests, to follow through on projects, to confront others. There is a related set of clients who feel unable to lead authentic lives, or who feel unworthy of achievement.

Many of the problems faced in psychotherapy suggest that the body is profoundly involved in the symptom picture, and that, therefore, we are somewhat closer to the traditional concept of disease. For example, anorexia and obsessive-compulsive disorder implicate the neurological and endocrine systems. It is hard to assert the sufficiency of working with narratives or interpretations when we know that drugs will often be powerfully effective in relieving depression or panic and that behavioral approaches are required to counteract deeply entrenched habits or powerful cravings.

Then there are patients who require more active management: severely depressed patients who cannot care for themselves or patients who are suicidal, schizophrenic, or sociopathic. In the past, hospitals have served as asylums, while currently they often function as temporary shelters for those in crisis, but that does not mean that the conditions of those they serve are best thought of as equivalent to cancers or broken limbs.

Though far from comprehensive, this discussion is sufficient to make the point that the complexity of human behavior rules out the adequacy of any single approach, which in turn implies that there is no single set of competencies, no single discipline that can hope to encompass all that is required of a psychotherapist. Neurologists have come back into the picture by virtue of the new discoveries being made about the functioning of the brain and nervous system. Behavioral psychologists have a role to play in reshaping destructive habits. Psychopharmacologists clearly have a powerful role to play by virtue of the complex array of new medications being developed for anxiety and depression. Traditional social workers often provide essential support. And the interpretive skills of psychodynamic psychotherapists and psychoanalysts continue to be essential.

We have come full circle: beginning by questioning the location of psychotherapy in medicine, we are now questioning the location of psychotherapy in any single discipline, the adequacy of any existing profession to encompass the knowledge and skills required to deal with the realm of personal problems. More than thirty-five years ago, a group of sociologists argued in *The Fifth Profession* that social workers, psychologists, psychiatrists, and psychoanalysts together constitute the beginnings of a new emergent profession of psychotherapy. They found that not only did the work of the four professions overlap, but also that there was significant overlap in their attitudes, values, and socioeconomic backgrounds.[8] Professional rivalries and ideological differences derailed any such emergence of a new profession of psychotherapy, but perhaps now, in the face of adversity, such a radical idea may have more appeal. Indeed, it may prove to be necessary. If so, it would have to incorporate the traditional psychotherapeutic professions in a manner that is cooperative and inclusive, not competitive.

Psychotherapy has been called a "cottage industry" because most of its work is accomplished piecemeal, in separate, informal locations. As an aggregate of outputs, it is a substantial industry, but as a means of production it looks anything but substantial. Psychotherapists operate out of home offices, for the most part, or in small professional spaces that are parceled out to individual practitioners. Waiting rooms, bathrooms, coffee machines, and water coolers are often shared, but the actual work is done in separate, isolated locations. Services are arranged on an individual basis, and there is little if any supervision or accountability.

Similarly, training takes place in a variety of small shops. Institutes that train psychotherapists sometimes consist of little more than a telephone number, a secretary or administrator, and a loose network of teachers and supervisors. Meetings are held, courses offered, and patients seen in an amalgam of private spaces. Even in the cases where training institutes have their own buildings and endowments, they are often struggling to pay the mortgage. Strapped for cash and riddled with uncertainty and worry about attracting enough trainees to keep going, they struggle to survive.

To be sure, for an industry that is primarily about the dilemmas of intimate personal relationships, there is a certain appropriateness to these conditions. Patients meet therapists under circumstances that are often not so different from how they live their lives, and this minimizes the risk of their being put off or intimidated. From the perspective of such established professions as law and medicine, however, this landscape resembles a kind of shantytown. Compared to the campuses of universities or the offices of engineers, lawyers, and consultants, it seems jerry-built, an array of temporary shelters that could be swept away in a storm or easily bulldozed. It could be argued that this informal diversity of arrangements makes the field more resil- ient and adaptable. On the other hand, it is not difficult to imagine the circumstances that could reduce this ramshackle landscape to rubble and require it to be drastically rebuilt.

The courts could decide, for example, that a therapist was culpable for not offering a treatment it believes the therapist should have known would have been more effective than the treatment actually offered. Such a ruling could quickly become a precedent, sending shock waves through the profession. Alternatively, new laws that mandate standards for training or requiring evidence for the effectiveness of treatments might well be enacted, rendering illegal or ineligible for insurance reimbursements those practitioners unable to demonstrate proficiency in a variety of proven methods. More established professions have cultivated friends in legislatures or paid lobbyists to protect against such sudden developments. The professional associations of psycho- therapy are not entirely without such resources, but they are relatively weak, and they often work at cross-purposes with each other, repre- senting the interests of one sector against another rather than work- ing together.

State legislatures could establish licenses for psychotherapists less fully trained than those who now practice, or licenses for others who would be required to work under the supervision of more senior prac- titioners.[9] Entrepreneurs, seeing profits to be made, could enter the field with aggressive marketing campaigns. The landscape of services that was drastically reshaped by the establishment of HMOs could be reshaped again.

Inevitably the profession of psychotherapy will become yet more stratified. Cost pressures are lowering barriers to participation. New York State has recently enacted a law calling for the new discipline of mental health worker, for example, requiring two years of prepa- ration. This stands in dramatic contrast with clinical psychologists, whose training takes a minimum of five years, including one year of clinical internship, usually in a hospital setting. Psychiatrists have an even more rigorous and lengthy set of requirements in preparing for their careers, starting with training in medicine. In accordance with traditional professional arrangements, there is already a significant tendency toward stratification: usually those who have more training have ended up with greater status and are able to charge higher fees. But market forces are squeezing the system. More and more, psychiatrists are being forced out of psychotherapy as their higher fees price them out of the market. Many turn their practices into medication consultations, seeing more patients less frequently and for briefer sessions. Insurance companies keep up the pressure by trying to reduce the fees for which they will reimburse clients. Increasingly, they negotiate directly with psychotherapists for what they assert are reasonable rates based on the market. Inevitably, those with briefer training, more willing to work for lower fees, come to define the market.

We are in the midst of a shakeout, in effect, with powerful long-term implications. Individual practitioners have increasingly little leverage under these circumstances. Market pressures are not likely to abate. Competitive services with shorter treatments will increase as more psychotherapists trained in them are licensed to practice. Even if universal health insurance is established and even if it includes services for mental health, that will only exacerbate pressures to contain costs. Sooner or later the resistance of established practitioners to these pressures will erode and they will adapt, either by reducing their fees or developing new competencies. Many will be forced to close their practices.

Or they will become entrepreneurial themselves, finding new ways to adapt and thrive. Some psychotherapists, not waiting to be swept up in the schemes of others, decentering from their traditional orientation as professionals, might devise ways to improve value and cut costs. Inevitably, they will discover that some trends in the commodification of services can be readily joined without compromise.

Specialized services could be set up where different sets of skills are brought together to treat particular problems: psychopharmacology, behavior modification, nutrition, neurology, endocrinology, as well as psychotherapy. Such services could utilize best practices as well as keep up with current research in order to establish and maintain a competitive advantage in the market. We already are seeing different services organized around specific clinical entities, such as eating disorders, depression, sexual dysfunction, and so forth. Some of these services would inevitably be more profitable than others, and they would be the ones more likely to be developed and enlarged first as this mode of delivering services proliferates. They could be managed by psychotherapists, but this would require, in turn, that those psychotherapists develop managerial skills and an understanding of how teams function.

In the diverse array of services now lumped together under psychotherapy, other initiatives are not difficult to imagine. Advisory services could be developed for those facing significant transitions in their lives, such as deaths, divorce, and empty nests. Many psychotherapists fully understand the ambivalence of those who seek advice: they want to be told how to solve their problems, but they resent being asked to change. Yet people seek advice, and they can use it, even if they resist it. We can envisage sophisticated advice that does not specify answers but helps clients think through their problems, clarifying their thoughts, assessing their strengths, becoming aware of some of the choices others have made in similar circumstances. Groups would be an option here.

Similar services might be developed for those who require counseling for problems with children, spouses, colleagues, friends, or parents, or for those going through difficult career transitions. Such problems could be separated out into particular services and characterized in ways that make them more readily accessible and acceptable to clients. If they were more clearly nonmedical, they might be easier for clients to accept.

Medical doctors or clinics could also benefit by having consultation with psychotherapists available on a regular basis. It is well known that people repetitively seek out medical help from physicians when in fact they are suffering from emotional problems they do not want to face. Conversely, patients often have difficulty accepting the diagnoses that their physicians arrive at. It could be useful and also less costly to have sophisticated means of dealing with such emotional issues available on the spot. In the case of incurable or terminal diseases, it would be invaluable to have consultation available to medical doctors who have to break the news to patients and their distraught families.

There is a need for services for executives or managers stressed or demoralized by the complex and contradictory demands of their work. Psychotherapists can help in grasping and reframing the meaning that clients attribute to their behavior and that of others. They are less likely to be taken in by their client's own preconceptions about their problems. Working on such problems would require additional training in understanding the current dilemmas of business and their cultural assumptions, but there is no inherent reason why psychotherapists should not be able to understand organizational life sufficiently to grasp the context of work issues for clients.[10]

There will be continued pressure to make services broader and cheaper by minimizing the costs of training. Inevitably that will lead to the development of two tiers of competence: those who know enough and have the basic skills to provide direct services; and those who can provide supervision, deal with exceptionally thorny problems, and manage. There are many laypeople, moreover, who could provide useful services dealing with problems in living but who would profit immensely from having guidance and supervision: mothers, retired businessmen, and political refugees. Psychotherapists could opt for training programs in order to serve as supervisors to providers of such services.

Psychotherapists need to help the public better understand the variety of what they can do beyond the medical model. To continue to link psychotherapy with medicine risks making psychotherapists seem relevant only in emergencies, oriented to suffering and disease—part of pathology, not part of life. More importantly, it lumps together a range of services and skills, obscuring the variety of needs that are being served. Some services will remain linked with medicine because some problems require interventions that physicians are best suited to provide, at least as part of the treatment. But distinguishing those treatments from the others will not only help the public better understand the appropriate range of services that is available, but also help to clarify what kinds of training are needed to provide them.

The specific individual initiatives that I just suggested—a small part of what creative and entrepreneurial practitioners might be able to come up with—will need to be matched and supported by an industry-wide effort to reposition psychotherapy as a distinct sector of medicine. A massive social marketing effort would be required to get the public, the government, and the private agencies currently supporting the existing system to grasp the meaning and importance of the change.[11] Some services currently provided might need to be reclassified as nonmedical, while still supported as before. Difficult as that would be, it would be easy compared with the problem of getting existing professional communities to cooperate with one another to carry out such a restructuring.

This would require redirected and newly vitalized professional associations. Today, the various organizations that represent the different profession dividing up the field are in competition with each other. Psychologists have the American Psychological Association, further divided into divisions representing psychoanalysts, counselors, family workers, psychotherapists, addiction specialists, and so forth. Social workers have the National Association for Social Workers, while psychiatrists have the American Psychiatric Association and pastoral counselors the American Association for Pastoral Counselors. Nurses have the American Association of Psychiatric Nurses, while newly accredited mental health workers will undoubtedly have their own organization shortly. And as we have already seen, there is a plethora of overlapping and competing professional associations within psychoanalysis alone.

It would be a daunting prospect to get these organizations to align their members for the effort required. Isolated in their own professional enclaves, professionals will inevitably think first about what they would be likely to lose in such a restructuring, what they would have to give up, and the advantages they fear would accrue to others. Leadership is needed that is able to focus attention on the danger of inaction and the larger opportunities to be gained. Facing a common enemy or standing to gain an obvious benefit might lead to cooperation.

The political direction of many professional organizations is usually vested in the elected professionals who preside for one year or two, tending to view those roles as stepping stones in their own careers. Often preoccupied with their own standing among their colleagues, they are uneasy if not threatened by the internal competition they face. Such circumstances make it more difficult to imagine how they can generate the vision and energy needed for these changes. And yet the pressure of developments may bring us closer to a tipping point where change will appear inevitable and the benefits of being proactive will be clearer.

NEEDED CAREERS: CONFLICT RESOLUTION, POLITICS, PREJUDICE, AND DIPLOMACY

We are beginning to understand what these new careers could be: careers that contribute to the understanding and solution of vitally important social problems, careers requiring consistent, knowledgeable, and professional preparation and training. Such careers have been foreshadowed by a few exceptional pioneers who have developed promising initiatives.

The career of Vamık Volkan is a case in point. When Anwar el-Sadat, in his unprecedented 1977 speech to the Israeli Knesset, suggested that a "psychological barrier" stood between Israel and Egypt, a barrier that accounted for 70 percent of the problems they faced, private funds were given to the American Psychiatric Association's Committee on Psychiatry and Foreign Affairs to investigate that barrier. That initial grant propelled Volkan on a new and unexpected path. An academic psychiatrist and psychoanalyst born in Cyprus, Volkan from 1979 to 1986 worked directly with Israelis, Egyptians, Palestinians, and others to understand the issues behind their conflicts and to design approaches for resolving them. When that project came to an end, he founded the Center for the Study of Mind and Human Interaction (CSMHI) in the School of Medicine at the University of Virginia to promote and develop what he had learned and to train others to use that knowledge.

Volkan and his colleagues have worked on international conflicts in Albania, Estonia, Greece, Germany, Cyprus, Georgia, and Kuwait, in addition to Israel and Egypt. They pursue what has been called "second-track diplomacy," an informal means of working behind the scenes with those who can influence public opinion. Bringing together representatives of groups in conflict, they try over time to clarify differences and identify new emergent interests. Such efforts do not aim to bring about dramatic change, but rather to begin to shift public opinion and open up new lines of thought. As a result, this method's effectiveness is difficult to measure. Moreover, it can elicit suspicion from those engaged in conventional diplomacy, who do not consider the roots of the conflicts they try to resolve so much as attempt pragmatically to exploit areas of compromise. Yet there is widespread agreement that such efforts have proved useful, particularly with conflicts emerging from clashing ethnic identities.

Highly honored for his work, Volkan retired in 2002, though he continues to write both about his experiences and about what he has come to understand on the nature of large group conflicts.[12] In 2005, demonstrating the difficulty of sustaining momentum in this work, the center he founded at the University of Virginia was closed. Volkan himself appears to have found a comfortable if remote base at Austen Riggs, a psychiatric residential facility in western Massachusetts. The work he pioneered is being sustained elsewhere, largely at universities where teaching programs can be offered for students and research orientations sustained. George Mason University has established the Institute for Conflict Analysis and Resolution (ICAR), where Joe Montville, a former associate of Volkan's, directs the Center for World Religions, Diplomacy, and Conflict Resolution (CRDCR).[13] Other universities that specialize in the training of diplomats and specialists in international services offer courses that draw upon his work. Elsewhere, think tanks that promote conflict resolution, sometimes associated with universities or located in academic centers like Cambridge, are keeping alive such concepts as multitrack diplomacy and the importance of grasping the roots of conflict.

Here is another example of an unplanned, unexpected career: As Jerrold Post was preparing to move to the Department of Psychiatry at Harvard, the CIA asked him to start a pilot project developing psychological profiles of foreign leaders. That project, initially housed in the Psychiatric Staff of the CIA's Office of Medical Services, led the CIA to establish the Center for the Analysis of Personality and Political Behavior (CAPPB), which Post headed for twenty-one years, from 1965 to 1986. A turning point in the center's work was their preparation of profiles of the Israeli and Egyptian leaders for the Camp David summit, profiles that President Carter later said were of the highest importance in guiding his negotiating strategy. After that, the CAPPB's profiles, as Post put it, were "considered a requisite for each summit meeting and a required resource for managing politico-military crises."

There were few precedents for such profiles. Various efforts were made to assess Hitler's personality during World War II, and, in 1961, at the start of the Kennedy administration, the CIA convened a panel of experts to create a psychological assessment of Khrushchev. Bryant Wedge, a psychoanalytically trained psychiatrist, summarized the conclusions of that conference for President Kennedy before the Vienna summit, but it is unclear how that information was used or the actual impact it had on Kennedy's thinking. Post's preparation for Carter's summit was the first time such profiles were known to be effective.[14]

Leaving government, Post went to George Washington University where, as professor of psychiatry, political psychology, and foreign affairs, he developed the Program in Political Psychology at the Elliott School of International Affairs. The State Department, the CIA, the Department of Defense's DIA, as well as nongovernmental organizations send mid-career employees to the program to learn to profile foreign leaders. The program offers tools for assessing the personalities of key political figures and for developing the skills needed to grasp how they think about issues and how they are likely to react to particular challenges.

The center at the CIA that Post founded went through a period of decline with the end of the cold war. With the lessening of hostilities, it lost much of its support as well as its interdisciplinary focus. It has become more active recently as the United States has engaged in Iraq and focused on the threat of international terrorism. Failures of conventional intelligence have spurred new interest in this approach.

The careers of Volkan and Post illustrate both the value of applying knowledge of unconscious dynamics to international affairs, but also the highly provisional—almost accidental—way that such careers unfold. Volkan and Post have been able to develop methods for pursuing such work effectively. They stress the clinical value of working to grasp the unconscious dimensions of behavior, in order to read behavior accurately in the context of real events. Grand interpretations or dramatic disclosures of repressed motives are beside the point. They have also emphasized the importance of interdisciplinary approaches, bringing political scientists, anthropologists, and historians together with psychiatrists and psychoanalysts in order to gain a detailed and accurate picture of the problems under review. Partly as a response to their work, a new discipline of political psychology has come into being.

But, their careers also indicate how unpredictable and precarious such careers inevitably are at this stage. The underlying problem is that as a society we are far from being able to acknowledge in a sustained way our need for this perspective, and just as far from finding a way to pay for it. Both Volkan and Post were dependent on individuals who took exceptional initiatives and made funds available. Both men were creative and courageous, but they were also lucky.

George Lakoff, the linguist at Berkeley discussed in Chapter Two, took a more entrepreneurial approach. He saw a way in which his theories were relevant to electoral politics and deliberately set out to play an influential role. In Lakoff's view, how policies and issues are framed by our language determines how we will respond to them. He traced the success of conservative Republicans in pulling together an unlikely coalition of Christian fundamentalists, fiscal conservatives, and social libertarians to their consistent and relentless use of the metaphor of the "strict-father family," as opposed to the metaphor of the "nurturant-parent family" favored by liberals. According to this metaphor, the world is a tough and dangerous place, requiring that children be taught to become disciplined and self-reliant in order to survive. He sees this metaphor as tying together policies of fiscal conservatism, religious fundamentalism, and curtailed social benefits, not only providing an underlying coherence to diverse policies but also mobilizing a strong allegiance from followers.

Lakoff's theories about the primacy of metaphor in perception have been criticized and are far from widely accepted in academic circles.[15] But on a practical level, he is calling attention to how metaphorical and narrative frames constrain thought and provoke responses, a fact that the advertising and public relations industries have been exploiting for years.

In 2000, Lakoff founded the Rockridge Institute in Berkeley, a think tank to promote his ideas about political discourse for progressive ends. The institute is avowedly nonpartisan and does not support candidates for public office, yet it is openly liberal and solicits members and donations to further its ends. It aims to drive a wedge into the role of conservative ideology in American politics—and in so doing provides new sophistication and training for political consultants. As a result, its support comes from those who want to shape electoral politics, whether for their own benefit or because of their commitment to progressive values. As a nonprofit organization, it depends on donations, grants, document sales, and membership fees. Like all such organizations, it cannot rely on an established demand for its services and must work constantly to keep afloat.

Virtually all the initiatives for applying knowledge of the unconscious to larger social issues struggle to maintain themselves. Those who want to do this kind of research and engage in projects that have a social impact must be somewhat entrepreneurial, good at gathering together resources, and adept at finding opportunities for action. Governments and universities, the two institutions that can provide more stable environments for such work, each have their drawbacks. Both Volkan and Lakoff began with university positions that allowed them to teach and support themselves while developing their ideas and undertaking their projects. But to undertake projects on a larger scale, universities are dependent on foundation grants or benefactors, and when the funds run out the programs they sustain come to an end, as happened in the case of the CSMHI at the University of Virginia. Post, working for the CIA, had the advantage of protected funding for a considerable period of time because his work was in the service of long-term strategic goals. The drawback of this arrangement, in the short-term, was that the results of his findings were not available to the public until well after they had served their purpose. Moreover, the projects might well have necessitated difficult compromises dictated by intelligence policies. The drawback in the long-term was that once the strategic goal no longer seemed important and policy shifted, funding was cut as well.

Lakoff's career illustrates an alternative pathway, the setting up of institutes or think tanks. Institutes and think tanks are by no means immune to changes in public perceptions or the pressure of circumstances, but they can offer a middle way. Gathering support for long-range goals from a wide variety of funding sources, a process managed by a part of the administrative staff, they can allow their professional staff opportunities to pursue the institute's mission—conducting research, seeking out projects, publishing papers and books, and training others. As institutes are always raising funds, they continually need to prove their value to those who support them. In this way they must be responsive to the public and accountable for their work. At the same time, they offer a space of reflection for the pursuit of long-range exploration.

No solution is reliable or ideal. Universities, institutes, and governments provide a mix of environments for such research and activities, and a range of shifting supports. Several other projects in this area and the careers of those who have initiated them make this point.

Much work is being done, for example, on violence in schools. William Pollack was hired by the Secret Service and the U.S. Department of Education to study the Columbine massacre as well as other incidents of school violence. A psychologist, he worked with a team of researchers and educators to interview students and teachers in order to find out how to assess threats of danger. They came up with a number of significant findings, including the fact that, in most cases of school violence, others knew about the plans of the attackers in advance, that previous actions indicated the existence of the danger, and that there is no accurate or consistent profile for those who launch such attacks. Needless to say, such research findings are of immense interest to educators and those who administer schools, and Pollack and his coworkers wrote a report that was published by the government and distributed widely.[16]

Pollack's career is grounded in a variety of positions: he directs the Center for Men at McLean Hospital in Massachusetts; he holds an academic position in the Department of Psychiatry at Harvard, where he is also a director of the National Violence Prevention and Study Center; he is director of the REAL BOYS® educational programs; he consults to the Secret Service; he writes books and articles, and gives talks; and he is a member of a consulting firm offering a wide variety of services to organizations. Through one lens, this is a highly impressive set of achievements. Through another, it is testimony to the multidirectional and exhausting efforts required to establish and maintain a career based on nontraditional methods and goals. It is his energy and drive that holds it together, but universities, government agencies, and free-standing programs combine to help Pollack keep his enterprise afloat.

A related career is that of Jonathan Cohen, a psychologist and psychoanalyst, who founded the Center for Social Emotional Education (CSEE) to promote the study of safe and flexible learning environments, often referred to as "school climates." The study of such climates involves being able to identify the individual and group factors, often operating outside awareness, that create safety and encourage exploration and collaboration in schools. The CSEE is a good example of a freestanding think tank, supporting research and offering programs to schools, school districts, and state and local departments of education. It has a strong fund-raising arm that enables its work to continue. Cohen runs the center, actively designing, implementing, and participating in its programs, as well as negotiating contracts to provide services to school systems. But he also maintains a private clinical practice, writes, and travels widely, giving talks and workshops. Like Pollack, he has embraced an entrepreneurial approach to his career in order to support it, as a result of which he has to devote much of his time and energy to more than research and its applications.

School violence has also engaged Stuart Twemlow, a psychiatrist and psychoanalyst at the Menninger Clinic. He helped start the Peaceful Schools and Communities research program in Topeka, before Menninger's moved to the Baylor Medical School in Houston. While it does research into incidents of school violence, his program focuses on prevention, seeking contracts with school systems in order to target and implement specific projects. Another entrepreneur of the unconscious, Twemlow has pursued a wide variety of socially important projects. He has consulted to the FBI on school violence, as well as to other government agencies about violence in communities. He undertook a program for the government of Jamaica to curtail community conflict in a midsized city. He has also written several books and numerous articles, and co-edits the *Journal of Applied Psychoanalysis* in order to promote thinking in this field and generate support for this kind of work.

There are many others who have ventured out into the trenches, trying to address social issues with an understanding of unconscious forces. Important work has been done not only in understanding prejudice but also in ameliorating it. Some have worked with police departments to help them deal with troubled families and children more effectively. Still others have helped to build cohesiveness in refugee and exile communities.[17]

An impressive amount of work has been done, but, for the most part, these are instances that stand in isolation from each other, remaining fragmented and disconnected. To be sure, those who concentrate on specific problems like school violence or community building tend to know of each other's work and work to assemble a common understanding of the underlying issues and the techniques that can be used. But at this stage, they cannot easily collaborate in deeper ways because they are constrained by the pressures of their own entrepreneurial roles, occupied with finding the opportunities to use their skills and the financial resources to sustain their projects.

For years, psychoanalysts, dynamic psychiatrists, social psychologists, and others have written about social issues, but the kinds of projects undertaken by these pioneers and others in recent years have shown what actually might be accomplished, how an understanding of the roots of those issues can suggest specific actions that might be undertaken. In the process, they have trail-blazed careers that might someday exist for others to pursue.

The application of unconscious knowledge to social problems and issues is poorly charted territory, not just because the paths are unpaved and poorly marked. The ground itself is broken and porous. It is the nature of the unconscious to be unknown and surprising, just as it is the fate of consciousness to claim more certainty than it can ever justify.

The public usually wants more certainty. It often expects the knowledge workers it consults to be precise, detailed, and reassuring. They have come to expect that of science as well as technologists and engineers. Though push-button control has increasingly become a feature of modern life, we have also come to understand in our postmodern world that nothing is absolutely fixed or certain. Yet the unconscious adds an additional layer of ambiguity. As we have seen, the unconscious seldom stands still and never yields to proof.

As a result, working with the unconscious can be frustrating for clients. It is frustrating for those of us who do it, but, by and large, we get used to the uncertainty and ambiguity of the work. We come to appreciate the value of our knowledge and the new perspectives that our awareness opens up. Scientific research that has been done on the unconscious shores up our conviction about its reality while adding to our strategies and concepts. The unconscious can no longer be ignored or treated as arcane or mystical.

Nevertheless, no scientific research can demonstrate the existence of any particular unconscious fact or prove the reality of any specific unconscious thought. We are always probing, constructing hypotheses, assessing and reassessing our work. Many of our clients may not like the fact that there is so much that they cannot know directly, and they may get annoyed and skeptical about our claims to help them. But that is how it is.

CHIMERAS AND ROBOTS

■

In the *Iliad*, Homer tells the story of how Bellerophon was sent by the king of Lykia on an impossible task, designed to ensure his death:

> *with orders to kill the Chimera*
> *none might approach; a thing of immortal make, not human*
> *lion-fronted and snake behind, a goat in the middle,*
> *and snorting out the breath of the terrible flame of bright fire.*[1]

As befitted a more civilized hero overcoming a more literate challenge, Oedipus destroyed the Sphinx by solving her riddle. The Chimera, fire breathing, represented many dangers in its implausible and contradictory forms, many ways to be terrified and threatened with death. It was thought to take other forms, different combinations of animal and human parts, and it cropped up again and again in ancient stories. Indeed, some have thought the Sphinx a version of a chimera, if not a descendant.

The landscape of Greek mythology was filled with hybrid monsters with supernatural powers: hydras, gorgons, medusas, minotaurs, harpies, griffins, centaurs—all terrifying and destructive. The Middle Ages added hippogriffs, manticores, unicorns, cockatrices, basilisks, gargoyles, and others to this beastiary, as well as a proliferation of variously formed dragons and leviathans. Composites of such beasts embodied overlapping categories, the disturbing and uncanny fusions and mergers that we have come to see as characteristic of unconscious thought—or, more precisely, the eruption of unconscious thought and perception into conscious awareness. As modern explorers surveyed and mapped the natural world, science proceeded to categorize the actual forms of life that lived in it, pushing such hybrid monsters back into the recesses of the human imagination where, clearly, they originated.[2]

But we have our modern equivalents. Our landscape is dotted with immense, intractable threats, monstrous abstractions distorting our political dialogues. The cold war produced the Evil Empire, while more recently we faced an Axis of Evil. For many years the twin ogres of capitalism and communism faced each other; more recently, infidels threaten Islam, and terrorists threaten the whole world. Enhanced and amplified by social forces operating out of awareness, the real dangers and difficult problems we face appear overwhelming. We dread facing them or avoid thinking about them altogether. Feeling helpless, we tend to abdicate any role we might play as citizens.

Fundamentalist subgroupings in our culture combat what they believe are "murderous" abortionists and "godless" evolutionists, while mainstream culture faces an insidious tide of immigration. The Iraq war can serve as a good example of how we recently constructed a modern-day chimera. Characteristically, we see these dangers as capitalized abstractions, not personifications, but they do transform persons into monsters. And surely they appear as dangerous and no less real in our social discourse than the chimeras that threatened earlier generations and other cultures.

In no way do I mean to minimize the importance of the underlying problems those abstractions often refer to, but I do want to point out that they are the imaginative constructions of our age, our modern means of attempting to describe the overwhelming and frightening issues that stalk our landscape and appear to threaten our security and our lives. To be sure, there are always real dangers or difficult sets of problems at the core of each looming abstraction. At the same time, they are inflated with projections that amplify and exploit our fears. Moreover, their fearfulness is often augmented by political leaders who promise to fight them on our behalf as well as pundits and commentators in the media who interpret their changing appearances and alert us to the risks we face.

Our societies are prone to declaring "war" on such complex abstract problems, because being assertive in the face of them reinforces our sense of gaining control. Having a plan of action is reassuring; it keeps anxiety at bay. Moreover, it helps to keep the problem "out there," at a distance in the world, in others, not in us. Such "wars," if actively engaged, we are led to believe, are sure to be won.

But there are significant difficulties with this approach. Attempts to find temporary relief from the unconscious pressures of helplessness and anxiety do not aid understanding in the long run. Nor do such "wars" often succeed in achieving their goals. On the contrary, our giant abstractions reinforce the sense that the dangers are too great for individuals to cope with. As solitary individuals, we have little choice but to be afraid, and we are inclined to turn to others for help. The threats appear too intractable to yield to anything but massive government or corporate intervention.

The Greeks believed that only heroes could overcome chimeras, a belief that was consistent with their cultural emphasis on the education and development of the privileged individuals who presided over their highly stratified societies. A need for heroes was, in part, at least, an incentive to become heroic; to become knowledgeable, strong, and courageous; to deserve your place in the community. Our chimeras, however, in a way that is entirely consistent with our contemporary culture, persuade us to let others act on our behalf. Generalized, abstract, widely distributed, they appear to require the subordination of individual thought and initiative to mass behavior. As a result, as citizens, we are prone to being persuaded of our helplessness, and thus we become more alienated and increasingly cynical. As we rely upon the giant enterprises that claim to be addressing such immense problems on our behalf, we note how they are inevitably infiltrated with other agendas involving profit and social control, how they lend themselves to corruption and exploitation, and how often they are ineffective at combating the dangers they were ostensibly brought into existence to defeat. We remain cowed and frightened—and vulnerable to those who use these modern chimeras as new ways of maintaining their social and economic power.

Our political leaders are often unreliable guides as they too are likely to be caught up in the dynamic forces that create such presences, if not all too eager to manipulate them in their own interests. They are likely to be convinced themselves of the reality of the abstract monsters they are trying to destroy, all too ready to identify external enemies and embrace aggressive solutions, convincing us to be frightened as well and to embrace their solutions. For them, too, the unknown easily becomes threatening, dangerous, mesmerizing, and monstrous.

In reality, it is unlikely that there will ever be simple answers to our riddles such as the answer that vanquished the Sphinx. We do face serious and complex problems that are often persistent and intractable. But we might reasonably hope to disentangle our projections and collusions from the beasts that haunt us. We might not need to succumb to the looming threats we collectively create and amplify. Courage will always be required and a certain freedom from conventional thought, a willingness to go beyond entrenched patterns of consciousness. We have to be willing to notice that something is amiss in what we are told, that there are anomalies, inconsistencies in what we see, and we need to maintain our curiosity and skepticism in the face of the explanations we are offered. But there will be hints and portents, and we can hope to find our way through the mountains past the signs of danger if we can be open to discovering more and more fully where we really are.

Most important of all, however, we need to be more informed and aware of how the unconscious drives us to join in these collective pressures. Collusions will inevitably occur as we share common anxieties and seek joint defenses, but we can also be more alert to those processes, more prepared to recognize them as they come into play. Without such awareness, we will continue to manipulate each other in the service of assuaging our fears. We will also be vulnerable to manipulation by the economic and political powers that find the means to profit from our fears, while they extend their control over political processes for their own ends.

A second specter looms over the modern world, a threat embodied in our new technologies. If chimeras can represent the intimidation of what we fear, the robot symbolizes the ways in which technology increasingly caters to our needs and desires. I use it to represent the myriad ways in which we construct objects and scenarios that offer the pleasures and services we come increasingly to expect and demand. Here the unconscious is no less implicated, but the danger is more obscure and indirect.

The danger represented by the chimera stems from fear; the danger of the robot stems from our expectations of convenience and comfort. Both threaten to weaken our ability to reflect on our future as a society and engage in informed political debate about our collective choices. This is a political issue because it strikes at the heart of what kind of polity are we likely to become: Informed, reflective, and engaged? Or passive and manipulated? Our stance toward the unconscious will profoundly affect the outcome of these struggles.

I single out the robot as the face of this new technology and a symbol of the danger we face because there now seems little doubt that the astounding advances in computers, artificial intelligence, and nanotechnologies will soon bring about an explosion of sophisticated robots programmed to serve our desires and needs. Robot dogs and dolls are already widely distributed, while books "talk" to our children, and computers make reservations on the Internet, handle our complaints, and answer most of our questions. Robot vehicles roam the surface of Mars, while automobile manufacturers are planning cars that will drive themselves. The Japanese are investing heavily in "carer" robots that will be able to provide essential services and companionship for an aging population, and there is little doubt that in less than twenty years reasonable facsimiles of human beings for that purpose will be available for purchase. Work is advanced on "fembots" and "malebots" programmed to provide sexual satisfaction; the projected time for their full development is about forty years.

The military, already skilled in the development of pilotless drones and smart bombs, is working on creating enhanced soldiers and, ultimately, armies of robots.

Sherry Turkle, in her groundbreaking work on our responses to computers and other "evocative objects," makes it clear how easily we project human qualities and traits onto computers and computer-assisted devices. She tells many stories of children who experience feelings and thoughts in computer animated objects, but she also notes how readily adults talk to their computers, and even engage in dialogue with computer-generated psychotherapy programs.

Consciousness, as we have seen, is all too cooperative in creating and sustaining such illusions of complete and consistent reality. At the same time, engineers and designers are working to make them ever-more lifelike and believable—and useful. There is little doubt that our minds will cooperate in making this a reality, filling the gaps in perception, sustaining plausible illusions, conferring humanity on these machines wherever that will make our experience of them more familiar and reassuring.[3]

Perhaps even more significant than robots are the various cyborg technologies that seek to supplement or enhance our minds and bodies. We already have artificial joints and limbs, pacemakers, and the like, but soon we will have far more sophisticated devices for enhancing human memory and perception, as well as drugs that combat fatigue and illness. We are at the point where professional athletes are routinely tested for performance-enhancing drugs that skew competitive achievements, but most of us will want the more and more sophisticated drugs that work without causing side effects. We will crave devices that enhance memory, reduce pain, increase concentration, and provide greater strength and endurance. The Defense Department's Advanced Research Projects Agency (DARPA) is investing heavily in research to develop metabolically enhanced soldiers. Just as it helped develop the Internet, speech recognition software, global positioning systems, night-vision sensors, spy satellites, and lasers, it will contribute to the burgeoning market in cyborg products that will augment and attract the ordinary consumer.

Few are suggesting that the machines themselves will become independent and autonomous agents, wreaking revenge on their creators, as in Mary Shelley's story of Dr. Frankenstein, or that they will threaten to take over the world, like Hal in Stanley Kubrick's film *2001: A Space Odyssey*. That is not the danger. The problem is, rather, that we will become increasingly adjusted to the conveniences, the pleasures, and the services they will be able seamlessly to provide. Living and interacting with robots will create new expectations of interactions that are without the frictions or disappointments inevitable in human relationships. They will create new images and ideals of smooth services and easy relationships.

Already many teenagers are preoccupied by if not addicted to their gameboys and other digital distractions, their cell phones, their Facebook communities. Adults who are shy, withdrawn, or socially inept are increasingly able to find or create digitized, virtual worlds that provide simulated responsiveness and engagement. On the Internet, they can create alternate identities for themselves and enjoy lively interactions with others. This is not all bad, Sherry Turkle argues, as it provides venues for experimentation and trial behaviors that liberate confined lives and may lead to new gratifications. It would not be useful for us to become twenty-first-century Luddites, opposing such developments simply because they displace existing jobs, take us into unchartered territory, and challenge established and comfortable assumptions. On the other hand, they will change us in ways we cannot foresee or may even notice.

This brave new world will have a paradoxical relationship with the new unconscious. On the one hand, it will be organized and programmed to respond to the inner logic of our behavior, not our conscious thoughts. Robots will know us better than we know ourselves. To serve us better, they and their programmers will detect and discriminate what we say and do, how our bodies actually respond to stimuli, not what we consciously believe we think. They will remember our inclinations and preferences.[4] As a result, they will be better able to anticipate our desires and to fend off what we want to avoid. In a sense, they will be more perfect slaves, but more perceptive and attuned, and they will be entirely without the onerous and guilty effects, for us, of violating human rights or depriving fellow humans of their basic needs. By taking over some of the more unpleasant and dangerous tasks, now usually assigned to the less well off in society, robots will make unambivalently positive contributions to our welfare.

Yet in creating new standards of service, inevitably they will also create new expectations for human behavior. Our unconscious will adapt to the new standards they exemplify. No doubt much of this will be seen as highly desirable, and, in fact, there is much to be said for more reliable services and higher levels of satisfaction. But as the robot increasingly overlaps with the human, because robots will both take on human activities as well as imitate human behavior, our expectations of one another will be irrevocably altered. The meaning of "human" will change.

Katherine Hayles, perhaps our most astute observer of the interface between these technologies and culture, notes, "Humans may enter into symbiotic relationships with intelligent machines (already the case, for example, in computer assisted surgery); they may be displaced by intelligent machines (already in effect, for example, at Japanese and American assembly plants that use robotic arms for labor); but there is a limit to how seamlessly humans can be articulated with intelligent machines, which remain distinctively different from humans in their embodiments."[5] John Pickering at Warwick University in the United Kingdom has worried that "agent technologies," those anticipating human needs or interacting with human requests, may "harmfully degrade how people value themselves and treat each other." To be sure, while being immensely useful, mimicking us literally, machines will not be able to take into account the unexpected or new changes in our thoughts that stem from deeper and more visceral experiences or the new perceptions that arise from spontaneous interactions with others.[6]

The mind is not a computer, as we saw in Chapter One. Part of the body, it responds in multivariant ways and constantly is adjusting and restructuring itself. The danger is that in relying more and more on computers to assist our agency, in responding to them as if they were human, we will neglect the vital data that comes from our own bodies and from each other. New standards and expectations will be set by the interactions between our computers and our bodies that will leave less and less room for variants on the status quo.

All of this will inevitably be in the service of the existing social order, and will reinforce existing fault lines of privilege and status. The new robots and the seamless gratifications they offer advance our individual goals as flattered selves, adding to the qualities and characteristics that enhance our individual value and self-esteem, and they will help to make us more competitive. But they will also advance the goals of our consumer society and the established corporations that serve it.

But this is the danger with chimeras as well. Outside threats and services provided by intelligent machines may seduce or distract us from the deeper knowledge of ourselves we could gain from being more reflective, more in touch with our bodies, more alert to the dynamics of the unconscious. We can easily become increasingly integrated into existing social structures without recognizing what is happening to us.

This is all the more urgent as the unconscious, as we have seen, is inherently conservative. Trying to repeat its old adaptations to the past, it almost automatically links with established forms of power and authority. All of us have adapted to the differentials of privilege and wealth we encounter well before we can begin to think they might be changed.

There is no doubt that much of the discoveries and insights of the new unconscious will be used to maintain the status quo. It will be employed to sell goods, promote candidates, and advance social goals, many of which no doubt will be of questionable social benefit. Indeed, knowledge of the unconscious will often end up in the service of those who can buy the best talent to exploit it and pay for the means to make it work on their behalf.

Education has been our historic answer to this problem—and it still is our primary resource against entrenched ideas and exploitative practices. Schools decenter us from traditional relationships, while teachers introduce new ideas. We are encouraged to compare and reflect, to question assumptions and be skeptical of others. Other worlds and other perspectives open up. So long as the marketplace for ideas remains open and vital we will be forced to think afresh and be less vulnerable to received opinion.

Moreover, the explosion of popular culture and communication constantly exposes us to new experience. So long as the cultural marketplace also remains open and alive, we will continue to be forced to think beyond familiar boundaries. To be sure, mass communication caters to the lowest common denominator. Still, over time, driven by competition, it will colonize new ideas and expose its consumers to new experience.

The new unconscious defines a new frontier, in effect, a limitless space of exploration. To realize its potential as well as guard against its abuse, we will all need to be better educated to understand its multiple forms, its varied presence in our lives. We will also need to be more effective at detecting its manifestations in ourselves as well as in others. And we will need consultants and commentators who will remind us that what we see and take for granted will, inevitably, be infiltrated with unconscious elements we do not see and do not understand. We will need continual help in being alert to how much of our perception is filtered out or how much never gets formulated from the start.

Is it too far a stretch for our imaginations to imagine television programs or newspaper columns that routinely assess the unconscious dimensions of our daily news? When will the chief information officers of corporations see the importance of mining their organizations for unconscious information or reflecting on its influence on their own roles? Can we imagine our presidents, governors, and mayors getting continual advice on the inattended dimensions of their policies or their interactions with each other or with their constituencies? And if we can imagine that, could we also conceive of watchdog institutions to counter the unconscious manipulations they engage in? At what point in the educational process will we start to develop awareness in children of the ubiquitous dangers of scapegoating and the tendency of peer groups to screen out uncomfortable facts? How will jurors be aided in factoring greater awareness into their deliberations, and how will judges and lawyers become more conscious of the unconscious ideas that enter into their assessments? Obviously those in public relations and advertising will want to know as much as they can about the unconscious motivations of the public. They will be in the vanguard, but how will the consumer and the citizen gain the benefits of a countervailing perspective? How will the public protect itself as the future of the unconscious unfolds?

Education continues to be the answer, both formal education and continuing public information campaigns. With luck, the dynamics of trade, economic competition, and free speech will ensure the dissemination of information about the unconscious and its applications. But, then, educators will have to be educated, and the public alerted and informed. It will take a very long time for us to become knowledgeable and proficient as a society, but there is really no alternative once the power and reach of the unconscious have been recognized.

Throughout the twentieth century, many social critics voiced concerns about the dangers that mass society posed through an increasing standardization of human experience. Other critics pointed out how our capacity for free thought has been debased by our culture's emphasis upon production and consumption.[7] We have an appearance of greater and greater freedom in the immense range of consumer products we have to choose from. Moreover, new technologies increasingly liberate us from the constraints of time and space as well as the ravages of disease. On the other hand, it is not clear that we are actually more free or more satisfied, and, as a result, more able to choose how to live in ways that matter. Do we enjoy life more? Do we think more creatively? Do we understand ourselves more fully?

As we saw at the outset of this book, the interest in the unconscious that propelled Freud to fame one hundred years ago came about because he exposed the power of hidden motivations, the limits to our control over our own behavior. Naive notions of progress and perfectibility could not be sustained. The unconscious he uncovered provided beginning ways to think about how the picture we had of ourselves was far more complex than we had wanted to believe.

Understanding the unconscious is still daunting and certainly dashing to simplistic hopes, but it remains compatible with the goals of expanding our capacity for thought and extending our freedom. Indeed, that belief has animated this book from the start. If we understand the hidden recesses of our minds, our social collusions as well as our vulnerabilities, if we recognize the hidden role of anxiety and insecurity in our behavior, the importance of meeting our emotional as well as our material needs, we are better placed to reach our long-range goals of safer, freer, and more productive lives.

A greater awareness of the unconscious can be of incalculable help to us all in the future. It will help us to know ourselves better, to make better choices, to work better with others, to join more effectively in collaborative enterprises, to be better citizens. But it will also be essential to combating the dangers posed by the chimera and the robot, to help us become aware of how external dangers and easy opportunities can be used to circumscribe our lives and move us in directions we will ultimately regret.

ACKNOWLEDGMENTS

Many have helped and encouraged me along the way. Jay Greenberg first planted the idea of a book in my mind, and though this has turned out to be a very different book from what he had expected, no doubt, I remember and appreciate the support he provided at the outset. Philip Blumberg was a frank and extraordinarily generous critic of many earlier proposals, helping to steer me in the direction I ultimately took. Sometimes I thought he knew better than I did what this book was going to be. Judith Gurewich, my publisher, also encouraged me along the path, helping me to discard some old ideas and sharpening my focus on what mattered more. I also want to acknowledge the support of Don Stern, who has been exceptionally helpful from the start, and Dick Pollak who, at the very beginning, helped me to grasp what a book proposal needed to be.

Many colleagues have read portions of this work in progress and suggested innumerable improvements: Paul Lippmann, Judith Rustin, Todd Essig, Jack Drescher, Marc Maltz, Ann D'Ercole, Marcia Cavell, Debra Noumair. My daughter, Elizabeth Blaylock, made shrewd and useful comments on Chapter Five. Two friends and colleagues in England, Julian Lousada and Jon Stokes, made very valuable comments on the tenor of earlier drafts. Toward the end of the process, two friends generously served as readers, Peter Marks and Victor Friedman. I also had a superb editor, Pat Cremins, who taught me much about being clear.

I owe a debt to the patients who took the risk of allowing me to describe their experiences in order to help me present my ideas more effectively: "Amos," "Vico," "Marilyn," and "Victor." I also want to acknowledge some of the many colleagues from whose work I have borrowed: Amy Frayer, Gordon Lawrence, Marc Maltz, Larry Hirsch-horn, Bill Kahn, Eric Miller, and George Gwynne.

It would be impossible to acknowledge all the colleagues who have shaped my thinking over the years. Many, no doubt, will find some of their own ideas embedded in mine throughout this book. It would be entirely accurate and fair to say: I don't begin to know all of what I have come to know through them.

NOTES

■

INTRODUCTION

1. Sigmund Freud, "On the History of the Psychoanalytic Movement," *Standard Edition* 14:7–66.
2. W. H. Auden, *The Age of Anxiety* (New York: Random House, 1947).
3. Sigmund Freud, "Studies on Hysteria," *Standard Edition* 2:157.
4. "The idea that the unconscious constituted an insatiable but also manipulable well of desire was crucial to the development of consumer culture." Eli Zaretsky, *Secrets of the Soul: A Social and Cultural History of Psychoanalysis* (New York: Knopf, 2004), p. 144.
5. R. F. Bornstein, "The Impending Death of Psychoanalysis," *Psychoanalytic Psychology*, 18 (2001): p. 5.
6. Newell Fisher made this point in 2004. The comments about the declining number of candidates worldwide is from a task force set up by the International Psychoanalytic Association (IPA): Report from the House of Delegates Committee on "The Actual Crisis of Psychoanalysis: Challenges and Perspectives" (1995). The statistics on candidates are from the two plenary talks given by Fisher as president, published in the newsletter of the American Psychoanalytic Association, *The American Psychoanalyst*, in 2002. For a trenchant and authoritative account of the decline in the publication of books and journals, see Paul Stepansky's article, "The Problem: Psychoanalytic 'Balkanization' and the Creation of Part-Professions with Part-Theories and Part-Journals," in his online seminar, *Uncommon Ground and the Creation of a Psychoanalytic Future*, offered in 2007 by the Psychoanalytic Connection.
7. See S. Fisher and R. P. Greenberg, *Freud Scientifically Reappraised* (New York: Wiley, 1996). Among philosophers of science, see Adolf Grunbaum, *The Foundations of Psychoanalysis* (Berkeley, CA: University of California Press, 1984); Karl Popper, *Conjectures and Refutations* (New York: Basic Books, 1962); Ernest Gellner, *The Psychoanalytic Movement* (London: Paladin, 1985).
8. For a fuller account of the internal problems of the psychoanalytic profession, see my article, "Psychoanalysis as a Profession: Past Failures and Future Possibilities," *Contemporary Psychoanalysis*, 39 (2003): pp. 557–582.

9. Hannah Arendt, "Authority," in *Between Past and Future* (New York: Viking, 1961).

10. An excellent account of how the profession of medicine achieved respect and standing is Paul Starr's *The Social Transformation of American Medicine* (New York: Basic Books, 1982).

11. See Ernest Jones, *The Life of Sigmund Freud*, 3 vols. (New York: Basic Books, 1953–1957); Vincent Brome, *Freud and His Disciples* (London: Caliban, 1984); Paul Roazen, *Freud and His Followers* (New York: New York University Press, 1984); Peter J. Swales, "Freud, Minna Bernays, and the Conquest of Rome," *New American Review* 1 (1982): 1–23; Peter J. Swales, "Freud, His Teacher, and the Birth of Psychoanalysis," in *Freud: Appraisals and Reappraisals*, P. Stepansky, ed. (New York: Analytic Press, 1986); Peter Gay, *Freud: A Life for Our Time* (New York: W. W. Norton, 1988). More recently, additional evidence has surfaced supporting the conjecture of Freud's affair with his sister-in-law. See *American Imago*.

12. Jeffrey M. Masson, *Final Analysis* (New York: Addison-Wesley, 1990); Janet Malcolm, *In the Freud Archives* (New York: Knopf, 1984). On Freud's precursors, see Henri Ellenberger's *The Discovery of the Unconscious* (New York: Basic Books, 1970). Ellenberger also refuted claims that Freud was a lonely pioneer who "discovered" the unconscious by himself. Frank Sulloway, in *Freud: Biologist of the Mind* (New York: Basic Books, 1979), pointed out that the myths of Freud's "splendid isolation" and early neglect were highly exaggerated.

13. Antonio Suman and Antonino Brignone, "Psychoanalytic Psychotherapy and Psychoanalysis: A Choice in Step with the Times," in *Psychoanalysis and Psychotherapy: The Controversies and the Future*, Sergio Frisch, ed. (London: Karnac, 2001), pp. 91–109, see p. 107. Interestingly, Freud criticized America precisely on this point: "the American has no time," he wrote in a passage he ultimately decided against including in *The Question of Lay Analysis*. "He has a passion for large numbers, for the magnification of all dimensions, but also for cutting the investment of time to an absolute minimum." Freud's words are to be found in Elizabeth Grubrich-Simitis, *Back to Freud's Texts: Making Silent Documents Speak* (New Haven, CT: Yale University Press, 1996), p. 181.

14. *New York Times*, June 7, 2005, p. A18.

15. B. L. Zacharias, *Strategic Marketing Initiative* (Chicago: American Psychoanalytic Association, 2002). See also Newell Fischer, "The Numbers Tell the Story," *American Psychoanalyst* 36 (2002): 3, 8.

16. See P. Fonagy, B. Roth, and A. Higgitt, "Psychodynamic Psychotherapies: Evidence-Based Practice and Clinical Wisdom," *Bulletin of the Menninger Clinic* 69 (2005): 1–58, for a current overview of the field.

17. See, for example, Michael J. Mahoney, *Constructive Psychotherapy* (New York: Guilford Press, 2005).
18. See Irving L. Janis, *Groupthink*, 2nd ed. (New York: Houghton Mifflin, 1986). The report of the senate committee was published on the front page of the *New York Times*, July 10, 2004.
19. An impressive array of professional organizations has been developed in the past twenty years to promote this expanded interest in the unconscious. The International Association for Applied Psychoanalytic Studies (IAAPS) has formed to encourage and support social and political applications of psychoanalysis. The International Society for the Psychoanalytic Study of Organizations (ISPSO), formed in 1985, helps academics, managers, and consultants exchange ideas about the psychodynamic aspects of businesses and other organizations. The Association for the Psychoanalysis of Culture and Society (APCS), founded in 1994, supports the study of the unconscious determinants of social and cultural problems. In the United Kingdom, the Organization for Promoting Understanding of Society (OPUS), attracts psychoanalysts and consultants to explore social and organizational issues.

ONE • THE NEW UNCONSCIOUS

1. John R. Searle, *The Mystery of Consciousness* (New York: New York Review of Books, 1997), p. 193.
2. See Tor Norretranders, *The User Illusion* (New York: Viking, 1998). For an account of recent work in academic psychology on the unconscious, see Timothy Wilson, *Strangers to Ourselves: Discovering the Adaptive Unconscious* (Cambridge, MA: Harvard Press, 2002). A perspective on such studies more sympathetic to psychoanalysis is in Drew Weston, "The Scientific Legacy of Sigmund Freud: Towards a Psychodynamically Informed Psychological Science," *Psychological Bulletin* 124 (1998): 333–371.
3. George Lakoff and Mark Johnson, *Philosophy in the Flesh* (New York: Basic Books, 1999), p. 13. See also P. Baumgartner and S. Payr, *Speaking Minds: Interviews with Twenty Eminent Cognitive Scientists* (Princeton: Princeton University Press, 1995); and Howard Gardner, *The Mind's New Science: A History of the Cognitive Revolution* (New York: Basic Books, 1985).
4. A useful early introduction to chaos theory is found in James Gleick, *Chaos: The Making of a New Science* (New York: Penguin, 1988). More recent discussions of this area include Steven Strogatz, *Sync: The Emergent Science of Spontaneous Order* (New York: Hyperion Books, 2003);

Albert-Laszlo Barabasi, *Linked: The New Science of Networks* (Cambridge, MA: Perseus, 2002); and Steven Johnson, *Emergence* (New York: Scribner, 2001).

5. Antonio Damasio, *The Feeling of What Happens* (New York: Harcourt Brace, 1999), p. 25.

6. Gerald M. Edelman, *Wider than the Sky* (New Haven, CT: Yale University Press, 2004), pp. 38–39.

7. Nicholas Humphrey has recently argued that consciousness "lifts the subject out of zombiedom," the condition in which we have the information we need about the world but without the sense of being engaged with it. He cites the example of those suffering from the neurological condition of "blindsight," in which they can "see" objects sufficiently to avoid bumping into them but do not know they are seeing them. *Seeing Red: A Study in Consciousness* (Cambridge, MA: Harvard, 2006), p. 124.

8. Damasio, *The Feeling of What Happens*, pp. 129, 125, 173.

9. Gerald M. Edelman, *Bright Air, Brilliant Fire* (New York: Basic Books, 1992).

10. See Chapter 7 in Daniel Dennett, *Consciousness Explained* (Boston: Little, Brown, 1991). The concept of "memes," the cultural equivalent of genes, is borrowed from Richard Dawkins.

11. Edelman, *Wider than the Sky,* p. 136.

12. Wilson, *Strangers to Ourselves: Discovering the Adaptive Unconscious*, p. 38.

13. Joseph LeDoux, *The Emotional Brain* (New York: Simon and Schuster, 1996). Damasio notes dryly, "The left cerebral hemisphere of humans is prone to fabricating verbal narratives that do not necessarily accord with the truth." *The Feeling of What Happens*, p. 187.

14. Walter J. Freeman, *Societies of Brains* (Hillsdale, NJ: Lawrence Erlbaum, 1995), p. 147. Dennett, *Consciousness Explained*, p. 229, has commented that we think that we are in the role of the executive, in command of our behavior somewhat as the president is in charge of the government, but in reality consciousness is more often in the role of a press secretary who explains and justifies what is being done.

15. LeDoux, *The Emotional Brain*, p. 175.

16. Reviewing a number of psychological studies of the link between behavior and consciousness, Timothy Wilson noted "we know less than we think we do about our own minds, and exert less control over our own minds than we think" (*Strangers to Ourselves*, p. 48). See Michael Polanyi, *Personal Knowledge* (London: Routledge and Kegan Paul, 1958).

17. Freeman, *Societies of Brains*, p. 154. Damasio, *The Feeling of What Happens*, p. 127. Edelman comments more dryly: "Consciousness is a

property of neural processes and cannot act causally in the world" (*Wider than the Sky*, p. 141).

18. Wilson cites J. G. Miller, *Unconsciousness* (London: Chapman and Hall, 1942).

19. Wilson, *Strangers to Ourselves*, p. 35. My account of the processes of categorization and concept formation is largely based on Edelman.

20. Freeman has suggested that the intense experience of love, along with the hormonal secretions that accompany it, may account for the dissipation of old patterns of neuronal activation, the "unlearning" required for new relationships.

21. N. S. Glassman and S. M. Anderson, "Activating Transference Without Consciousness," *Journal of Personality and Social Psychology*, 77 (1999): 1146–1162. See also Wilson, *Strangers to Ourselves*, pp. 77–79.

22. Charles Spezzano, *Affect in Psychoanalysis* (Hillsdale, NJ: Analytic Press, 1993). Drew Westen has noted this in his "Towards a Clinically and Empirically Sound Theory of Motivation," *International Journal of Psychoanalysis*, 78 (1997): 521–549. The work of Bowlby and his colleagues on attachment patterns was something of an exception as it focused on emotional attunement rather than drives, but that work was kept on the periphery of psychoanalysis. More recently Allan Shore has explored links between neurobiology and psychoanalysis; see his *Affect Regulation and the Origin of the Self* (Hillsdale, NJ: Analytic Press, 1994). In both cases, however, the focus has been on the earlier phases of the mother–child relationship.

23. Damasio, *The Feeling of What Happens*, p. 54. Joseph LeDoux has also explored the pervasive role of the emotions in the activity of the brain in *The Emotional Brain* (New York: Simon and Schuster, 1996).

24. See LeDoux, *The Emotional Brain*, pp. 112–114, for a detailed account of the controversies about the classification of the emotions. His statement on recognizing them retrospectively is on p. 44. In *The Synaptic Self* (New York: Penguin, 2002), p. 201, he notes that James's theory was discredited, but it remains true that the recognition of the emotion follows its arousal and the behaviors it gives rise to. LeDoux makes the distinction, implicit in the passage just quoted, between emotions and feelings, seeing the latter as belonging to consciousness. See also John F. Kihlstrom, Shelagh Mulvany, Betsy A. Tobias, and Irene P. Tobias, "The Emotional Unconscious," in *Cognition and Emotion*, Eric Eich, ed. (New York: Oxford, 2000), pp. 30–86.

25. Damasio, *The Feeling of What Happens*, p. 58. The term *schema* has been proposed to describe integrated patterns of response that involve both the cognitive and emotional unconscious systems, patterns that approximate what psychoanalysts call transference. See Dan J. Stein and Jeffrey E. Young, "Rethinking Repression," in *Cognitive Science and*

the Unconscious, D. J. Stein, ed. (Washington, DC: American Psychiatric Press, 1997), pp. 147–175.

26. As Damasio has pointed out, "The alleged vagueness, elusiveness and intangibility of the emotions and feelings is probably a symptom . . . of how much we cover the representation of our bodies, of how much mental imagery based on nonbody objects and events masks the reality of the body. Otherwise we would easily know that emotions and feelings are tangibly about the body" (*The Feeling of What Happens*, p. 29).

27. Paul Ekman, *Emotions Revealed* (New York: Henry Holt, 2003). See also the pioneering work of Silvan Tomkins, *Exploring Affect*, E. Virginia Demos, ed. (Cambridge University Press, 1995).

28. See Arvid Kappas, "What Facial Activity Can and Cannot Tell Us About Emotions," in *The Human Face: Measurement and Meaning*, M. Katsikitis, ed. (Dordrecht: Kluwer Academic Publishers, 2003), pp. 215–234.

29. David McClelland, "How Motives, Skills and Values Determine What People Do," *American Psychologist*, 40 (1985): 812–825; David Kenny, *Interpersonal Perception: A Social Relations Analysis* (New York: Guilford, 1994); Wilson, *Strangers to Ourselves*, p. 90.

30. Harry Stack Sullivan, *The Interpersonal Theory of Psychiatry* (New York: Norton, 1953), p. 373; Donnel Stern, *Unformulated Experience* (Hillsdale, NJ: Analytic Press, 1997), p. 55.

TWO • THE NEW UNCONSCIOUS

1. Joseph LeDoux points out that the concept is based upon Donald Hebb's work on cell assemblies, but the slogan was coined by Carla Schatz. LeDoux, *Synaptic Self* (New York: Penguin, 2002), pp. 79, 334, footnote 43.

2. George Lakoff and Mark Johnson, *Metaphors We Live By* (Chicago: University of Chicago Press, 1980).

3. George Lakoff and Mark Johnson, *Philosophy in the Flesh* (New York: Basic Books, 1999), p. 63.

4. Michel Foucault, *The Order of Things* (New York: Vintage, 1994), p. xi.

5. For Foucault on mental health, see *Madness and Civilization: A History of Insanity in the Age of Reason* (New York; Random House, 1965). On homosexuality: "Homosexuality appeared as one of the forms of sexuality when it was transposed from the practice of sodomy onto a kind of interior androgyny, a hermaphrodism of the soul. The sodomite had been a temporary aberration; the homosexual was now a species." *The His-*

tory of Sexuality, Volume 1: An Introduction (New York: Pantheon, 1978), p. 43.

6. See George Lakoff, *Don't Think of an Elephant* (White River Junction, VT: Chelsea Green, 2004).

7. Steven Pinker wrote a sharply critical review of Lakoff's ideas in *The New Republic*. Drew Westen, in his recent book, *The Political Brain* (New York: Perseus, 2007), emphasizes the role of the emotional unconscious in shaping political outcomes.

8. See Steven Pinker's discussion of this question in *The Stuff of Thought* (New York: Viking, 2007), particularly his chapter "Fifty Thousand Innate Concepts."

9. For accounts of the intergenerational transmission of trauma, see Arnold Wilson, "On Silence and the Holocaust," *Psychoanalytic Inquiry* 5 (1985): 63–84; Peter Fonagy, Miriam Steele, George Moran, Howard Steele, and Anna Higgitt, "Measuring the Ghost in the Nursery," *Journal of the American Psychoanalytic Association* 41 (1993): 957–989.

10. Selma Fraiberg, S. Adelson, and V. Shapiro, "Ghosts in the Nursery: A Psychoanalytic Approach to the Problem of Impaired Infant-Mother Relationships," *Journal of the American Academy of Child Psychiatry* 14 (1975): 387–422, see p. 387.

11. Vamık Volkan, *Killing in the Name of Identity* (Charlottesville, VA: Pitchstone, 2006), pp. 157–172.

12. Drew Westen has argued, "Freud wanted to distinguish two systems, one unconscious and repressed and the other unconscious but not repressed, but he also wanted to distinguish rational from associationist thinking. He fused these two classification systems into one, but the two are not isomorphic." In "The Scientific Status of Unconscious Processes," *Journal of the American Psychoanalytic Association*, 47 (1999): 1061–1106. For additional comments on "primary process," see Marcia Cavell, "The Social Character of Thinking," *Journal of the American Psychoanalytic Association*, 51 (2003): 803–824. Lakoff has argued that the logic of dreams is no different from how all language is constituted: "What Freud called *symbolization*, *displacement*, *condensation*, and *reversal* appear to be the same mechanisms that cognitive scientists refer to as *conceptual metaphor*, *conceptual metonymy*, *conceptual blending*, and *irony*. But where Freud saw these as irrational modes of primary-process thinking, cognitive scientists have found that they are an indispensable part of ordinary rational thought, which is largely unconscious." "How Unconscious Metaphorical Thought Shapes Dreams," in *Cognitive Science and the Unconscious*, D. J. Stein, ed. (Washington, DC: American Psychiatric Press, 1997), p. 90.

13. Mark J. Blechner, *The Dream Frontier* (Hillsdale, NJ: Analytic Press, 2001).

14. Irving L. Janis, *Groupthink*, 2nd ed. (New York: Houghton Mifflin, 1986).

15. Charles Darwin, *The Descent of Man*, 2nd ed. (New York: American Home Library, 1974), p. 179.

16. See Howard Gardiner, *The Mind's New Science* (New York: Basic Books, 1985), pp. 89–91. According to Gardiner, Miller's essay, "The Magical Number Seven, Plus or Minus Two: Some Limits on our Capacity for Processing Information," was published in *The Psychological Review* in 1956. Pierre Turquet has also called attention to this phenomenon in "Threats to Identity in the Large Group," in *The Large Group*, L. Kreeger, ed. (London: Constable, 1975). (Reprinted by Maresfield Reprints.) The seminal paper on this phenomenon is Freud's *Massenpsychologie*, somewhat mistranslated as *Group Psychology and the Analysis of the Ego. Standard Edition* XVIII: 67–143.

17. Ralph D. Stacey, *Complexity and Group Process* (New York: Bruner-Routlege, 2003), pp. 47, 48. The concept of "conversational gestures" is borrowed from the work of George Herbert Mead.

18. James Surowiecki, *The Wisdom of Crowds* (New York: Doubleday, 2004).

19. William Kahn, "The Revelation of Organizational Trauma," *Journal of Applied Behavioral Science*, 39 (2003): 364–380.

20. Chapter Five provides a more extended discussion of the concept of social defenses.

21. Quoted in Vamık Volkan, *Bloodlines: From Ethnic Pride to Ethnic Terrorism* (Boulder, CO: Westview Press, 1997), pp. 33–34.

22. See Chapter Four, "The Development of Prejudice," in *The Future of Prejudice*, Henri Parens, Afaf Mafouz, Stuart Twenlow, and David Scharff, eds. (Lanham, MD: Jason Aronson, 2007), p. 71.

23. Charlotte Beradt, *The Third Reich of Dreams* (Chicago: Quadrangle Books, 1968). See also Gordon Lawrence's work on Social Dreaming: *Social Dreaming at Work* (London: Karnac, 1998).

24. A beginning study of this is Sherry Turkle's *Life on the Screen* (New York: Simon and Schuster, 1995).

25. See footnote 13, above, and particularly Drew Westen's "The Scientific Status of Unconscious Processes." But it is also clear that the unconsicous contains a variety of nonverbal or preverbal forms of information. A very useful guide to this realm is Wilma Bucci's *Psychoanalysis and Cognitive Science: A Multiple Code Theory* (New York: Guilford Press, 1997). She posits a range of symbolic and subsymbolic modes of recording experience in the brain.

THREE • A SHORT ACCOUNT OF THE SELF

1. *Principles of Psychology* (New York: Henry Holt, 1890), vol. 1, p. 291. Joseph LeDoux, citing James, opts for a comparable definition: "In my

view, the self is the totality of what an organism is physically, biologically, psychologically, socially, and culturally. Though it is a unit, it is not unitary. It includes things that we know and things that we do not know, things that others know about us that we do not realize. It includes features that we express and hide, and some that we simply don't call upon. It includes what we would like to be as well as what we hope we never become." *The Synaptic Self* (New York: Penguin, 2002), p. 31.

2. Colin B. MacPherson has argued that the idea that we are in possession of ourselves is the foundation of modern capitalism, which in turn is linked to modern notions of democracy. See *Political Theory of Possessive Individualism* (London: Oxford, 1962).

3. For a comprehensive survey of the development of the self throughout the history of western civilization, see Charles Taylor, *Sources of the Self* (Cambridge, MA: Harvard University Press, 1989). Taylor's focus is not on the self as a concept but on the larger issue of how the individual person has been thought about throughout our cultural history. His work requires that he conflate all relevant signifiers to gain an historical perspective on what I would call, using the concepts developed in the next chapter, the "person."

4. Clearly, the idea that the self or the mind survives death is based on a belief in an immutable core, but some contemporary philosophers still subscribe to this essentialist idea of a self without believing in immortality. See, for example, Richard Sorabji, *Self: Ancient and Modern Insights About Individuality, Life and Death* (Chicago: University of Chicago Press, 2006).

5. I am referring here to efforts to objectify the self as a distinct, privileged object. There is a somewhat parallel set of efforts to describe a sense of self, an awareness of being separate, having a boundary, capable of introspection and agency, and so forth. This is entirely legitimate, I think, and supported by a number of researchers, theorists, and clinicians. A "sense of self" is most likely indispensable to development and what young children are expressing their fledgling awareness of when they discover "I am me." Antonio Damasio theorizes the existence of a "proto-self," a collection of neural patterns concerned with regulating the state of the organism, that is, keeping it alive. This is consistent with the "sense of self." See *The Feeling of What Happens* (New York: Harcourt Brace, 1999), pp. 139–167. The conceptual difficulty arises when the sense of self, which is inherently open and based on processes, becomes reified, presumed to reflect the existence of a special and unique thing.

6. Christopher Lasch, *The Culture of Narcissism* (New York: W.W. Norton, 1991); Robert Jay Lifton, *The Protean Self* (New York: Basic Books, 1993); Kenneth J. Gergen, *The Saturated Self* (New York: Basic Books, 1991), p. 7; Philip Cushman, *Constructing the Self, Constructing America*

(New York: Da Capo Press, 1995), p. 6; Thomas de Zengotita, *Mediated* (New York: Simon and Schuster, 2005).

7. Walter J. Freeman, *Societies of Brains* (Hillsdale, NJ: Lawrence Erlbaum, 1995).

8. This is the strategy adopted by the psychoanalytic school of self psychology with its concept of the selfobject, another self that is incorporated on the boundary, so to speak, of the self.

9. I am indebted here to Amelie Oksenberg Rorty's "A Literary Postscript," in the book she edited, *The Identities of Persons* (Berkeley: University of California Press, 1976), pp. 301–323. I have constructed my own definitions and descriptions, but her work has proved influential and invaluable. A somewhat parallel effort is to be found in Raymond Williams, *Keywords*, 2nd ed. (New York: Oxford, 1985).

10. *Character Analysis* was first published in German in 1933. An expanded edition was translated and published by the Orgone Institute Press in 1945.

11. For an early critique of this strategy, though one that invokes "soul" tendentiously, see Bruno Bettleheim's "Reflections: Freud and the Soul," in *The New Yorker*, March 1, 1982, pp. 59–93. A useful overview of Freud's changing definition of the ego can be found in J. LaPlanche and J.-B. Pontalise, *The Language of Psycho-Analysis*, New York: W. W. Norton, 1973. The ego psychologists debated the relationship between the ego and the self in a literature that now seems substantially outdated. Heinz Hartmann, perhaps the most renowned theorist of ego psychology, saw the self as a collection of self-representations within the ego. But as Steven Mitchell and Jay Greenberg point out in *Object Relations in Psychoanalytic Theory* (Boston: Harvard University Press, 1983), subsequent efforts to transform the self into playing a more significant role in the psyche undermined the coherence of Freud's drive model and led to mixed and uncertain results.

12. For an account of folk psychology or folk theories, see Alison Gopnik and Andrew Wellman, *Words, Thoughts and Theories* (Cambridge, MA: MIT Press, 1997).

FOUR • PERSONS, IDENTITIES, AND ROLES

1. See Locke's *Essay Concerning Human Understanding*, Book II, Chapter XXVII.

2. *Hamlet*, Act V, Scene i, lines 150–151; Act V, Scene ii, lines 215–220. Quoted from The Arden Shakespeare, *Hamlet*, ed. H. Jenkins (London & New York: Methuen, 1981).

3. In *Gender as Soft Assembly* (Hillsdale, NY: Analytic Press, 2005), Adrienne Harris has explored how gender identity is *assembled*, a term

she prefers to *constructed*, as it does not imply purposefulness or intentionality. She relies on the concept of emergent structures popularized by complexity or chaos theory.

4. See Chapter Three, pp. 77–92. Acknowledging the adaptive variability of the self, Sullivan suggested that we have as many selves as we have relationships. This improbable idea does make a kind of sense, however, if we think of it in terms of identity. Erik Erikson, the first psychoanalyst to recognize the importance of identity, focused largely on detecting failures to form identity in youth and early adulthood. Well known and recognized by the public for addressing significant, practical issues, he was neglected by other theorists who could not link up his findings with more entrenched concepts such as ego and self. See *Identity: Youth, and Crisis* (New York: W. W. Norton, 1968).

5. Many coaches do not think psychologically, and, among those who do, it is not at all unusual for a psychologically minded coach to assert that his work is not psychotherapy. I see the distinction in terms of the purpose or goal of the work, not the method. The need that many executive coaches feel to assert the distinction stems from the anxiety of clients to be labeled as mentally disturbed. The popularity of the term *coaching* carries no such implication or stigma. Everyone—even the best athletes—can use coaching. Indeed, it is widely believed that, to be at the top of your form, you require it. That is an advantage for executives who find it difficult to acknowledge the need for help or ask for it.

6. An earlier and I think preferable term to describe this work is *role analysis*. This tradition, originating in England, is still alive, though the idea of coaching seems to be fast supplanting it. See, for example, Bruce Reed, *An Exploration of Role* (London: Grubb Institute, 2000).

FIVE • ORGANIZATIONAL LIFE

1. Early critics of "mass society" included José Ortega y Gasset, Gabriel Marcel, Karl Jaspers, and Karl Mannheim.

2. Thomas L. Friedman's *The World Is Flat* (New York: Farrar, Straus and Giroux, 2005) is a good guide to these developments, though I believe it is overly optimistic about its effects.

3. See Michael Useem, *Investor Capitalism* (New York: Perseus, 1996), for a good sketch of this development. Kurt Eichenwald's massive account of the rise and demise of Enron, *Conspiracy of Fools* (New York: Broadway Books, 2005) gives an inside look at how an exclusive focus on its share price led a major corporation to inflate profits and disguise losses, using dubious and ultimately dangerous accounting practices. Real profits and growth were entirely subordinate to statements of

profitability that were used in turn to attract investors and drive up the price of Enron's shares.

4. Peter M. Senge, *The Leader's New Work: Building the Learning Organization* (Boston: Harvard Business School Press, 1990), and more recently *The Fifth Discipline: The Art and Practice of the Learning Organization* (New York: Doubleday, 2006); Charles Handy, *The Age of Unreason* (Boston: Harvard Business School Press, 1990), and *The Age of Paradox* (Boston: Harvard Business School Press, 1995); Peter Drucker, *Age of Discontinuity* (New York: Transaction, 1992), and more recently *Management Challenges for the 21st Century* (New York: Harper Business, 2001).

5. See Rakesh Khurana, *Searching for a Corporate Savior: The Irrational Quest for Charismatic CEO's* (Princeton, NJ: Princeton Unversity Press, 2002), for an impressively researched and reasoned account of this phenomenon. For an example of such thinking brought to a disastrous end, see John A. Byrne, *Chainsaw* (New York: Harper Business, 1999).

6. This discussion is based on Frayer's presentation at the International Society for the Psychoanalytic Study of Organizations (ISPSO) symposium in Baltimore, June 2004, "AeroDynamics," as well as her paper "Team Resources Management (TRM): A Tavistock Approach to Leadership in High Risk Environments," *Organizational and Social Dynamics* 5 (2005): pp. 163–182.

7. Irving Janis's concept of groupthink was introduced in the Introduction.

8. Most of the vast literature on leadership focuses on the qualities of the leader in isolation from followers. Some pioneers have looked at individual leaders with a serious attention to unconscious factors, most notably Abraham Zaleznick, *Learning Leadership* (New York: Beard Books, 1993).

9. I described this case in two articles that give a somewhat fuller account: "The Task of Leadership: Leadership as an Attribute of Group Life," *ADE Bulletin* (Spring 1997), No. 116, pp. 33–37; and "Leadership and the Creation of Authority," in *Group Relations Reader III*, Solomon Cytrynbaum and Debra Noumair, eds. (Jupiter, FL: A. K. Rice Institute, 2004), pp. 289–302. The task of the consultation, which I undertook with my colleague Marvin Geller, was to help the senior faculty members talk to each other and, eventually, prepare for the new dean.

10. In using the term *projection* I am following an old convention. The perceptions or feelings are not literally transferred or projected from one to the other, but attributed differently: disclaimed on the one hand and reattributed on the other.

11. There are innumerable examples of this in the recent literature on corporate change. For an unflattering account of Jack Welch's leadership at General Electric see Thomas F. O'Boyle, *At Any Cost: Jack Welch,*

General Electric, and the Pursuit of Profit (New York: Vintage Books, 1998).

12. This case is taken from Larry Hirschhorn, *The Workplace Within* (Cambridge, MA: MIT Press, 1988).

13. *The Workplace Within*, p. 168.

14. The concept of social defenses was first put forward by Elliott Jacques in "Social Systems as a Defense Against Persecutory and Depressive Anxiety," in *New Directions in Psychoanalysis*, M. Klein, P. Heimann, and R. Money-Kyrle, eds. (London: Tavistock, 1955). The classic paper on the subject, including an analysis of bureaucracy as a social defense, is by Isabel Menzies-Lyth, "The Functioning of Social Systems as a Defense Against Anxiety," Tavistock Pamphlet No. 3 (1967). Reprinted in Menzies Lyth, *Containing Anxiety in Institutions* (London: Free Association Books, 1988).

15. Elliott Jacques, *Requisite Organization* (Green Cove Spring, FL: Cason Hall, 1989).

16. See Eric Miller and G. V. Gwynne, "Dependence, Independence and Counter-Dependence in Residential Institutions for Incurables," in *Support, Innovation and Autonomy*, R. H. Gosling, ed. (London: Tavistock, 1973). Reprinted in Eric Miller, *From Dependency to Autonomy* (London: Free Association Books, 1993). A full account of this project can be found in their book, *A Place Apart.*

17. In this account I am relying on several sources: Steven F. Freeman, Larry Hirshhorn, and Marc Maltz, "The Power of Moral Purpose: Sandler O'Neill and Partners, LLP, in the Aftermath of September 11, 2001," *Organization Development Journal* 22 (Winter 2004): pp. 69–81. Marc Maltz, "'Finding You in Me': The Organizational Clinician," *Contemporary Psychoanalysis* 41 (2005): pp. 471–498. I am grateful to Marc Maltz for several lengthy conversations about his work on this project. See also Diane Coutu, "How Resilience Works," *Harvard Business Review*, June 3, 2002, pp. 48–55.

18. This reflects the discovery of Wilfred Bion's about the therapeutic value of work during World War II. See Bion's "Preview" in *Experiences in Groups* (New York: Routledge, 1991).

19. For a retrospective account of this work, see Joe Nocera, "After 5 Years, His Voice Can Still Crack," *New York Times* September 10, 2006, p. D1.

SIX • PSYCHOTHERAPY TODAY

1. For a good account of this prehistory, see Henri Ellenberger, *The Discovery of the Unconscious* (New York: Basic Books, 1970).

2. The statistics on practitioners come from Gary R. VandenBos, Nicholas

A. Cummings, and Patrick H. DeLeon, "A Century of Psychotherapy: Economic and Environmental Influences," in *History of Psychotherapy*, Donald K. Freedheim, ed. (Washington, DC: American Psychological Association, 1992). For reports on the NIMH study, see the following news stories: Benedict Carey, "Most Will Be Mentally Ill at Some Point, Study Shows," *New York Times*, June 7, 2005, p. A18; Leila Abboud, "Mental Illness Said to Affect One-Quarter of Americans," *Wall Street Journal*, June 7, 2005, p. D1. On preventive uses of psychotherapy, see Corey L. M. Keyes, "Promoting and Protecting Mental Health as Flourishing," *American Psychologist* 62 (February-March 2007): 95–108.

3. Jack M. Gorman, *The New Psychiatry* (New York: St. Martin's Press, 1996), p. xviii.

4. John B. Watson, "Psychology as the Behaviorist Views It," *Psychological Review* 20 (1913): 158–177.

5. Irene Martin, quoted in Eysenck's autobiography, *Rebel with a Cause*, revised and expanded edition (New Brunswick: Transaction Publishers, 1997), p. 155. For a lively account of the internal battles Eysenck fought at the Maudsley, see the chapter entitled "The Battle for Behavior Therapy," pp. 120–161.

6. This was revealed by Lazarus himself. See Carol R. Glass and Diane B. Arnkoff, "Behavior Therapy," in *History of Psychotherapy*, pp. 587–628.

7. See Diane B. Arnkoff and Carol R. Glass, "Cognitive and Interactive Therapies," in *History of Psychotherapy*, pp. 657–694.

8. See Edward Erwin, *Behavior Therapy: Scientific, Philosophical and Moral Foundations* (New York: Cambridge University Press, 1978).

9. K. S. Bowers and Donald Meichenbaum, eds., *The Unconscious Reconsidered* (New York: Wiley: 1984). Wilson's comments are in his "Clinical Issues and Strategies in the Practice of Behavior Therapy," in *Review of Behavior Therapy*, vol. 12, Cyril M. Franks, G. Terence Wilson, Philip C. Kendall, John P. Foreyt, eds. (New York: Guilford, 1990), pp. 271–301, see p. 296.

10. Described in G. Terence Wilson, "Clinical Issues and Strategies in the Practice of Behavior Therapy," in *Review of Behavior Therapy*, vol. 12, pp. 271–301.

11. Diane B. Arnkoff and Carol R. Glass have made this point in "Cognitive and Interactive Therapies," in *History of Psychotherapy*, pp. 657–694. They cite the work of M. R. Goldfried, "The Challenge of Psychotherapy Integration," in *Progress in Psychotherapy Research*, W. Huber, ed. (Louvain-la-Neuve, Belgium: Presses Universitaires de Louvin, 1987). The Lazarus comment is in A. A. Lazarus, "From the Ashes," *International Journal of Eclectic Psychotherapy*, 5 (1986): 241–242, see p. 241.

12. Westen's observation is found in "Transference and Information Processing," in *Clinical Psychology Review*, 8 (1988): 161–179. J. Safran and Z. V. Segal, *Interpersonal Process in Cognitive Therapy* (New York: Guilford Press, 1990).

13. Stephen C. Hayes, "Acceptance and Commitment Therapy and the New Behavior Therapies: Mindfulness, Acceptance, and Relationship," in *Mindfulness and Acceptance*, S. C. Hayes, V. M. Follette, M. M. Linehan, eds. (New York: Guilford Press, 2004), pp. 1–29, see p. 5. The comment by researchers is in Susan M. Orsillo, Lizabeth Roemer, Jennifer Block Jerner, and Mathew T. Tull, "Acceptance, Mindfulness, and Cognitive-Behavioral Therapy," in *Mindfulness and Acceptance*, pp. 66–95, see p. 72.

14. See Robert J. Kohlenberg, Jonathan W. Kanter, Madelon Bolling, Reo Wexner, Chauncey Parker, and Mavis Tsai, "Functional Analytic Psychotherapy, Cognitive Therapy, and Acceptance," in *Mindfulness and Acceptance*, pp. 96–119, see pp. 116–117. Also Clive J. Robins, Henry Schmitt III, and Marsha Linehan, "Dialectical Behavior Therapy: Synthesizing Radical Acceptance with Skillful Means," in *Mindfulness and Acceptance,* pp. 30–44, see p. 37.

15. See Zanvel A. Liff, "Psychoanalysis and Dynamic Techniques," in *History of Psychotherapy*, Donald K. Freedheim, ed. (Washington, DC: American Psychological Association, 1992), pp. 571–586.

16. Freud's comment, delivered in a speech to the Budapest Society in 1919, can be found in his "Lines of Advances in Psycho-Analytic Therapy." *Standard Edition*, 17: 159–168. Franz A. Alexander and Theodore M. French, *Psychoanalytic Therapy: Principles and Applications* (New York: Ronald Press, 1946).

17. At the Tavistock Institute in London, David Malan began experimenting with what he called "focal psychotherapy"; in Boston, Peter Sifneos at Beth Israel Hospital developed short-term anxiety-provoking psychotherapy (STAPP), while James Mann at Boston University developed a twelve-session model that emphasized issues of loss and separation; at Montreal General Hospital, Habib Davanloo devised short-term dynamic psychotherapy (STDP), a somewhat more flexible model.

18. Hans Strupp at Vanderbilt developed time-limited dynamic psychotherapy (TLDP); Lester Luborsky and Paul Crits-Christof, working at the University of Pennsylvania, researched the core conflictual relationship theme (CCRT) method, and more recently an approach they call supportive-expressive (SE) treatment, working with patients at a VA hospital; Mardi Horowitz working with a group at the Langley Porter Institute in San Francisco developed stress response therapy, now called short-term dynamic therapy for stress response syndromes (STDT-SRS). Also in San Francisco, at Mt. Zion Hospital, Joseph Weiss and Harold

Samson developed an approach based on exposing and disconfirming what they called the "pathogenic beliefs" of patients. Brief adaptive therapy was developed at Beth Israel Hospital in New York, as was dynamic supportive therapy.

19. For accounts of the development of these approaches, there are several useful sources: Paul Crits-Christoph, Jacques P. Barber, and Julie Kurcias, "Introduction and Historical Background," in *Handbook of Short-Term Dynamic Therapy*, P. Crits-Christoph and J. P. Barber, eds. (New York: Basic Books, 1991), pp. 1–16; "Brief Psychotherapies," in *Essential Psychotherapies*, 2nd ed., A. S. Gurman and S. B. Messer, eds. (New York: Guilford Press, 2003), pp. 350–399; "General Issues in Brief Dynamic Therapy," in Hanna Levenson, *Time-Limited Dynamic Psychotherapy* (New York: Basic Books, 1995).

20. See Paul Crits-Christoph and Jacques P. Barber, "Comparison of the Brief Psychotherapies," in *Handbook of Short-Term Dynamic Therapy*, P. Crits-Christoph and J. P. Barber, eds. (New York: Basic Books, 1991), pp. 323–355.

21. Hoyt's comments on brevity are in "Brief Psychotherapies," in *Essential Psychotherapies*, p. 351, who also cites "Survival of the Shortest." Levenson's comments are in *Time-Limited Dynamic Psychotherapy*, p. 10. Hoyt also comments at length on single-session therapy, pp. 383–385.

22. Cited in Levenson, pp. 18–22. See also Hoyt, pp. 388–389.

23. Wachtel's comments are from his "Preface: Psychoanalysis and Behavior Therapy," quoted in the revised and expanded version of his original book, *Psychoanalysis. Behavior Therapy, and the Relational World* (Washington, DC: American Psychological Association, 1997), p. xix. See also Gerald C. Davidson's Foreword in the same volume, pp. xiii–xv.

24. See Stanley B. Messer's "A Critical Examination of Belief Structures in Integrative and Eclectic Psychotherapy," in *Handbook of Psychotherapy Integration*, John C. Norcross and Marvin R. Goldfried, eds., 2nd ed. (New York: Oxford, 2003), pp. 130–165.

25. See, for example, "New Age Therapies," by Margaret Thaler Singer and Abraham Nievod, in *Science and Pseudoscience in Clinical Psychology*, Scott O. Lilienfeld, Steven Jay Lynn, and Jeffrey M. Lohr, eds. (New York: Guilford Press, 2003), pp. 176–204.

26. See Arthur Janov, *The Primal Scream* (New York: Putnam, 1970). A critical look at this work and some of its spinoffs can be found in Margaret Thaler Singer and Janja Lalich, *"Crazy" Therapies* (San Francisco: Jossey-Bass, 1996), as well as Martin Gardiner, "Primal Scream: A Persistent New Age Therapy," *Skeptical Inquirer*, May/June (2001): 17–19.

27. See Myron R. Sharaf, *Fury on Earth: A Biography of Wilhelm Reich* (New York: St. Martins Press, 1983).

28. A fuller account of this rich array can be found on the Web site of the U.S. Association for Body Psychotherapy: www.usabp.org. For a more contemporary view of body therapy, see Robert Shaw, *The Embodied Therapist* (New York: Brunner-Routledge, 2003).

29. See Jay Haley, *Uncommon Therapy: The Psychiatric Techniques of Milton H. Erikson* (New York: W. W. Norton, 1973). A good account of the man is to be found in Sidney Rosen, *My Voice Will Go with You: The Teaching Tales of Milton H. Erikson* (New York: W. W. Norton, 1982).

30. Andre M. Weitzenhoffer, *The Practice of Hypnotism*, Vol. I (New York: John Wiley, 2000), p. 592.

31. See Francine Shapiro, *Eye Movement Desensitization and Reprocessing: Basic Principles, Protocols and Procedures*, 2nd ed. (New York: Guilford, 2001), p. 18.

32. See Gerald M. Rosen and Jeffrey Lohr, "Can Eye Movements Cure Mental Ailments?" *National Council Against Health Fraud Newsletter*, January–February 1997.

33. See Nadine J. Kaslow, Barbara M. Dausch, and Marianne Celano, "Family Therapies," in *Essential Psychotherapies*, 2nd ed. pp. 400–462.

34. Robert R. Dies, "Group Psychotherapies," in *Essential Psychotherapies*, 2nd ed., pp. 515–550. For a good overview of the history and variety of group psychotherapies, see Max Rosenbaum, Martin Lakin, and Howard B. Roback, "Psychotherapy in Groups," in *History of Psychotherapy*, pp. 695–724.

35. The systemic aspects of groups are explored in work groups, about which there is an extensive related literature we touched on in Chapter Five. For an overview of group dynamics at work, see Clayton Alderfer, "An Intergroup Perspective on Group Dynamics," in *Handbook of Organizational Behavior*, Jay William Lorsch, ed. (Englewood Cliffs: Prentice-Hall, 1987).

36. Yvonne M. Agazarian, *System-Centered Therapy for Groups* (New York: Guilford, 1997), p. 9.

SEVEN • THINKING IN A POST-PROFESSIONAL WORLD

1. For some recent sociological discussions about the nature of the professions, see Keith M. Macdonald, *The Sociology of the Professions* (London: Sage, 1995); Magali S. Larson, *The Rise of Professionalism* (London: University of California Press, 1977); and Andrew Abbott, *The System of Professions* (Chicago: University of Chicago Press, 1988). In

this view, the professional compact went something like this: a group of experts, entrusted with a body of socially useful but complex knowledge, assumed the responsibility to develop and protect that knowledge and train new practitioners in its use. They became the gatekeepers to their profession, regulating access to practice and monitoring ethical standards. In return, they were granted a monopoly by the state, with the ability to establish standards, define the conditions of work, and set fees. Society benefited because the development of specialized knowledge and skills was turned over to those who best understood what is required to foster and protect them, while practitioners were immunized from the excesses of ruthless market competition. Because their knowledge is socially important, professionals came to have exceptional control over the conditions for their work. They assumed an idealized social status.

2. For a useful set of discussions on this issue, see Jane Broadbent, Michael Dietrich, and Jennifer Robert, eds., *The End of the Professions?* (London: Routledge, 1997).

3. Experiential conferences to study the dynamic issues around leadership are offered in the United States by the A. K. Rice Institute, as well as various university departments. See www.akriceinstitute.org. In the United Kingdom, where they are more established, they are offered by the Tavistock Institute for Human Relations, the Bayswater Institute, and the Grubb Institute.

4. Henry Mintzberg, "Third-Generation Management Development," *Training and Development* (March 2004): 28–36, see p. 36. See also Mintzberg's *Managers Not MBAs* (San Francisco: Berrett-Koehler, 2005) and Jennifer Reingold's account of Mintzberg's work in "You Can't Create a Leader in a Classroom," *Fast Company* 40 (November 2000): 286. Mintzberg and Gosling, forging an alliance with schools of management in Canada, England, France, Japan, and India, established the International Masters Program in Practicing Management (IMPM) to implement this new approach. Other programs, similarly oriented to real experience, reflection, and exploration, have been set up elsewhere.

5. Cynthia Kurtz and David J. Snowden, "The New Dynamics of Strategy: Sense Making in a Complex-complicated World," *IBM Systems Journal* 42 (2003): 462–483, see p. 462. See also Snowden's "Complex Acts of Knowing," in a special edition of *Knowledge Management* 5 (Spring 2002): 1–28, and his "Multi-ontology Sense Making," *Management Today*, Yearbook 2005, vol. 20. Useful also is Gary Hamel and Lisa Valikangas's article, "The Quest for Resiliance," *Harvard Business Review* (September 2003): 52–63. See also Ralph Stacy's *Complex Responsive Processes in Organizations: Learning and Knowledge Creation* (London: Routledge, 2001).

6. Andrew Abbott, *The System of Professions*, p. 281.
7. See Thomas T. Szasz, *The Myth of Mental Illness* (New York: Harper and Row, 1961), p. 4. For definitions of illness, see R. E. Kendell, "The Myth of Mental Illness," in *Szasz Under Fire*, J. A. Schaler, ed. (Chicago: Open Court Press, 2004), p. 35.
8. W. E. Henry, J. H. Sims, et al. *The Fifth Profession* (San Francisco: Jossey-Bass, 1971).
9. Recently New York State enacted a law that provides for the licensing of psychoanalysis, introducing confusion and consternation in the profession. For a partisan account of this, see Laurel Bass Wagner, "The Culture of Psychoanalysis in the United States: The Use of State and Federal Government to Advance Psychoanalysis," *Psychoanalysis, Culture and Society* 12 (2007): 51–64.
10. There is a growing literature on psychodynamic coaching, some of it written by therapists who have retrained themselves. See, for example, John Newton, Susan Long, and Burkard Sievers, eds., *Coaching-in-Depth: The Organizational Role Analysis Approach* (London: Karnac, 2006), as well as Ruth Ornstein *Multidimensional Executive Coaching* (New York: Springer, 2007).
11. Social marketing is the effort to get the public to buy into new social policies and change their behaviors; see Alan R. Andreasen, *Social Marketing in the 21st Century* (New York: Sage, 2005).
12. Volkan's own brief account of his career is to be found in his Introductions to *Blind Trust* (Charlottesville, VA: Pitchstone Publishing, 2004) and *Killing in the Name of Identity* (Charlottesville, VA: Pitchstone Publishing, 2006).
13. See J. Montville, "The Arrow and the Olive Branch: A Case of Track Two Diplomacy," and "Psychodynamic Enlightenment and the Greening of Diplomacy," both in V. Volkan, D. Julius, and J. Montville, eds. *The Psychodynamics of International Relationships, Vol. II: Unofficial Diplomacy at Work* (Lexington, MA: Lexington Books, 1991), pp. 161–175, 177–192.
14. Jerrold M. Post, "Leader Personality Assessments in Support of Government Policy," in *The Psychological Assessment of Political Leaders*, Jerrold M. Post, ed. (Ann Arbor: University of Michigan Press, 2003), p. 59. See also *Leaders and Their Followers in a Dangerous World* (Ithaca: Cornell University Press, 2004). An account of the Camp David profiles is found in the appendix to that book. Wedge's account was published in "Khrushchev at a Distance—A Study of Public Personality," *Trans-Action* 5 (October 1968): 24–28.
15. Lakoff outlined his theory about the conservative message in *Don't Think of an Elephant* (White River Junction, VT: Chelsea Green Publishing, 2004), with a foreword by Howard Dean. His ideas were sharply

challenged by Steven Pinker in "Block That Metaphor," *The New Republic*, October 9, 2006. For a thoughtful appraisal of Lakoff's ideas and the controversy with Pinker, see Geoffrey Nunberg, "Frame Game," on the Web site of *The New Republic* (posted November 4, 2006).

16. R. Fein, B. Vossekuil, W. Pollack, R. Borum, W. Modzeleski, and M. Reddy, *Threat Assessment in Schools: A Guide to Managing Threatening Situations and to Creating Safe School Climates* (Washington, DC: U.S. Department of Education, Office of Elementary and Secondary Education, Safe and Drug Free Schools Program and U.S. Secret Service, National Threat Assessment Center, 2002).

17. On prejudice, see Henri Parens, "Malignant Prejudice—Guidelines Toward Its Prevention," in *The Future of Prejudice*, Henri Parens, Afaf Mahfouz, Stuart W. Twemlow, and David E. Scharff, eds. (Lanham, MD: Jason Aronson for Rowman and Littlefield, 2007), pp. 269–289. For the project on police working with families and children, see Steven Marans, "Psychoanalytic Responses to Violent Trauma: The Child Development–Community Policing Partnership," in *Analysts in the Trenches*, Bruce Sklarew, Stuart W. Twemlow, and Sallye M. Wilkinson, eds. (Hillsdale, NJ: Analytic Press, 2004), pp. 211–236. For a project providing assistance to the African National Congress (ANC) in maintaining communities in exile, see Freddy G. Reddy and Sigmund W. Karterud, "Must the Revolution Eat Its Children? Working with the ANC in Exile and Following its Return," in *Group Process and Political Dynamics*, Mark F. Ettin, Jay W. Fidler, and Bertram D. Cohen, eds. (Madison CT: International Universities Press, 1995), pp. 217–238.

POLITICAL POSTSCRIPT

1. Book VI, lines 179–182 (Lattimore translation). *The Iliad of Homer* (Chicago: University of Chicago Press, 1951), p. 214.

2. Interestingly, Egyptian mythology is also replete with hybrid creatures, but they lack the threatening or monstrous qualities found in Greek myths. The Sphinx itself was considered benign in Egypt, its presence beside the great pyramids at Geza a symbol of strength and wisdom. Can it be that the Greek discoveries of rationality and order in the universe had the paradoxical effect of intensifying their fears of irrationality, causing them to personify them in such monsters?

3. See Turkle's *Life on the Screen* (New York: Simon & Schuster, 1997). A few of the more thoughtful and balanced texts I have found useful in the vast literature on this subject are the following: William J. Mitchell, *Me++: The Cyborg Self and the Networked City* (Cambridge, MA: MIT

Press, 2003); David Levy, *Love + Sex with Robots* (New York: Harper, 2007); Joel Garreau, *Radical Evolution* (New York: Doubleday, 2004).

4. See John Letzing's report in *MarketWatch* (Jan 18, 2008) on Microsoft's researcher Desney Tan: "It's our fundamental belief that computers are still relatively dumb, no matter how smart they act," Tan said. "We're trying to make computers smarter, and provide them with a mechanism to understand the user more deeply." Following up on the initial brain-sorting method described in last year's patent application, Tan's team is planning to present two more related innovations at an April conference. One involves "cognitive load," Tan said, or "measuring how hard you're thinking in order to perform a task." By tracking that, a computer could "adapt itself in real time to what you're doing," Tan said, and "present you information so you learn it in an optimal manner." The second innovation, Tan said, involves tapping a computer user's brain signals to rapidly sort and classify images as they appear, without the user even realizing what he or she is doing. Microsoft's research groups are relatively sheltered from the commercial needs of the company, and Tan is not sure when his team's innovations might appear in a product. "Obviously we'd like to get this out to the mass market," he said. (http: //www.marketwatch.com/news/story/why-microsoft-so-interested-our/ story.aspx?guid=%7b5FC1EC89-A444–4BD9-B436-FD8BBE879E26 %7d&dist=TNMostRead&print=true&dist=printTop)

5. See *How We Became Post-Human* (Chicago: University of Chicago Press, 1999), p. 284.

6. From "Human Identity in an Age of Software Agents," cited by Andy Clark in his *Natural-Born Cyborgs* (New York: Oxford, 2003), p. 178.

7. On the issue of standardization and conformity, see Ortega y Gasset, *The Revolt of the Masses* (New York: W. W. Norton, 1957); Gabriel Marcel, *Man Against Mass Society* (South Bend, IN: Gateway, 1978); and Karl Jaspers, *Man in the Modern Age* (New York: Doubleday, 1957). The critique of thinking emerged largely out of the Frankfort School; see, for example, Karl Mannheim, *Ideology and Utopia* (New York: Harcourt, Brace, and World, 1966); Max Horkheimer, *Eclipse of Reason* (New York: Oxford, 1947); and Herbert Marcuse, *One Dimensional Man* (New York: Routledge, 2006).

INDEX

behavioral therapies, 18, 155–156, 158, 164, 168. *See also* cognitive behavioral therapy (CBT)
behaviorism
  history of, 156–159
  psychoanalysis *vs.,* 160–161, 168
  response to cognitivists, 158–159
Bertalanffy, L. von, 176
bioenergetic analysis, 171
biofeedback, in conscious control of autonomic systems, 31–32
blame
  in groups' culture, 65–67, 190
  of self *vs.* others, 45–47
Blechner, M., 59
Blink (Gladwell), 15
body
  arguing for isolation of self, 83–85
  autonomic processes of, 31
  computers not accounting for data from, 225
  difficulty managing needs of, 37
  effects of meditation on, 31–32
  effects of trauma on, 37
  emotions and, 234n26
  role in symptom picture, 198–199
  therapies focused on, 171
Bowlby, J., 161, 233n22
brain
  computers *vs.,* 24–25, 224–225, 249n4
  emotions in activity of, 41, 233n23
  limited information-processing capacity of, 23–24
  neural pathways in, 50–52
  plasticity of, 26–27, 49
  split brain research on, 28, 232n13
  trying to maintain order, 24, 122
Breuer, W., 43
Brignone, A., 15
business
  advertising and, 55, 70, 210, 227
  effects of groupthink in, 21
  explorations of unconscious dynamics in, 19–20
  need for adaptability in, 123–125
  webs of organizations in, 121

Carter, J., 208–209
Cartesian theater, 27–28
catharsis, in early radical psychotherapies, 170–171
censorship, self-, 43, 73
Center for Social Emotional Education (CSEE), 213

Center for the Analysis of Personality and Political Behavior (CAPPB), 208
Center for the Study of Mind and Human Interaction (CSMHI), 207
Center for World Religions, Diplomacy, and Conflict Resolution (CRDCR), 208
cerebral cortex, processing fear responses, 41
character, *vs.* self, 88–89
childhood. *See also* families, of childhood
  discovery of self in, 78–79, 87–88
  effects on adult personalities, 6, 46–47, 72
  efforts to reduce anxieties of, 6–7
  formation of identity in, 103–104, 109–111
CIA, and psychological profiles of foreign leaders, 208–209, 211
clergy, as consultants or therapists, 197–198
coaching, 126
  to improve work roles, 107–116
  to realign roles and identity, 115–116
cognition
  cognitive behavioral therapy and, 158–163
  mediating behavior, 29–30, 32, 162
Cognition and Behavior Modification (Mahoney), 158–159
cognitive behavioral therapy (CBT)
  effectiveness of, 164
  offshoots of, 161–163
  therapeutic relationship in, 159–161
  third wave of, 161–162, 169
cognitive science, 24
cognitive therapies, 18, 158–159, 164
cognitive unconscious, 162–163, 174, 233n25
  categorization of perception in, 50, 69
  changing patterns of, 34–37
  information processing by, 32–35
  linking issues to metaphors and images, 70–71
Cohen, J., 213
communication
  in cyberspace, 71
  as marketplace of ideas, 226
  patterns in families, 176
  primary metaphors of language in, 51–52
  through facial expressions of emotions, 42–43
competition
  among psychotherapies, 16–18, 202
  economic, 124–125

legal system, 227
  meaning of persons in, 96–97
  potential threats to psychotherapists in, 201
Levenson, H., 166
Lewin, K., 176
Lifton, R. J., 82
Linehan, M., 162
Lowen, A., 171
Luborsky, L., 243n18

MacPherson, C. B., 237n2
"The Magical Number Seven, Plus or Minus Two" (Miller), 61
Mahoney, M., 158–159
Malan, D., 243n17
Malcolm, J., 13
Maltz, M., 144–151
managed care companies, 164, 201
management
  in-house advisors for, 192
  need for counseling and support, 204, 239n4
  the professions and, 182–183
  reconstructing for Sandler O'Neill after 9/11, 146–147
  studies of, 123, 125–126
  training for, 193–196, 239n4
  value of understanding unconscious processes for, 193–195
management consulting, 184
  possible functions of, 190–192
  as profession, 189–190
  on technical *vs.* social issues, 191–192
  uncertain results of, 186–187
Mann, J., 243n17
Marilyn, case study of, 36–37, 40, 58
Masson, J., 13
Mayo, E., 123
McClelland, D., 43–44
meaning
  constructing, 39
  of dreams, 59
  language conferring, 50
medications. *See* drugs
medicine
  psychotherapies in model of, 196–199, 205
  psychotherapists as consultants for doctors and clinics, 204
meditation, 31–32, 162
memory, 28, 56
  autobiographical, 26, 41
  implicit *vs.* explicit, 29

procedural, 72
  of trauma, 171, 174–175
Menninger Clinic, 213
mental functioning. *See also* information processing
  concept of self and, 77
mental health, 53–54, 197–198
mental health field, 10–11, 17
mental health worker, as proposed new discipline, 201–202, 205
mental illness, 3, 197
  management of, 153, 157
  as personal problems, 196–198
  prevalence of, 16–18, 153
Mesmer, A., 153
metaphors
  cognitive unconscious linking issues to, 70–71
  of culture, 58
  in dreams, 58–59
  families sharing, 56–57
  used in politics and advertising, 210–211
Miller, E., 141–143
Miller, G., 61
mindfulness, 161–162
minds, 77, 232n16
  as "black box," 157–158, 184
  Cartesian theater view of, 27–28
  connections among, 62, 83–84
  deprogramming through, 174–175
  difference from computers, 224–225
  jumping from association to association, 185–186
  organizations compared to, 122–124
Mintzberg, H., 195
Montville, J., 208
mood-dependent memory, 161
motivations
  effects of individuals' on group dynamics, 63–64
  implicit *vs.* conscious, 43–44
  need to defend against damaging, 43, 45
  unconscious, 1–4, 187
myths
  cultural, 166
  families', 166
  of family, 54–55, 210
  Greek, 217, 219, 248n2

narcissism, 81
National Association for Social Workers, 205
National Institute of Mental Health (NIMH), 10